DEH313
Social Sciences/School of Education/Institute of Educational Te
An Interfaculty Third Level Course

PRINCIPLE
OF SOCIAL AND EDUCATIONAL
RESEARCH

BLOCK 2

UNIT 5
PROBLEMS, CASES AND THE LOGIC OF RESEARCH STUDIES
Roger Sapsford

UNIT 6
EXPERIMENTS AND THE LOGIC OF COMPARISON
Roger Sapsford

UNIT 7
CASE STUDY
Martyn Hammersley

UNIT 8
SAMPLE SURVEYS
William Schofield

UNIT 9
VARIETIES OF SURVEY AND THEIR PROBLEMS
Victor Jupp

UNIT 10
ASSESSING RESEARCH DESIGNS
Ruth Finnegan

The Open University

DEH313 Course Team

Roger Sapsford, Senior Lecturer in Research Methods, Faculty of Social Sciences, and Course Team Chair

Michele Aylard, Course Secretary, Psychology

Andrew Bertie, Academic Computing Services

Judith Calder, Deputy Director, Institute of Educational Technology

Tim Clark, Research Fellow, School of Management

Jack Clegg, Producer, Audio-visual Services

Stephen Clift, Editor, Social Sciences

Sarah Crompton, Graphic Designer

Ruth Finnegan, Professor in Comparative Social Institutions, Faculty of Social Sciences

Adam Gawronski, Academic Computing Services

Martyn Hammersley, Reader in Educational and Social Research, School of Education

Fiona Harris, Editor, Social Sciences

Kevin McConway, Senior Lecturer in Statistics, Faculty of Mathematics

Ann Macfarlane, Secretary, School of Education

Sheila Peace, Lecturer, Department of Health and Social Welfare, Institute of Health, Welfare and Community Education

David Scott-Macnab, Editor, Social Sciences

Paul Smith, Media Librarian

Keith Stribley, Course Manager, Faculty of Social Sciences

Betty Swift, Lecturer in Research Methods, Institute of Educational Technology

Ray Thomas, Senior Lecturer in Applied Social Sciences, Faculty of Social Sciences

Pat Vasiliou, Discipline Secretary, Psychology

Steve Wilkinson, Producer, BBC

Michael Wilson, Senior Lecturer in Social Sciences, Faculty of Social Sciences

Consultant Authors

Pamela Abbott, Principal Lecturer in Sociology and Social Policy, University of Plymouth

David Boulton, Lecturer, Faculty of Community Studies and Education, Manchester Polytechnic

Peter Foster, Senior Lecturer in Education, Crewe and Alsager College of Higher Education

Victor Jupp, Principal Lecturer in Sociology, Polytechnic of Newcastle upon Tyne

William Schofield, Lecturer, Department of Experimental Psychology, University of Cambridge

External Assessor

Robert Burgess, Professor of Sociology, University of Warwick

Advisory Panel

Peter Aggleton, Senior Lecturer in Policy and Management in Education, Goldsmiths' College, University of London

Jeanette James, Consultant Psychologist and Open University Tutor

Elizabeth Murphy, Research Fellow, University of Nottingham

The Open University
Walton Hall, Milton Keynes
MK7 6AA

First published 1993. Reprinted 1995

Edited, designed and typeset by the Open University.

Printed in the United Kingdom by the Alden Press, Oxford

ISBN 0 7492 0154 1

This text forms part of an Open University Third Level Course. If you would like a copy of *Studying with the Open University*, please write to the Central Enquiry Service, P.O. Box 200, The Open University, Walton Hall, Milton Keynes MK7 6YZ, United Kingdom. If you have not already enrolled on the course and would like to buy this or other Open University material, please write to Open University Educational Enterprises Ltd, 12 Cofferidge Close, Stony Stratford, Milton Keynes MK11 1BY, United Kingdom.

1.2

4412/deh313b2u5i1.2

UNIT 5 PROBLEMS, CASES AND THE LOGIC OF RESEARCH STUDIES

Prepared for the Course Team by Roger Sapsford

CONTENTS

ASSOCIATED STUDY MATERIALS

Offprints Booklet 2, 'Leaving it to Mum', by Pamela Abbott and Roger Sapsford.

Offprints Booklet 2, 'Working with women's health groups', by Jean Orr.

Offprints Booklet 2, 'Health visitors' and social workers' perceptions of child care problems', by Robert Dingwall and Susan Fox.

1   INTRODUCTION

If the goal of research is discovering truth, then validity is the study of how to obtain research evidence which is plausible and credible. The next three blocks of the course are about how data are collected and analysed, the strengths of various research strategies and the pitfalls against which the researcher (and the reader of research) must guard.

In this block we shall be looking at three related questions: how problems are formulated, how cases are selected for investigation, and the 'design' or 'logic' which underlies research reports and should underlie research studies, helping the report to move validly from clear initial questions via appropriate evidence to credible conclusions. Unit 6 looks at experiments as an example of comparative method — learning about a group by looking at similarities with and differences from other groups — and at how the same logic is expressed in other kinds of research. Unit 7 looks at case selection and the relative merits of broad, representative coverage of a population versus deeper study on a smaller scale. Units 8 and 9 look at different kinds of survey design and their relative merits for answering different kinds of question. Throughout the block the emphasis is on being able to present appropriate evidence to support conclusions: whether and in what ways the cases studied are appropriate to the problem under investigation and whether the comparisons which are presented are appropriate to cast light on it.

The major concern of this unit, and the block, is with the question of *validity*. By this we mean the design of research to provide credible conclusions: whether the evidence which the research offers can bear the weight of the interpretation that is put on it. Every report of research is not just a 'factual report' but embodies an argument: '... on the basis of this evidence, I argue that these conclusions are true'. This holds just as much for the 'descriptive' paper, which aims only to say how many of a certain kind of person are to be found in a population, as for papers which try to explore people's conceptual frameworks or to test general law-like propositions about the human species. Moreover, the evidence which is cited is again not just a 'factual report', but the product of an argument; the authors collected certain information in a certain way from or about certain people, and the paper argues that this information may be interpreted in certain ways to lead to true conclusions about a certain population. What has to be established in order that the report's conclusions can be believed is that the arguments embodied in the report are *valid* ones: that the data do measure or characterize what the authors claim, and that the interpretations do follow from them.

In the rest of this section of the unit we shall be looking in more detail at the three issues of the block: problem formulation, case selection and the logic of comparison. After that we look at some of the questions these issues raise in relation to particular pieces of research. Section 2 examines the 'secondary' use of a variety of government statistics to answer research questions, and particularly at the statistics of unemployment. Here the three issues tend to become muddled, because reports based on the analysis of existing statistics are not presenting evidence specifically designed to be appropriate for the problem under investigation but have to do the best they can with what is available. The section illustrates the crucial importance of clear definition and critical appraisal of the extent to which evidence is appropriate. In Section 3 we look at three reports of 'primary' research: an interview study of mothers of children with learning difficulties, an account of health discussion groups for women, and a more structured study of health visitors' and social workers' reactions to aspects of child care and neglect. Here the issues are more distinct and we can look at the particular strengths and problems of individual studies. Finally we consider 'action research' as something superficially dissimilar to 'fact-finding' studies but sharing the same problems and having the same need to establish evidence as credible.

We shall be looking, therefore, at questions which must be asked about the design of any piece of research. We shall be asking who were researched and whether the research population is fairly represented by what was studied — in other words, whether the results can validly be generalized to the extent which the authors claim. Beyond this, we shall be looking also at the structure of research studies as a whole, conceived of as *arguments* from initial ideas to conclusions about them *via* the collection and analysis of data, and asking whether the argument expressed in any given research report is a valid one. These questions will be considered not just in the abstract but by reference to a wide range of particular studies. The block organizes research under the headings of 'case study', 'experiments' and 'surveys', each with its own design issues, but you should be warned that this is an over-simplification. These three headings do not by any means exhaust the possibilities of what can be done in a research project, and (as we saw in Block 1) it is not at all uncommon for a given study to be made up of a combination of them. We also pointed out in the previous block that researchers sometimes show a loyalty to a particular research approach and allow it to determine the way in which they formulate problems. In this course we do not regard these three approaches as competing paradigms, however, but as ways of structuring the questions we ask about research reports. Researchers are not compelled to adopt one in preference to another, and the problems of each are relevant to the assessment of all research.

The issues of this unit and this block are what are often termed 'design' issues, and we tend to think of 'design' as something that is done at the beginning of the study. It is worth stressing that design, in the sense in which we are using it, is not a phase of the research process nor something that is done only at the start of a research project before moving on to data-collection and analysis. Rather, it is an aspect of the research, something which forms part of a critique of a research report, and it is relevant to one degree or another throughout the research process. Early in a research project, of course, we give a great deal of thought to precisely what problem lies at the root of the study, what cases are to be investigated and what shape the 'argument' of the eventual report will take. However, the researcher will return to the issue at various points in the course of the research, and sometimes the initial problem under investigation will be reformulated on the basis of subsequent data analysis, and further cases may be selected for investigation on the basis of analysis of the earlier ones. Research is frequently an iterative process — it cycles through the different stages, sometimes several times. None the less, the distinction between design, execution and analysis is a useful way of ordering our ideas in this course. This block looks at the design issues of what/who forms the focus of the research, and at how research studies are structured to make possible the kinds of conclusion that the researchers want to draw from them.

1.1 PROBLEM FORMULATION

As we saw in Block 1, research may be undertaken for a wide variety of reasons, and so research reports may embody a wide range of goals.

- Some of the research reports you will read during this course and elsewhere may fairly be described as 'academic'. That is, their main purpose is to contribute to the study of an area of theory (using the term 'theory' loosely, to mean any coherent body of ideas and/or knowledge about some identified 'problem'). Such work will typically be carried out by people identified as 'academics'. Some will be teachers or researchers at institutions of higher education whose terms of service include an expectation that they will contribute to the development of their subject area (or research students); others will be full-time members of research institutes which have some measure of independence from those who supply their funds. Large-scale projects are typically funded by specific grants from research councils or elsewhere; smaller-scale ones are carried out by academics 'in their spare time', without specific funding.

- Other research may be commissioned to solve some specific problem or to explore a general area of practical interest to practitioners or policy-makers. Such research may again be carried out by academics, or by full-time researchers (including agencies specifically set up, perhaps by the commissioning body, to perform such tasks), or by practitioners themselves.

- Other kinds of exploration are carried out by practitioners themselves, not with the intention of providing general illumination, but to improve their own practice and as part of the routine handling of their day-to-day work. (The concept of 'the reflexive practitioner' is relevant here.) You will seldom see a research report based on this kind of work, but on occasions it generates results of sufficient interest that someone decides to write it up and publish it (more frequently in the areas of medicine and psychotherapy than elsewhere).

Each of these kinds of research generates its own typical kinds of 'problem', whose relevance will be judged according to the context of the research. Commissioned research or practitioner research typically accepts the 'problem' as being what practitioners, management or policy-makers conceive of it as being, and its relevance to the area of work is very evident. Whether it is formulated in the most illuminating way will sometimes be less evident. Often what academics have to contribute to areas of applied research is an ability to side-step the 'traditional' ways of looking at a problem and show that some other way of framing it may be more fruitful — or sometimes, even, to uncover the political or ethical presuppositions which lie behind the traditional way of formulating it. As an example of this we might take research into theft and vandalism. A great deal of research has been carried out in this area during this century, some by academics interested in the psychology or sociology of youth and crime, some by practitioners or commissioned academics. Most of it shares the presupposition implicit in 'folk wisdom' about crime and embodied in the institutions of our criminal justice system: that crime is most fruitfully tackled at the level of individual morality and behaviour, by punishing, treating or training offenders. It took a team of academic researchers (in the Home Office Research Unit) to stand back from this research tradition and realize that the root 'practitioner' question for the Home Office was not 'How do we cure offenders?' but 'How do we prevent crime?' Given this conceptual reorientation they were able to shift their attention from the reform of offenders (which has not been a conspicuously successful line of strategy) to the environment and making crime difficult or impossible. A number of studies have been carried out on 'target hardening' — rendering theft and vandalism more difficult or more conspicuous — and some success is reported for this line of action. (For details of some of the early studies see Mayhew et al., 1976, 1979; Clarke, 1978.)

In general, research initially conceived for an academic audience is likely, at its best, to pay a great deal of attention to how the initial problem is formulated and what kinds of theory or presupposition are buried in its formulation, but to be less concerned with, and less aware of, what a practitioner or policy-maker actually finds useful and applicable. This bipartite division into academics on the one hand and practitioners/policy-makers on the other — the traditional division between 'pure' and 'applied' research — is of course far too simple, however. Many practitioners are academically trained and/or would regard themselves as academics. Many academics are also practitioners, or have been, or are very familiar with some area of practice or policy through their years of research. Also, most academic areas have practical implications, and most areas of practice embody theory. Thus research projects are capable of being 'written up' for two quite different kinds of audience who would identify different kinds of 'problem' as important, but the two areas overlap. Indeed, many research reports are written for both audiences and try to answer both practical/policy and theoretical/academic questions.

In all cases, what comes first in any research is a 'problem' — a question to be answered, a problem to be solved, an unknown area to be explored. The conclusions of research reports can be valid and useful only to the extent that the problem(s) that they address are clearly formulated and expressed, and followed through in a consistent manner during the research. The nature of the problem should imply what *kind* of answer will be acceptable, even before the research has been carried out. The art of research design is then employed in carrying out research which can provide credible answers of this kind and in presenting the results in a logical and plausible way. Conversely, the art of problem formulation lies in constructing problems which can lead *via* valid research to credible answers. (In some of the best research the researchers' understanding of the nature of the problem develops as the research progresses and as a result of the research, as we have noted already. This is possible, however, only if the researchers are aware of the importance of clear formulation and alert to how their formulation is changing.)

'Problems', in this sense, are not necessarily 'things which require solutions': research is carried out in a variety of styles and for a variety of purposes.

- Some research is descriptive — trying to supply information in an area of interest or concern, without necessarily trying to supply 'solutions', and/or exploring an area in a descriptive way to see what of more general interest can sensibly be said about it. Descriptive survey work is of this kind (e.g. the decennial UK Census, which tries to provide a complete description of the population of the UK under a range of headings). We should note, however, that even description is seldom a neutral matter. The most supposedly neutral of descriptive surveys asks particular questions which are very likely to express how the researcher has conceptualized the field of study, so to an extent they constrain the description to the researcher's categories. 'Qualitative' or 'appreciative' research which aims to describe — observing what goes on or asking questions among a group or in a setting — may allow the participants' own views to come forward, often in their own words, but they do so through the analysis which is carried out by the researcher, and so again the researcher's preconceptions can all too often shape the conclusions. None the less, some studies set out to describe, not to explain or to solve.

- Other descriptive studies may be undertaken with the intention of influencing policy or practice. Surveys of prison populations, for example, are often undertaken to demonstrate how many 'petty' criminals finish up (expensively) in prison, and ethnographic studies of prison life often have as their aim the exposure of unsatisfactory living conditions. The researcher who is involved in an area of research will often have views on what should be done within it and carry out research with the aim of supporting these views. There is nothing wrong in this, but good research will always be designed to make it equally as possible for the results to disprove or unsettle the views of the researcher as to support them.

- At another extreme, some research sets out explicitly to test theories or try out preformulated solutions to problems. We tend to think of quantitative, rigorously controlled and often experimental studies when asked for examples of hypothesis-testing research, but in fact all manner of research styles can be employed both for theory-testing and for evaluating practical solutions to problems.

- Another conceptually different kind of research is 'action research', which develops and implements a solution to a problem and describes the process of doing so with the aim of evaluating the solution's success.

Each of these 'kinds of research' may also be seen as a kind of problem — 'What is out there?', 'Does this theory hold true?', or 'What happens if I do this?' Because they are not really distinct but blur into each other, however, and because a single programme of research may entail elements of two or even three of them, a research programme may have more than one 'problem' as its focus. In evaluating published reports we want to be clear precisely what the problems (or problem) of the research are as presented in the reports, and of what kind, before we can judge whether the research that follows from them uses valid methods to provide plausible answers.

1.2   CASE SELECTION

A second aspect of design, and one of the two main topic areas of this block, is the way in which cases are selected for research and what part this plays in the overall argument which leads to the research conclusions. If the research is concerned with providing information about a single case — the treatment of a single patient, the evaluation of a single experimental institution and whether it meets its aims — then case-selection is obviously unproblematic. More often, however, the research will be making claims about a *population* — about a class or group or kind of person or event or setting. When this is so, a part of the argument in the research paper entails showing that the subjects or cases investigated can be taken as typical or representative of this population.

The simplest way of making this argument, clearly, is to investigate every case within the population. An example would be the government's Census, run by the Office of Population Censuses and Surveys (OPCS). The Census is taken every ten years, and it aims to record information about every person who is in the United Kingdom on a particular night. Enumerators are hired across the country and carefully briefed in standard format by local Census officers — that is, every Enumerator receives an identical briefing, as far as is possible. In the few days before Census night the Enumerators identify every private home in their district (counting buildings shared by more than one family, or by a number of single people or couples, as one household or several according to whether the people in the building share meals), and they deliver Census forms personally to one person in every household. (Institutions such as hotels, boarding houses, residential schools and hospitals are dealt with separately but in essentially the same way.) On Census night one person in the household is required to fill in details about the household's accommodation and about every person in the household on the night — basic demographic information such as gender, age, occupation, educational qualifications, plus sufficient information for the person's migration around the country since the last Census to be worked out, plus a few other questions. After Census night the Enumerator calls back (several times if necessary, until she or he makes contact with the household) to collect the form, check that it has been filled in correctly and, if need be, help with its completion. Completion of the form is required by law, and the head of the household can be prosecuted if he or she fails to do so. The aim is to describe the UK population, at least in part for planning purposes — provision of schools, hospitals, medical services, etc.

ACTIVITY I

What strengths and weaknesses do you see in the Census? What does it do well? What kinds of criticism might be made of the data it produces?

Spend a few minutes thinking about how it is carried out and what it can and cannot produce. Compare your answer with mine, below.

The greatest strength of the Census is that no inference is required in relating the results to the whole population — it collects information about everyone. (This is not *quite* true, because some people live neither in households nor in institutions, but an attempt is also made to assess the numbers and the kinds of people 'sleeping rough' by sending the police round with a questionnaire on Census night.) Because Enumerators check it in the presence of the householder and are able to help those who find it difficult, the information is collected in a reasonably reliable way.

The weaknesses of the Census are twofold. First, because it is legally compulsory and people cannot refuse to fill it in, there are limits to the kinds of information that can be asked without spawning too great a clutch of prosecutions for refusal to comply. At each Census the question of whether and how information about ethnic origins should be collected, for example, is much debated. The second drawback is that it is very expensive indeed — which is why it happens only once every ten years.

If you do not have the resources to mount a census — a complete count of population — then a reasonable alternative is to do a *sample survey*. One such, again with the purpose of describing the UK population, is the General Household Survey, which is run by the OPCS every year. A large sample of addresses (over 10,000) is selected randomly from a complete list, and trained interviewers ask questions every year about the numbers and kinds of people in the household(s) at the address, the resources and facilities available to them, and certain other topics on an *ad hoc* basis — smoking and burglary victimization have been two recurrent topics in the past. The presence of a trained interviewer again assures reliability of responses, and because informants are free to refuse it is possible to ask more searching and personal questions than in something compulsory such as the Census.

ACTIVITY 2

What is the key problem with the General Household Survey and other surveys of this kind?

Again, spend a few minutes thinking about this, and compare your answer with mine, below.

Clearly the main difference between the General Household Survey and the Census is that the former does not reach everyone in the UK, but only a sample. However accurate its information about that sample, we can use it as a description of the UK population only to the extent that we can be reasonably confident that the sample is typical — representative — of the population. We should want to be assured that the sample is made up of the same kinds of people, in the same proportions, as the population which it purports to represent; then, and only then, do we feel safe in taking its answers to, for example, attitude questions as likely to represent what we would have obtained if we could have asked everyone in the population. (A large, randomly selected sample from a complete list of the population is very likely to meet these conditions, as we shall see in Unit 8.)

Even where only a small number of cases are investigated, or a single case, there are often implicit claims to representation — that the person, school, or city location is typical of others, and therefore that what is said about it can be applied in other contexts. You cannot guarantee that a small sample or a single case will be *representative* — that it will represent the attributes of the population in the same proportions as are found in the population. (This is obviously particularly true of single-case research.) However, the researcher should generally try to establish for the reader that the case or small sample is at least *typical* — that other cases are likely to resemble it enough for general conclusions to be drawn. A part of the task of the reader of research reports is to deploy an analytic imagination in trying to see ways in which the cases investigated might *not* be typical and the conclusions drawn from them therefore subject to qualification.

There is one circumstance under which it is not necessary to demonstrate that a sample is representative, and this is where it can be taken to be part of a population which is homogeneous — which does not vary in ways which might affect the conclusions. When chemists investigate a chemical compound, they do not have to establish the typicality of the sample — pure copper sulphate *is* copper sulphate, and once you have established that what you have in front of you *is* copper sulphate and nothing else, then this part of the argument has been made. Some social scientists, particularly psychologists, tend to use readily available samples which might be thought untypical of the population (e.g. students) and to justify them, implicitly, by this kind of argument. They would claim, if pressed, that what they are studying is the capabilities of the human species, and that one member of it is as good as another for this purpose. As we come to realize just how much of our psychological performance is culturally defined and determined, however, this kind of argument becomes less plausible.

A final kind of sampling which does not necessarily have to demonstrate typicality or representation is theoretical sampling. Sometimes an extreme case, or a case of a particular kind, will be studied for theoretical reasons, because it will cast light on a particular point of theory. In *The Affluent Worker in the Class Structure*, for example, John Goldthorpe and his colleagues investigated workers at a car factory in Luton in the late 1950s and early 1960s. Luton was by no means a typical manufacturing town, but a new town shorn of traditional roots, and car production was selected not as a typical kind of factory work but as one which was well paid at the time. Goldthorpe *et al.* (1969) were looking at a certain kind of predicted behaviour, which included withdrawal from 'the public sphere' and concern with individual interests rather than public and collective concerns, valuing affluence and the trappings of affluence above most other things, and treating paid work not as a source of satisfaction in itself but as a source of money. They reasoned that Luton and the motor industry provided a *critical case* in the sense that if this behaviour and way of looking at the social world was not found in Luton car factories then it was unlikely to be found anywhere.

1.3   THE LOGIC OF RESEARCH STUDIES

The major topic of this block is the structure or logic of the argument presented in a research report. We have looked already, briefly, at how the 'problem' is formulated and what cases are selected for investigation. How the data are collected and how they are analysed are also vital aspects of judging the validity of the paper's 'argument'; these are discussed in the next two blocks. Linking them all together, however, is the overall argument of the paper: that this problem, investigated in this way using these cases, leads inescapably to these conclusions. This block looks at forms of argument — logics — as expressed in research designs.

It will be a contingent matter whether the overall argument of a research paper is specific to the paper or inherent in the study or studies which it describes. Some studies are structured beforehand — large-scale survey projects, for example, and experiments — while others proceed a little at a time. All research reports embody an argument, however — that such and such is the case, on the basis of evidence presented — whether the argument is structured from the initial stages of the research or imposed *post hoc* in the process of making sense of the data. The basic point is that research depends on *comparisons* to establish its conclusions. Some research, of course, is purely descriptive: the Census, for example, sets out quite simply to describe the population. Some research depends on comparison with an absolute standard (e.g. of morality): Amnesty International, for example, are not concerned with whether there is *more* torture in the prisons of country *x* than in British prisons, but with whether there is *any* torture in either. Mostly, however, even descriptive surveys and secondary analyses of descriptive statistics such as the Census are carried out with the intention of comparison: we want to know whether there are more or less of certain kinds of people than elsewhere in the country, or more of them than can be covered by available resources. We describe areas, settings, or people as being like others in certain ways and unlike them in other ways. (Where the comparison is not explicit, it may be being made with 'common-sense' notions.) Finally all conclusions about causes or influences or preconditions are established by arguments based on comparisons.

We shall be looking at experiments — studies which attempt to control all factors other than one which the experimenter manipulates, and thereby guaranteeing that it is that particular factor which is responsible for changes in outcome. We shall be looking at different kinds of surveys and what can be concluded from them about causal influences — including the use of the logic of the experiment on survey data. We shall also be looking at studies of one or a small number of cases, at what they are capable of doing which is beyond the scope of the more controlled study and at the price which is paid for exploring a smaller area in greater depth. Throughout all these, however, the same logical questions will keep recurring:

1   how do some cases differ from others, and what can be concluded from the difference?, and

2   with what population are the research cases comparable, and what can be concluded from the comparison?

2   EXAMPLES FROM GOVERNMENT STATISTICS

Government statistics always look authoritative and are frequently presented as carrying authority; they are, after all, prepared by government statisticians and used by ministers for planning purposes. In fact, however, they differ very much in their quality; it is always relevant to ask whether they represent what the analyst needs in order to establish his or her argument. We may always relevantly ask whether the population which they in fact represent is the same as the population about which we wish to draw conclusions. Of the research arguments which are based on them, in other words, we need to ask whether the statistics in themselves are appropriate for the purpose and whether they are used appropriately to make the points which need to be made.

At one extreme we might look at the statistics of births and deaths, collected by the OPCS and presented in a variety of more or less detailed formats monthly, yearly and at other intervals. (See the Central Statistical Office publication *A Guide to Official Statistics* for places where these and other government statistics may be found.) These statistics are like the Census — they may on the whole be relied on. Births have to be registered, both by the parent(s) and by the hospital or doctor; this includes not only live births but also still births and abortions. Deaths have to be registered before a funeral may take place. There are, presumably, some births and deaths which are concealed — cases of murder or infanticide — but we may reasonably suppose these to be a very small proportion indeed of the total, given how difficult it is to do so. Birth and death statistics may therefore be taken as virtually accurate counts of what is occurring — as an accurate representation of the 'populations' of births and deaths. (To a statistician the term 'population' means not just a collection of people, but any collection of objects about which generalizations are to be made.)

At the other extreme, let us consider criminal statistics. These are published annually by the Home Office, and they contain (among other things) a supposedly complete count of crimes recorded by the police. We may be tempted to take this as a valid measure of what crimes have been committed during a year — as a 'census of the population of crimes' — but it would be a mistake to do so without careful thought. We know that some crimes are uncovered mostly by police action (e.g. traffic offences), but that others (e.g. burglary, car theft, rape, violent assault on the streets) depend mostly on private individuals reporting them to the police. There is, therefore, an element of personal discretion in what comes to the notice of police in the first place. (We know from other evidence, for example, that most car thefts are reported — because of the need to do so in order to claim on insurance — but that only a minority of rapes are reported.) Once the complaint reaches the police, a further level of discretion comes into action: the police officer may decide to record or not depending on whether he or she decides that a crime actually has been committed on the basis of the complaint, or to initiate further investigation before recording. Thus at least two levels of individual discretion are involved before an actual occurrence appears as a crime statistic. *What* crime is recorded, where several possible legal categories may apply, will depend partly on the discretion of the reporting officer, and partly on the local policy in this matter. Thus, what appears in *Criminal Statistics*, is not an unedited record of events, but one that has been filtered through two or three decision-making processes, any of which can prevent an event achieving the status of a statistic. We would handle 'crimes recorded by the police' with some caution as a measure of the 'population of crimes committed'; their *validity* in this respect is in doubt.

There are very many sets of official statistics which have this 'discretionary' character — more than there are statistics which may safely be taken as neutral records of events. To take one more example, death statistics may be a valid and reliable measure, but we cannot say the same for the 'cause of death' tables. These depend on decisions made by GPs, hospital staff, or coroners, and are prone to human error and the uneven working of discretion as to what to record in the case of multiple causation.

As a third and more complex example we might take government statistics of unemployment. Table 1 shows statistics on employment and unemployment from 1841 to 1951, based on Census statistics. As we can see, nearly a quarter of the male population were not in employment in 1841, but half that proportion in 1951; the years between show substantial variation, with no clear trend emerging. Table 2 shows statistics of male employment and unemployment from 1951 to 1991 collected on a different basis — figures derived from the records of the Department of Employment and the Department of Social Security. A general increase is noticeable from 1951 to 1991. Much more obvious, however, when comparing the two tables is that the figure for proportion of men unemployed is very different: about 12 per cent in 1951 on the basis of Census figures and less than 1 per cent on the basis of departmental figures. Table 3 summarizes the difference in that year.

Table 1   Male unemployment in Great Britain, 1841–1951: Census data

	Employable population[a] (thousands) (A)	Unoccupied[b] (thousands) (B)	(B) as % of (A)
1841	6,697	1,604	24.0
1871	9,351	1,169	12.5
1901	13,790	2,242	16.3
1931	16,342	1,552	9.5
1951	17,862	2,213	12.4

[a] The 'employable population' is the sum of people in employment plus unoccupied adults; it includes children aged less than 10 in employment.
[b] The 'unoccupied' figure does not include unoccupied children aged less than 10.

(Source: Department of Employment and Productivity, 1971)

There are two reasons for the difference. One is that the figures are collected in different ways. Census records depend on people answering questions about whether they were employed or not on a particular day, and they could have lied or given mistaken answers. (Census figures from the earlier years are also suspect for other reasons, given the greater incidence of illiteracy, the greater amount of vagrancy and the fact that all counts had to be conducted and analysed by hand.) The departmental figures for registration as unemployed are an exact count of persons so registered and may be taken as reliable. (The count of persons in employment is more difficult to achieve, but it is successively approximated in stages: monthly estimates based on returns from major employers are revised in the light of a quarterly sample survey, which in turn yields results which are

Table 2 Male unemployment in Great Britain, June, 1951–91: departmental data

	Employable population (thousands) (A)	Unoccupied (thousands) (B)	(B) as % of (A)
1951	16,187	139	0.86
1961	24,739	287	1.16
1971	22,139	751	3.39
1981	22,189	2,520	11.36
1986	21,594	3,294	15.25
1991	22,855	1,636	7.16

(Sources: Department of Employment, 1978; Office of Population Censuses and Surveys, 1987, 1988, 1992)

Table 3 Comparison of 'unemployment' rates for 1951

	Employable population (thousands) (A)	Unoccupied (thousands) (B)	(B) as % of (A)
Census data	17,862	2,213	12.4
Departmental data	16,187	139	0.9

revised annually in the light of the international Labour Force Survey, and every three or four years checked against a Census of Employment. The monthly estimates have proved unreliable in recent years (Thomas, 1991), but the overall estimation procedure probably provides reasonably accurate counts.)

The main reason for the difference between Census and registration figures lies not in the mode of collection, however, but in the definition of 'unemployment'. The Census figures for 'unoccupied' men include all men who do not have a job. Some will be out of work and seeking work; others will be out of work and not seeking work; others will be students; others will be school leavers who have not yet obtained employment; others will be permanently sick or disabled and *unable* to seek work. If I used this as a source of figures on unemployment, it would be because I was interested in the population of men not in paid employment, whatever the reason. The departmental statistics come closer to what we usually mean by 'unemployment' — people who could be in work but are not currently employed. The count of the unemployed is taken from the numbers who register themselves as unemployed with the Department of Social Security in order to obtain unemployment benefit, other forms of income support or access to the department's file of job vacancies. If we wanted a count of the men available for work but not currently employed, however, the register underestimates this number. Registration is partly discretionary — the department will register you only if you fulfil certain conditions. Registration is not compulsory, and some men do not register as unemployed, particularly those whose normal work is of a casual and intermittent but highly paid nature. The self-employed would also not appear on the register, even though some of them might consider themselves unemployed — for example, men who have been made redundant and are doing window-cleaning and other odd jobs for pay while looking for permanent employment. Thus the two sources describe quite different though overlapping populations and would be appropriate for different research questions, but neither is unimpeachably accurate.

Counting unemployment is not an easy task, because it is difficult to decide who counts as unemployed. The category itself is a socially constructed one — or rather, the word embodies *several* concepts, each constructed for a different purpose.

> Where ... should the line be drawn between employment and unemployment? If someone is in full-time paid employment it seems obvious that they cannot be regarded as unemployed. But what if they are in paid employment but only work part-time? Is one day's work a week enough to count ... ? And what about one hour?
>
> Where should the line be drawn in terms of wanting to be employed? What about individuals who say they would like to be in employment but don't try to get a job? ... What if individuals say they would like to have a job, but are not willing to take the jobs which are on offer because they are not regarded as suitable?
>
> Where should the line be drawn in terms of 'availability' for employment? What about individuals who say they would like to work if they could find someone to take care of the children ... ?
>
> ... What if someone is 75 years old and says he or she is unemployed? Should they be registered as unemployed or as retired? ... Asking these questions indicates that statistics of unemployment are unavoidably based on social and organisational attitudes.
>
> (Thomas, 1991)

One problem of using the count of registered unemployed as an indicator of unemployment over time is that the basis on which the figures are collected has changed quite substantially from time to time. Before 1911 there was no state relief for unemployment and therefore no registration of the unemployed in the modern sense; any figures you see for this period are likely to be estimates based on the percentage of their membership to which certain trade unions were paying unemployment relief. Three Unemployment Insurance Acts (of 1911, 1916 and 1920) gradually extended state relief to a widening group of people. In 1939 the scope of the 1920 Act was extended to cover juveniles, and from the National Insurance Act of 1948 the system assumed roughly its present shape. Figures from before 1948 are therefore not strictly comparable with later ones. Changes have continued to be made *ad hoc*, however. In the 1980s, for example, there were 30 separate changes to the way that unemployment was defined. The major ones were: (a) exclusion of young people on special employment training schemes (in 1981), (b) exclusion from the count of those actively seeking work but not collecting benefit (in 1982), and (c) removal of 16- and 17-year-olds from the register (in 1988). As Thomas (1991) comments,

> The Thatcher government set about reducing the unemployment figure by changing the definition ... Fiddling with important statistical series in this kind of way is unusual, not because politicians are above doing such things, but because politicians are usually intelligent enough to recognise the need for consistency ... and imaginative enough to recognise the likelihood of undesired repercussions if this consistency is lost. In this case the undesired repercussion was the loss of an important economic indicator of the state of the economy — a loss which contributed directly to the mismanagement of the economy in 1988 and 1989 leading to the recession centred on 1991.
>
> (Thomas, 1991)

Comparing two different sources which express similar concepts but pick out different populations can cast light on the shortcomings of one of them and provide interesting insight into research questions. In Table 4, for example, the count of registered unemployed for 1990 is compared with the Labour Force Survey for the same year — a sample survey which asks people whether they are in work or not and whether they are seeking work.

Table 4 Unemployment in 1990: 'registered unemployed' vs. Labour Force Survey figures

	Labour Force Survey (thousands)	Registered unemployed (thousands)	
	(A)	(B)	(B) as % of (A)
Men			
Total[a]	1,089	1,125	103.3
16–19	144	78	54.2
20–24	194	223	114.9
25–34	278	319	114.8
35–49	227	277	122.0
50–59	162	200	123.5
60+	83	27	32.5
Women			
Total	780	404	51.8
16–19	105	48	45.7
20–24	132	92	69.7
25–34	222	101	45.5
35–49	217	90	41.5
50–59	85	73	85.9
60+	19	0	0.0

[a] The 'age-group' figures may not quite add up to the totals, because of rounding to the nearest thousand.

(Source: Department of Employment, 1991)

ACTIVITY 3

Look carefully at Table 4 and see what you can deduce from it.

The total figures for men in Table 4 are fairly similar — within about 3 per cent of each other — though this similarity masks more substantial variation by age. The count of registered unemployed produces much lower figures than the Labour Force Survey for men aged less than 20 or more than 59, for technical reasons to do with the way the count is made up: people aged 16 or 17 are now excluded from it, being ineligible for benefit, and people over 65 receive income support in the form of a pension and therefore cannot register as claimants.

The figures for women are very dissimilar; about twice as many women show up as unemployed in the survey as the number registered. This reflects three facets of women's lives:

1 a tendency for many to take a 'career break' to bear and raise children, with a subsequent risk that it will be difficult to get back into the labour market at an appropriate level when they want to do so;

2 some tendency for women to 'retire' from work at an earlier age than men, if they are married and the husband's income is sufficient to support both of them; and

3   the difficulty married women with children experience in registering as unemployed, because of the social presumption that their break in employment is deliberate and the tendency of the officials to apply more stringent tests of 'availability for work', e.g. that child care shall already be available, before the job whose wages will pay for it has been obtained.

In addition, the same effects as we discussed above for men are also present for women (remembering that the pensionable age for women is 60).

A more detailed comparison of how the two sets of figures are made up is available for 1989 and is shown in Table 5.

Table 5   Unemployment in 1989: 'registered unemployed' vs. Labour Force Survey figures, and reasons for not seeking work

		Registered unemployed	Labour Force Survey
Total unemployed		1,780,000	1,860,000
		%	%
Counted as unemployed by both methods	1,270,000	71.4	68.3
Included in count of registered unemployed but not Labour Force Survey	510,000	28.7	
employed[a]	170,000	9.6	
does not want work	130,000	7.3	
not available in next 2 weeks	90,000	5.1	
other[b]	120,000	6.7	
Included by Labour Force Survey but not in count of registered unemployed[c]	590,000		31.7

[a] The Labour Force Survey includes as employed people who are working such a small number of hours per week that they also qualify for unemployment benefit.
[b] The largest categories of reasons are looking after home or family, believing no jobs are available, or long-term sickness or disability.
[c] Note that some of these are excluded from the count on grounds of age.

(Source: Department of Employment, 1990)

So what you can validly conclude from governmental statistics depends crucially on how they are collected, how this has changed over time and what 'discretionary stages' are built in to the collection procedures. The 'population' which is being described — in other words, what precisely the statistics can be taken as measuring — has always to be determined and justified. Different statistical sources may delineate very different populations within the same general area of enquiry. Precisely the same holds for any other kind of measurement, along with the data used by studies which would characterize themselves as describing rather than measuring what is going on (e.g. the papers by Orr and by Abbott and Sapsford which you will be reading in association with Section 3). The validity of the conclusions depend crucially on the extent to which the evidence can be taken as meaning what the authors of the report take it to mean.

3 DESIGN ISSUES IN THREE RESEARCH STUDIES

3.1 EXTERNAL VALIDITY

READING

You should now read 'Leaving it to Mum', by Pamela Abbott and Roger Sapsford, reproduced in Offprints Booklet 2. Take notes as you go along on how the authors attempt to establish that their 'cases' are typical, and of what.

This paper on mothers of children with special learning difficulties (or 'mental handicap', as it was called at the time), pays a fair amount of attention to representing its population. This kind of research, concentrating in detail on a small number of cases, is not generally able to say much about how well these cases represent the population for which they purport to stand. It is an obvious problem of 'small sample' research that a small number of cases are more likely to differ from the general population in idiosyncratic ways than a large sample, all other things being equal. However, the authors did take some trouble to show that their samples at least 'covered the range' and were reasonably 'typical' of what you might expect if you drew samples elsewhere. They drew samples of children with special learning difficulties from one of each of the two types of school which catered for them, at a time when the vast majority of such children went to 'special schools'. Their comparison sample of 'normal' families is roughly matched (within the constraints of what was available) by number of children, chronological age of children and area of residence (which in the town where the study took place was fairly well correlated with social class). Even this 'qualitative' piece of research, therefore, has tried to show that the mothers that were interviewed who had children with learning difficulties were reasonably typical of such mothers in the general population, and that the comparison group was indeed comparable.

We should note, however, that the paper cannot claim to be typical of *all* mothers whose children have learning difficulties — the research population is more limited than this, strictly speaking. There are a few notes on grown-up 'children', from Abbott's earlier work, but by and large the paper does not purport to describe what it is like to have an adult with learning difficulties in the family. Also, because the source of the main sample was schools, the paper does not deal directly with families whose children are too young to go to school. There is information about that period of a family's life, but it is retrospective information, collected when the children were older, not at the time when they were babies, and it therefore suffers from problems of memory and from the fact that we all reconstruct our understanding of our past lives in the light of present circumstances. (The problems of retrospective studies are discussed in Unit 9.)

Thus, pieces of research which differ as markedly in their methods as the General Household Survey and a small-scale interviewing project on mothers of children with learning difficulties may share a concern to demonstrate that what they say about a subset of the population from whom they collected data holds true of the rest of the population from whom they did not — though they do so in different ways. The General Household Survey, unable for reasons of cost (among other things) to question every member of the population, guarantees that it represents that population by taking a large and random sample. The interview study which compares two groups of less than 20 mothers in some depth is unable to sample systematically in this manner, but at least it takes some trouble to show that its criterion sample is *typical* and covers the expected range and that its comparison sample is comparable in respects which are known to be important in this context. These two studies, in other words, are concerned to show the *validity* of their results, in the sense of showing that what they say about the *population* which is the focus of their conclusions may validly be derived from their research.

Where representing the population is concerned, 'representative sampling' is on the whole a stronger concept than 'typicality'. If you claim that your sample is representative, you claim that it is a small copy of the larger population likely to reproduce in the same proportions any distribution of traits to be found in that population within calculable limits of sampling error. If you say that your informants were typical you are only saying that they were not abnormal in some detectable way. You cannot state with any degree of confidence that about three-quarters of the population will behave in a certain way because three-quarters of your sample do so — you have not been able to establish that your sample 'maps onto' the population in this way. This is precisely the aim of large-scale random sampling — to draw a microcosm of the population, such that everything which is true of the sample will be true of the population. (Estimating the validity of the sampling involves testing the likelihood that a true representation of the population has indeed been found; we shall look at this in more detail in Unit 8.) With single cases the concept of typicality is even more tenuous: your single case will be typical of the population in some respects, but undoubtedly not in all. None the less, typicality is the minimum towards which research generally strives.

The two exceptions to this principle, as we saw above, are the study of extremes and the study of 'critical cases'. Some research will concern itself not with average cases but with extremes, in order to understand a phenomenon better by studying it in 'pure form'. Thus, some research on memory will consider not how average people remember things but what is possible for a trained mnemonist, and some research on institutions will consider not average prisoners or patients but the long-stay cases whose lives are most affected by institutional living. Other research may concern itself with the 'critical case', the situation which tests the efficacy of a general principle.

READING

Now read 'Working with women's health groups', by Jean Orr, in Offprints Booklet 2.

This paper pays very little attention to sampling but just presents two 'cases' of groups which Jean Orr has run and on which she has taken notes. We have no real idea of whether they are in any way typical of such groups, though they do illustrate the diversity of groups and perhaps their unpredictability. In that sense the paper's conclusion might be said to rest on the logic of 'critical case' sampling. That is, the 'unconventional' Group A in particular is used to justify the conclusions in the final paragraphs, and to indicate that it is possible for a health visitor to reach the women in such groups even though they would consider themselves marginal to and alienated from the formal health service. Group B adds to that conclusion by illustrating a group in which younger women could be involved in problems which were not yet their own but which they would eventually encounter, and how they could be brought to interact fruitfully with older women. None the less there is an implicit appeal to typicality in this paper. Jean Orr would deny this — 'every group was like no other group' — but we are none the less to understand that the groups are at least not *un*typical of women's groups in general, and thus that conclusions drawn from them have some validity.

Thus an important part of our assessment of a research report's conclusions rests on our assessment of whether the right cases have been investigated to make the points that need to be made. In technical terms this is referred to as *external validity* — the extent to which the conclusions of the study generalize beyond the immediate subjects and circumstances of the investigation.

There is also some research which does *not* feel the need to establish this kind of validity, because it does not seek to generalize beyond the immediate case. Because most of what we think of as 'research' is presented in the form of articles or reports to be read after the event, we tend to think of research as being concerned with 'finding out' or 'trying out', for the benefit of a wider audience. Quite a lot of activity which might be thought of as research, however, is not concerned with informing the wider audience. If you introduce a new policy into your school, your hospital, or your office — a new way of organizing some part of the work, or a new machine intended to save labour — then you will want to see whether the innovation delivers what was promised, and exploring this question systematically is a form of research. The boundaries of what is to be counted as 'research' become blurred when we consider the analysis of professional practice. If you are in the habit of monitoring your own professional practice systematically (perhaps including feedback from other people, noting bad habits which tend to develop and changing your practice to correct them), then this is something akin to research and the same principles of good practice are invoked to judge the outcome. Indeed, wherever there is a goal, a systematic treatment or style of working applied to achieve that goal, and systematic monitoring to see whether the goal is being achieved, then what is done will benefit from the same kind of systematic thought and planning as is brought to the best of research studies.

3.2 INTERNAL VALIDITY

The other aspect of validation is *internal validity* — the extent to which the 'argument' which a study embodies is adequate to sustain its conclusion. A part of this rests on how the data were collected, whether any measuring instruments which were used do indeed measure what the authors say they do, and whether the data have been correctly analysed; these areas are discussed at length in Blocks 3 and 4. An even more fundamental question, however, is whether the design of the study overall is capable of supporting the conclusions to which it leads — whether the logic of the design will support the logic of the argument. In this sub-section we shall look at the *structure* of research studies and how this contributes to the plausibility of their conclusions.

If we asked the person in the street to describe what he or she meant by research, then what was described might well be a classic experimental design. We are all familiar with experiments from our schooldays in the chemistry laboratories: taking a substance, applying a 'treatment', and noting what results our treatment has caused. The popular stereotype of research (carried out in laboratories by people in white coats) echoes this experience. Drug trials, for example, involve giving a substance to a group of sufferers, withholding it from a precisely similar group of sufferers, and noting the extent to which the first group do better than the second. 'Experimental' regimes in schools, prisons, or hospitals work by making a change in one place, maintaining the old regime in a precisely similar place, and seeing whether the change leads to a noticeable improvement. (This, at least, describes a *well designed* social experiment; many studies that go by this name are *not* well designed.) We shall be looking in more detail at this kind of research design in Unit 6. For the present, the point to note is that the experimental design represents one kind of ideal, the form of research best designed to establish causal connections and so to test the value of innovations, and that its value in this respect rests in the degree of structure in its design. If two identical groups can be established, a treatment applied to one of them and not to the other, and every other factor can be held constant, then in simple logic one *must* conclude that any subsequent difference between the two is due to the treatment. (Note, however, the impossibility even in theory of obtaining two *identical* groups and controlling *every* conceivable alternative explanation; every true experiment approximates to this ideal more or less closely, but it is impossible in principle for any to achieve it perfectly.)

READING

You should now read 'Health visitors' and social workers' perceptions of child care problems' by Robert Dingwall and Susan Fox, in Offprints Booklet 2. Take notes on the way that the argument is structured — how structural features of the design contribute to the conclusion, and where the logic is weak. Think similarly about the other two papers you have read for this unit (looking back at them if necessary).

At one end of a continuum lies the controlled trial of medical research or the social experiment. At the other lie studies such as those you have read by Orr or Abbott and Sapsford, where there is no particular attempt to establish causal connections (except perhaps anecdotally), but rather an emphasis on holistic description (trying to describe the full range of what is occurring or what is being said, without identifying 'variables' at all, let alone 'causal variables'). In between come studies which imitate the logic of the experiment by contrasting 'naturally occurring' groups such as men and women, or older and younger people, to see the effects of gender or age on some attitude or behaviour — or, in the Dingwall and Fox paper, two professional groups and their attitudes to a topic area with which they are both concerned.

Why do I describe this study as imitating experimental logic, rather than as displaying it?

The study on which Dingwall and Fox report is set up something like an experiment in that it contrasts two groups which differ on the variable of 'professional status' — they are health visitors or social workers. They are both set the same task, to react to brief descriptions of things which might be done to children. The underlying logic is that to the extent that the two groups differ on nothing but their professional status, and there is a difference between them in reaction, then the difference must be due to professional status. However, the study differs from a true experiment by facing a major problem of *confounded variables*. As well as differing on professional status the groups differ in educational level (the entrance qualifications for the two professions are different), in professional training and in professional socialization, and any of these may as easily be the explanation for any difference which is observed. Indeed, there may well be a number of other respects in which the groups differ, of which we are unaware, any of which could as easily be the explanation. Thus, the study mimics the logic of the experiment but does not wholly achieve it. A similar point holds for the Abbott and Sapsford paper: we cannot tell in what respects mothers of children with learning difficulties differed from the other mothers we interviewed, except in respect of those characteristics we checked, and we cannot tell what it is about their situation and experience which makes the differences which we observed, because many differences between the two groups (some of which we may not know) are probably confounded in the design.

A similar kind of structuring principle can be seen at work, however, in a wide range of research papers which differ very widely in other ways. The essence of the experiment lies in the comparison of one group with another, to tie down changes or differences to the groups which experienced the 'treatment'. The Abbott and Sapsford paper compares the lives of mothers whose children have special learning difficulties with the lives of other mothers, to see what is specific to the former and what can be seen as general problems of motherhood. The same principle of controlled contrast underlies many of the best-known sociological studies. Durkheim (1897), looking at the incidence of suicide, compares Catholic countries with Protestant ones, and then Catholic and Protestant populations within countries where the religious groups are mixed. Durkheim posited that a state of solidarity with community and family existed to a greater extent among Catholics than Protestants, mitigating against the alienation which leads to suicide. The argument is that where two otherwise similar regions differ in their religious affiliation, and suicide is rife in one area but not another, then something associated with that religious affiliation may be connected with the rate of suicide. We might want to argue that Durkheim was wrong in what it was, associated with religious affiliation, which affected suicide rates. We might argue, for example, that the different social conditions of Catholic and Protestant countries greatly affected the likelihood of any given death being recorded as suicide. None the less, the comparative principle is sound in itself. Comparison and contrast are very common structuring principles in research arguments. One could almost assert, indeed, that you do not know what is true of a group until you know of what groups it is *not* true. In our research on special learning difficulties, for example, anything we found out about the mothers of children with learning difficulties could as well have been true of all parents. It is only by comparing them with mothers whose children did *not* have learning difficulties that we began to be able to say what was special about *their* lives.

4 ACTION RESEARCH

All three of the papers which you have read could be characterized as 'applied research' in the sense that they deal with practical problems of one kind or another. Two of them, however, take a distinctly 'academic' stance to those problems. In Abbott and Sapsford's paper on bringing up children with special learning difficulties, the descriptions and conclusions are intended to be useful to those whom they interview by adding to the general stock of knowledge about what their lives are like and so informing policy-makers, health visitors and social workers. The Dingwall and Fox paper looks for differences between health visitors and social workers in the area of 'child abuse'. In both studies the research is distinctly separate from the problems and the professional practice of those involved; researchers come in to explore an area of interest and 'leave the field' to report on it. The third paper is of a more strictly applied nature: Jean Orr describes educational discussion groups which she organizes as part of her work as a health visitor. The research is still separate from the practice, however, even in Orr's case — the investigation is not part of the job, but something superimposed on the job because of 'outside' interests.

This provides one end of another dimension on which research studies might be classified. At the other end come studies such as one that Edna Conlan and I are carrying out in Milton Keynes at the time of writing (1992). A local closed mental health facility is under an obligation to demonstrate its value, at a time when regular monitoring of quality of service is becoming an acceptable concept within the health services. Most of the available 'quality of service' measures depend on structured questionnaires, and we have our doubts about the relevance of this approach to institutions with only a dozen or so beds. What we have done is to put together a qualitative package for quality assurance, consisting of:

1   a baseline study in which an experienced interviewer will hold a group meeting of residents, talk to each resident individually, interview every member of staff and also talk to a sample of 'outside users' — those who refer patients, provide funds or have an interest in the overall management; and

2   continuation studies, on a smaller scale, every six months — a subset of the interviews or meetings, extended if problems come to light which need further investigation.

The agenda for the study is not set, but rather left to be discovered within the study itself. We are equally happy to deal with questions of whether the 'philosophy' of the institution is being actualized or whether the institution is providing the service that outsiders expect of it, problems of changing use and the impact on staff and patients, or specific complaints about food or comfort.

Three points are worth making about this study.

1   First, it is *action research* — that is, its purpose is not to describe the insti-
    tution but to change it. The immediate aim is to detect problems (at whatever
    level) before they have developed to crisis proportions and to bring them to
    the attention of those most able to deal with them. On a longer-term basis, the
    aim is to build a 'culture of openness' within the institution, such that the
    research becomes at least partly redundant because residents, staff and out-
    siders are able to bring their concerns to each other's attention without the
    need for outside monitoring.

2   Secondly, and related to the second aim, the research is *collaborative* to a very
    large extent. The aim is not to interrogate residents, staff and outsiders, but to
    involve each group in exploring their own problems, with the researchers act-
    ing less as auditors and more as facilitators for each group to formulate its
    own concerns. We are particularly concerned to build this understanding of
    the research among the residents, as part of the general movement towards
    self-advocacy on the part of mental health patients. The researchers retain cer-
    tain personal 'freedoms of action' — to interview residents and staff individu-
    ally, so that minority views can be expressed as well as those of the majority,
    and to formulate the eventual report — but otherwise the research is intended
    not as something done *to* or *on* people, but something done *with* them.

3   None the less, despite the difference of aims and approaches between this
    and 'fact-finding' research, similar principles apply. We still need a basis of
    comparison: evaluation is meaningless unless there are measurements from
    which change can be shown. Further, we are sampling into all the interested
    parties not just in the interests of 'justice' but also to be sure of representing
    all relevant sides of the institution.

5   CONCLUSION

A final point is that our research inevitably reflects the way we have conceptualized the 'problem', which in turn determines the agenda of the research argument
and the scope of what is available to be discovered. With imagination we may
identify some biases of this kind and, if necessary and desirable, deal with them,
but inevitably some element of the 'taken for granted' will remain. Not everything
taken for granted is a bias, but whatever assumptions remain unexamined may
shape the conclusions in unintended ways. The reader of research should be alert
for such assumptions.

ACTIVITY 4

Looking back at the paper by Abbott and Sapsford which you read earlier, what might
you characterize as the agenda which is taken for granted — researchable questions
which are closed off by the way in which the research has been designed?

Your list will undoubtedly be different from mine; this kind of analysis is a very
personal process. What occurs to me is that the paper takes for granted the nature
of 'mental handicap' as identified at the time. What it actually explores is the
experience of mothers whose children are *labelled* as mentally handicapped by
one of a range of state agents — doctors, health visitors, educational psychologists, etc. — and what it is like to bring up a child who carries this public label.
A study of bringing up children of markedly less than average IQ would have to
be differently designed, starting from some kind of sampling of the general population.

In other words, the researcher's focus of interest, reflecting his or her interests,
world-view, politics and/or preconceived solution to the 'problem' are reflected in
the research studies which are carried out.

So, to finish, in this unit we have identified a three-point check-list against which the design of a piece of research might be judged. (The list resembles the one Martyn Hammersley gave in the concluding section of Unit 1/2 but is not identical to it.)

1   *To what population may the results be generalized?*

In other words, are the informants or subjects typical of a broader class (is it possible to use them as an indicator of what the broader class is probably like) or representative of a broader class (made up of the same kinds of people or objects, in the same proportions)? There are perhaps two separate questions to be considered here:

(a) to what population do *the authors* claim the results may be generalized?, and

(b) to what population do *you* consider the results may be generalized?

We noted that while virtually all published research makes some claim to generality, even if only implicitly, not all research is published or publishable. Some local evaluation studies make no claims to hold for anything other than the immediate target of the research.

We also noted that not all research sets out simply to describe or even to test or evaluate. Some research studies are inseparably bound up with attempts to *change* the situation which is being researched.

2   *How is the argument structured?*

Looking at a piece of research as a stage in a logical argument — from a set of questions via evidence to a set of conclusions — to what extent does the design of the research allow the conclusions to be drawn validly from the evidence?

We noted that it is also possible to structure a piece of research to the extent where the argument may be valid in formal terms, but at the cost of such artificiality that the authors may not be able to claim to represent what happens in 'real-life' situations. (The alternative is also possible — research which represents the real situation very well, but whose 'argument' is so flawed as to be useless.)

3   *To what extent are the conclusions of the research structured into the way it is conducted?*

All research is likely to suffer from preconceptions and prejudices, which are likely to be expressed in the way the questions are posed, the research designed and the data collection conducted. Preconceptions and assumptions are inevitable, but the reader must remain alert to their implications.

ACTIVITY 5

Compare this list with the one given in the Conclusion to Unit 1/2. How do they cover the same ground?

Item 1 on my list relates to item 2 of Martyn Hammersley's: to ask to what population the results may be generalized is to ask what cases were studied and why. It is also relevant to item 4 on the Unit 1/2 list, however: the basis of generalization is part of the evidence for the main claims.

Items 2 and 3 on my list cut across all the items on the list in Unit 1/2: they concern the basis on which a research question is formulated, the reasons why particular evidence is collected, and the soundness of conclusions inferred from the evidence.

REFERENCES

Abbott, P. and Sapsford, R. (1987) 'Leaving it to Mum', in *Community Care for Mentally Handicapped Children*, Chap. 2, Milton Keynes, Open University Press (reproduced in Offprints Booklet 2).

Central Statistical Office (irregularly) *A Guide to Official Statistics*, London, HMSO.

Clarke, R.V.G. (ed.) (1978) *Tackling Vandalism*, London, HMSO, Home Office Research Study no. 47.

Department of Employment (1978) *British Labour Statistics Year Book 1976*, London, HMSO.

Department of Employment (1990) 'Measures of unemployment: the claimant count and the Labour Force Survey', *Employment Gazette*, October, pp.507–13.

Department of Employment (1991) *Unemployment Unit Working Brief, April*, London, DOE.

Department of Employment and Productivity (1971) *British Labour Statistics: Historical Abstract 1886–1968*, London, HMSO.

Dingwall, R. and Fox, S. (1986) 'Health visitors' and social workers' perceptions of child care problems', in While, A. (ed.) *Research in Preventive Community Nursing Care: Fifteen Studies in Health Visiting*, Chap. 12, Chichester, Wiley (reproduced in Offprints Booklet 2).

Durkheim, E. (1897) *Suicide: a Study in Sociology*, New York, Free Press (1951).

Goldthorpe, J., Lockwood, D., Bechhofer, F. and Platt, J. (1969) *The Affluent Worker in the Class Structure*, Oxford, Oxford University Press.

Mayhew, P., Clarke, R.V.G., Sturman, A. and Hough, J.M. (1976) *Crime as Opportunity*, London, HMSO, Home Office Research Study no. 34.

Mayhew, P., Clarke, R.V.G., Burrows, J.N., Hough, J.M. and Winchester, S.W.C. (1979) *Crime in Public View*, London, HMSO, Home Office Research Study no. 49.

Office of Population Censuses and Surveys (1987, 1988, 1992) *Social Trends*, London, HMSO (annual).

Orr, J. (1986) 'Working with women's health groups', in While, A. (ed.) *Research in Preventive Community Nursing Care: Fifteen Studies in Health Visiting*, Chap. 13, Chichester, Wiley (reproduced in Offprints Booklet 2).

Thomas, R. (1991) 'Employment and unemployment', unpublished paper.

UNIT 6 EXPERIMENTS AND THE LOGIC OF COMPARISON

Prepared for the Course Team by Roger Sapsford

CONTENTS

ASSOCIATED STUDY MATERIALS

Offprints Booklet 2, 'Leaving it to Mum', by Pamela Abbott and Roger Sapsford.

Offprints Booklet 2, 'Health visitors' and social workers' perceptions of child care problems', by Robert Dingwall and Susan Fox.

Offprints Booklet 2, 'Treatment of depressed women by nurses in Britain and the USA', by Verona Gordon.

1   INTRODUCTION

This unit is the first of three which look at, among other things, the selection of cases. In Unit 7 we shall look at 'case studies' — projects involving one or a small number of cases, picked to make a point. In Unit 8 we shall be reading about cross-sectional surveys and the selection of samples of cases to represent a population. The current unit leads up to experimental research, where the cases (or, at least, the situations in which they find themselves) are created by the experimenter as part of the structure of his or her argument.

In this unit we first look briefly at how conclusions are drawn from figures by comparing groups or areas or years, and the problem of comparing like with like. The major example here is a study of health status and material deprivation, comparing small areas in order to describe a Health District. Following on from this, we look at how research studies are structured to draw conclusions from the comparison of naturally occurring groups and the logical problems associated with such conclusions. Here the major example is the study comparing social workers' and health visitors' attitudes to child-rearing practices and child neglect which you read in association with the last unit. Next we look at the most highly structured of all research designs, the *experiment* or *controlled trial*, and consider the strengths of such designs, their logical problems, and their associated weaknesses. (The main example is an experimental study on the treatment of women's depression.) Finally, we consider how systematic comparison can be built even into studies which are not set up to 'compare figures', and how doing so adds to the interpretability of results. One major example here is a study describing the lives of mothers of children with learning difficulties (which, again, you have already read).

Most of the examples in this unit are of 'quantitative' research — i.e. using the kind of research that takes measurements and uses statistical analysis to reach its conclusions — but we shall look briefly, at the end, at the application of the same principles to more 'qualitative' research. As we saw in Unit 5, a single logic runs through any study, determining design factors, how data are collected, and how the analysis is to proceed. The structure of a piece of research determines the conclusions that can be drawn from it (and, more importantly, the conclusions that *should not* be drawn from it). This holds as much for research commonly called 'unstructured' — participant observation and interview studies which do not have a predetermined questionnaire — as for more quantitative work; every piece of research has an underlying structure.

We commence, in Section 2, with the kinds of comparison generally carried out on figures which are already available — e.g. government statistics. We are looking at the kinds of question which we would generally want to ask of such statistics: have things changed from one year to another, or are things different in one area compared with another, or do the figures differ from one group to another? These are not casual questions, but generally causal ones. That is, the question is generally asked on the basis of some theory, to test some conclusion — that one variable is responsible for the change in another. The immediate question, on which the section focuses, is whether like is compared with like — whether observed differences can reasonably be attributed to a causal factor, or whether they may be 'written off' as due to the way that the comparison is made. For example, if we looked at the number of people in prison over time and correlated it with the number of people unemployed, we might want to conclude that unemployment causes an increase in crime. This may be true — there is some evidence to support such a proposition. It cannot be derived from the simple comparison of numbers in prison, however, without making some allowance for the growth in the size of the general population (which means that there are more people available to be sent to prison), and for any changes over time in police or court policy, or in the law, which made it more or less likely that someone who committed an offence would be apprehended, charged, brought before the court, convicted and sentenced to a term of imprisonment.

Sections 3 and 4 continue the examination of research designed to demonstrate causal influences. The basic logic of such research involves identifying one or more variables (aspects of the situation) as *independent* or *explanatory* variables, showing that when they are altered, the values of one or more *dependent* variables are also altered. Beyond this, the researcher needs also to be able to demonstrate that the changes *are* indeed due to the effects of the independent variable and not to something else in the situation which happened to be changing at the same time (*extraneous* variation). In the prison example in the last paragraph, for instance, the independent variable is the level of unemployment and the dependent variable is the extent of imprisonment. The extraneous variables which might have provided an alternative explanation for why rates of imprisonment varied include such factors as the efficiency of the police in detecting offenders, trends in the likelihood of their charging rather than cautioning them, the willingness of the courts to sentence people to imprisonment, and the state of the law on the use of imprisonment as a penalty.

A great deal of 'causal' or 'hypothesis-testing' research proceeds by comparing one group with another. An experiment, for example, consists in the comparison of people before and after treatment, and/or the comparison of a treated group with an untreated one. True experiments are comparatively rare in the social sciences, except in social psychology and as a means of evaluating small-scale changes of professional practice, but many other studies which compare 'naturally occurring' groups which differ in some respect are making use of the same kind of logic in their arguments.

Finally, in Section 5, we look at the essential part that comparison plays even in studies which might be seen as having the purpose of describing 'what is going on' rather than testing hypotheses about causal influences. It is argued that any competent description delineates an object or a situation by showing what it is like and what it is *not* like. When we describe something we do not reproduce it, but select or summarize particular aspects of it; reality is inexhaustible, and in describing it we abstract from reality. All descriptions are from a particular point of view, and usually the point of view is based on a comparison of some sort. For instance, when social anthropologists set out to describe 'the culture' of a society, they focus on certain aspects of it, the ones which are known to vary between societies: forms of economic organization, religious beliefs and institutions, the role of kinship, etc. The descriptions that are produced are based on an explicit or implicit comparison with other societies. Because most of the practitioners of social anthropology have until recently been European or North American, the primary comparison has tended to be with Western cultures. And because most social anthropologists are middle class by origin, when studies are carried out within Western culture the comparison point tends to be Western middle-class values and practices.

Another kind of comparison often involved in description involves reference to an implicit or explicit evaluative standard. For example, when Atkinson *et al.* (1985) provide a description of life in an Adult Training Centre, their description is structured in terms of a largely implicit standard of how things *ought* to be in such centres — based in turn on how things are 'outside'.

What comparative standard we adopt, and being aware of what standard we are adopting, is, of course, of considerable importance for the argument of a research paper. Different standards will necessarily produce different descriptions, and probably focus on different aspects of the phenomena studied. Even where the same aspects are being studied, the purpose of the description affects the standard of comparison and therefore the conclusions drawn. If we are interested in whether we have enough petrol in the car to get to Crewe, then we may describe the petrol can which we forgot to refill as 'empty'. If we are interested in our own safety, however, we handle it as if it is *not* empty — we do not expose it to naked flame, for example. So comparisons are made for a purpose. This unit is particularly concerned with comparisons made in order to identify causal influences or preconditions: with comparing groups in order to see why one differs from another in some interesting way. Comparison also lies at the heart of many studies which do not have this as an aim, however.

2   STANDARDIZING DATA

In all 'quantitative' research reports which go beyond describing populations in terms of the frequency of characteristics, comparison is the first stage of analysis. Simple tables are a form of comparison — comparing, for the same subjects, their position on two dimensions. For example, when we make up a table comparing two groups on different values of some variable (e.g. social class and preferred political party) we are trying to make points about, say, how the parties compare in terms of the class make-up of their voters. Comparisons are often, however, bedevilled by the fact of different group sizes: we are comparing, say, fifty labour voters out of a hundred with 65 conservative voters out of two hundred. We obviously need some way of *standardizing* our figures — getting over the fact, in this case, that they are derived from samples of different sizes — before we and the reader can readily grasp the point that is being made. Putting it another way, we need to be able to *compare like with like*, to control irrelevant differences so that the differences which are perceived are those which matter. This principle of *comparing like with like* is at the heart of the logic of comparison.

The simplest form of standardization, at which we looked very early in the course, is to express the data in the form of percentages — to eliminate sample size by expressing everything as if it were derived from a sample of a hundred. The strength of percentaging is that we can use it to express figures derived from groups of different sizes as if they came from groups of the same size, and thus comparison between groups is easy. Ratios or proportions could be used in the same way. We also use this kind of standardization routinely to look at changes over time — expressing figures as percentages of the value for a given year, or setting one year arbitrarily to equal 100 and looking at the other years in terms of percentage change. We can also use similar devices to 'get rid of' unwanted variation to reveal underlying trends. Economists routinely express their figures 'at constant prices', adding or subtracting the effects of inflation before or since a given year, so that we can see what has happened to types of income or spending without being confused by changes in amounts of money which are due to the inflation of the currency. Statistics of sales or unemployment are 'seasonally adjusted' as a matter of routine — the tendency for people to spend more at certain times of the year, or for jobs to be more available at some times of the year than others, is subtracted from the figures so that underlying trends can be seen.

Where the two variables to be compared are both measured on an integer or ratio scale (in other words, where four is twice two and the distance between 1 and 2 is the same as between 3 and 4), a more compact and in some ways neater way of expressing the same thing is through the *correlation coefficient* (r). This is a statistical device, a number which varies between +1 and −1, and it expresses the extent to which one variable predicts another. If high values on one variable perfectly predict high values on the other, and low values predict low values, then r will come out at or near +1.00. And if high values on one variable perfectly predict low values on the other, and low values predict high values, then r will come out at or near −1.00. If values on the first variable do not at all predict values on the other, then r will be zero. Values between zero and +1 or −1 mean a degree of association, the association being higher the further from zero the value of r. The correlation between two variables is called a *bivariate* or *zero-order r*. It is also possible to calculate a multiple correlation coefficient (R), which measures the extent to which a given variable is predicted by values on *several* other variables.

More complex forms of standardization are used for more complex problems to render figures from different years or different places comparable with each other. A major example of this is the *Standardized Mortality Ratio* (SMR), a form of standardization devised to offer a fair comparison of death-rates between different areas of the country. The death-rate in any given area is partly determined by the health risks in that area, partly by the quality of medical services provided, and partly by the area's demographic composition. More older people die each year, proportionately, than those in their middle years, and at any age men are statistically less likely to survive than women. Places like Bournemouth and Hastings, which are popular places for retirement, have a high crude death-rate (number of deaths per thousand of population) just because they have an elderly population. Therefore, to assess the effectiveness of the health services in such areas, it is necessary to *standardize*, to eliminate the effects of population structure so that like can be compared with like on an equitable basis. The SMR is calculated by working out, for each age-group and separately for each gender, the number of deaths that would be expected if the area in question had the same age and gender structure as the country as a whole. We can then take the actual number of deaths, divide it by this expected number of deaths, and multiply by 100 so that the resultant SMR will come out at 100 if the area has precisely the number of deaths that would be expected. A smaller number indicates a lower than average death-rate, controlling for the structure of the population, and a figure larger than 100 indicates a higher death-rate than would be expected.

Standardization is one important way in which the comparison of like with like is facilitated. What we gain from it are figures that can more validly be compared, and thus comparisons which can form more valid evidence in a chain of argument. There are also corresponding losses, however: every time we standardize, we lose information. Even in straightforward percentaging we lose information about the absolute size of each category, unless we also report the totals (percentages take samples of different sizes and render them comparable by reducing each total to a hundred). The same can be said of the SMR: by relating each area to the national average, it discards information about the actual rates at which deaths are occurring. (Two years will by definition have the same overall SMR nationwide — 100 — even if they differ greatly in the extent of death.) In assessing research designs and techniques, this is one aspect to which you will need to pay attention: whether they deliver what is needed for the purpose of the argument, and what information they discard or obscure in order to do so. This is one case of a general principle: that the strengths of each research design or technique or procedure are bought at the cost of corresponding weaknesses. In general, standardization has two weaknesses as a tool of argument:

1   It controls only those variables which are collected and used — the SMR, for example, controls for the effects of age and gender balance, but it does not control for social class or incidence of unemployment, both of which are known to be related to health status.

2   Once we have eliminated a variable by standardization, we cannot then use it in the argument — if the SMR did control for unemployment, we could not use it to contrast areas with different unemployment rates and look for effects on health.

2.1   A STUDY OF HEALTH AND MATERIAL DEPRIVATION

To round out this section and introduce the subject-matter of the next, let us consider an epidemiological study carried out in one Health Authority District (Abbott, 1988; Abbott *et al.*, 1992). It is intended to illustrate two kinds of research design — two ways in which figures may be compared in order to yield useful information. The 'subjects' of the paper are not individuals but wards (small geographical areas), and it compares figures on two indicators of social state — material deprivation (poverty etc.) and health status (death-rates and rates of chronic illness).

Material deprivation and health status are both 'concepts' — things which are not directly visible, but inferred from indicators which *are* visible — and they have to be operationalized for the sake of the research (that is, visible indicators have to be chosen which would be agreed to represent the concepts reasonably well). This study was carried out using 1981 Census small area statistics and health statistics available from the Office of Population Censuses and Surveys (OPCS), as the most readily available and the most reliable sources, though for this topic they have their limitations. Neither directly measures poverty: the census collects data about households from which poverty can be inferred, but it does not ask for any direct measure of income or wealth. There is also no good measure of morbidity (illness not amounting to death) in either, except for a question in the Census on whether the informant or others in his or her household is registered as permanently sick or disabled. The study followed earlier research and picked the following as indicators:

Material deprivation:

- Unemployment: from the Census, the proportion of employable adults in each ward who described themselves as unemployed.

- Car ownership: the percentage of private households in the ward without the use of a car.

- Home ownership: the percentage of private households in the ward not in owner occupation of their premises.

- Overcrowding: the percentage of private households with more than one person per room.

(The first, third and fourth of these have substantial face validity — they are fairly obvious measures of the concept, and plausible in themselves. The second, car ownership, is less immediately obvious, but it has appeared in other studies (e.g. Townsend *et al.*, 1986) to be a fairly good general indicator of household income levels.)

Health status:

- Mortality statistics: Standardized Mortality Ratios for each ward for deaths of persons aged 1–65 (i.e. number of deaths divided by the expected number if the ward's population were distributed in the same way in the UK as a whole in terms of age and gender), averaged over a five-year period (to eliminate chance fluctuations).

- Disablement: the proportion of residents in private households described in the Census as permanently sick or disabled.

- Infant mortality: the rate of infant deaths (aged less than 1 year) per thousand live births in a ward, averaged over a five-year period.

The first of these is a measure of 'avoidable' death rate — excluding older people, whose death rates would be expected to be higher whatever ward they lived in. The second is the only straightforward morbidity indicator in either source. The third is a measure of maternal health as well as of the health of infants — healthier infants are born to healthier mothers. All three are very similar to indicators used in earlier studies (e.g. Townsend *et al.*, 1986).

The Plymouth Health District, the subject of this study, was made up at this time of 85 wards, ranging from inner-city wards in Plymouth itself, through affluent suburbs, small country towns and rural wards close to towns, to rural wards remote from any sort of town and not well served by public transport. The indicators which were selected were already to some extent standardized for comparison — expressed as percentages or rates per thousand or, for mortality, as Standardized Mortality Ratios. Looking at the relationships between four indicators of deprivation and three indicators of health, however, would be a long and tedious job both for the analyst and for the reader of the report, so some way was needed of adding them together into two composite indexes — of material deprivation and of health status — which could then be compared quite straightforwardly.

Simply adding the figures together would obviously not produce meaningful results, so what the authors did was to use a process of standardization called *normalization*, to rate each ward on each indicator by how extreme its score was in comparison with the overall mean for the area. This draws on the mathematical properties of the 'normal curve' (see Figure 1), which you will meet again when you are looking at statistical analysis later in the course. This curve is the distribution of random numbers — any set of figures which vary randomly around a mean value. Some values will be on the mean, most will be quite close to it, but some will be further away from it; there will be fewer such cases, the further you travel from the mean. The normal curve is mathematically constructed so that a unit called a 'standard deviation' will mark out a given proportion of cases: two thirds of cases (roughly) will lie within plus or minus one standard deviation from the mean, 95 per cent within about plus or minus two standard deviations, and 99 per cent within about plus or minus 2.5 standard deviations. One way of comparing figures based on very different units therefore (percentage of households lacking some amenity, percentage of sick people, death rates) is to convert each to standard deviation units, so that all have the same mean and in principle the same spread around the mean.

Having scored each ward for each indicator in units which all signify the same thing — they all measure how extreme the ward is from the mean for the District as a whole — we are in a position to build composite indicators. The authors added together the scores for the four deprivation indicators to build a single Index of Material Deprivation, and the scores for the three health indicators were summed to build an Index of Health Status. As a final refinement, each of these was then normalized again: on each index, each ward's score was expressed as a distance in standard deviations from the District mean for the Index. This made it possible to put an interpretation on the size of the scores. If the scores were randomly distributed, then 95 per cent of them should lie within about plus or minus two standard deviations from the mean, and 99 per cent within about plus or minus 2.5 standard deviations. If there were many figures greater than this, then they could reasonably be interpreted as more extreme than one would expect by chance alone.

What was found was as follows:

1   On both Indices the majority of wards fell roughly within a normal distribution pattern, compatible with random distribution of the traits, but more wards were extreme on the positive side (poor health status, high material deprivation) than could reasonably be expected by chance.

2   There was a marked tendency for the wards with the highest scores on material deprivation also to have the worst scores on health status, and for the least deprived wards to have the best health scores.

3   Overall the two Indices yielded a correlation coefficient of 0.64, indicating that they shared around forty per cent of their variance. In other words, allowing for the crudity of the measures used, health status is predictable to a very substantial degree from level of material deprivation.

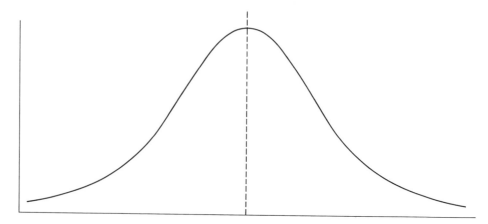

Figure 1   *The normal curve*

Maps 1–4 illustrate the location of the best and worst 17 wards (one fifth of the total wards) on the Index of Material Deprivation and the Index of Health Status. The degree of overlap between the two should be readily apparent.

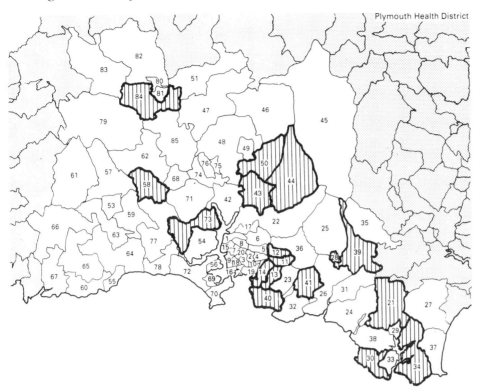

Map 1 *Plymouth Health District: 17 wards with the lowest Deprivation Index scores*
(Source: Abbott et al., 1992, p.142)

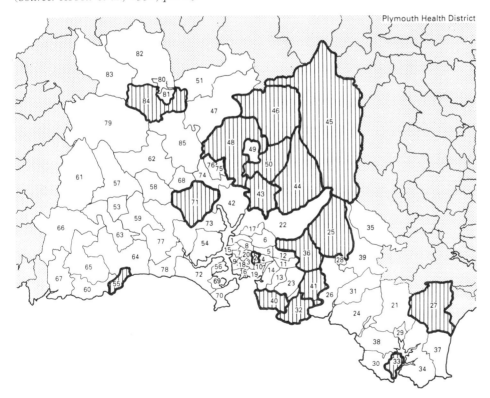

Map 2 *Plymouth Health District: 17 wards with the best Health Index scores*
(Source: Abbott et al., 1992, p.143)

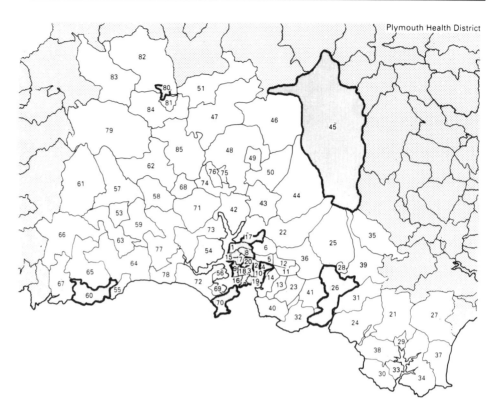

Map 3   *Plymouth Health District: 17 wards with the highest Deprivation Index scores*
(Source: Abbott et al., *1992, p.144)*

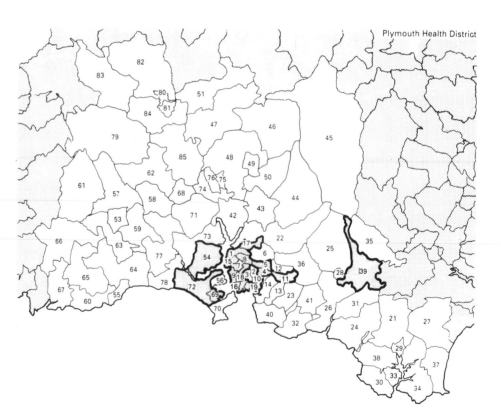

Map 4   *Plymouth Health District: 17 wards with the worst Health Index scores*
(Source: Abbott et al., *1992, p.145)*

As a further stage of analysis, the authors of this study looked separately at the urban and rural wards within the Plymouth District, and an intriguing pattern emerged. Among the urban wards the two Indices show a high correlation. Looking at the rural wards by themselves, however, the correlation decreases to such an extent that the association might be a product of chance alone. One possible explanation could be that material deprivation is *not* predictive of health status in rural areas. This is a logical possibility, but it does not seem plausible on the face of it. More probably, the authors suggest, one or both of two other explanations should be accepted, both of which are criticisms of the methods of the study:

1   The indicators, particularly of deprivation, may not be as appropriate in rural areas as in urban ones. For example, car ownership may be a good indicator of income in urban areas, but in rural areas it is an economic necessity for anyone who wishes to travel more than a mile or so to work, however poor, in the absence of public transport.

2   The census ward may not be an appropriate unit of analysis in rural areas. The ward is determined in part by population size, and in towns the wards are geographically fairly small and therefore stand some chance of being socially homogeneous. In rural areas, the wards have to be geographically larger to 'capture' the same number of inhabitants, which increases the chances of there being wards inhabited by both affluent and impoverished people.

Both of these conclusions rest on comparisons between one set of scores and another, and both stand up only to the extent that the scores come from groups which are comparable with each other. We shall be looking at how comparisons between groups are structured as part of research arguments in the sections which follow. It is worth pausing at this point, however, to think about the two sorts of comparisons which are being made in this study, and how they differ. One may argue that in one of them the groups whose scores are being compared are 'naturally' more comparable than in the other.

ACTIVITY 1

Look back over the description of the study and see what 'logics of comparison' are being employed and how they function within the argument leading to the conclusions. What is being compared with what, (a) to establish that material deprivation and health status are associated (and therefore to suggest that the one may be a cause of the other), and (b) to show that material deprivation does not predict health status as well in rural areas as in urban ones? Why do I describe one of the comparisons as being stronger than the other?

3   COMPARING GROUPS

The study we have just been considering uses 'public data' to examine the relationship of health and material deprivation in one health area. (It is worth remembering, in a course which necessarily spends a lot of time talking about studies which collect fresh data, that a great deal of research can be done using data which have already been collected — the 'secondary' use of official surveys and official administrative statistics.) The overall design is a *same subjects* comparison — charting the extent to which high values of 'material deprivation' predict poor health status, and the extent to which the materially advantaged areas also enjoy good health. In terms of overall distribution it was discovered that there were no *exceptionally* prosperous areas but that at the poorer end of the dimension a group of areas could be identified which were as materially disadvantaged as the worst areas of London.

Overall there was a good degree of correlation between health status and material deprivation, suggesting a causal connection. You can never *prove* causation in this kind of study — there could always be some other (unmeasured) factor responsible for both material deprivation and health status. For example, there could be class-related eating habits, as a health minister was suggesting at the end of the 1980s, so that poorer people (clustered in the wards which show high material deprivation) could tend towards ill-health because of poorly planned diet. However, while correlation is not *sufficient* for causation, it is *necessary* for it — if there is no correlation, there can be no possibility of a causal connection.

There is little problem in same-subject designs of comparing like with like; it is the same subjects who form both sides of the comparison. One hesitation about interpreting the results was raised in the paper, however, and this stems from the fact that the 'subjects' of this study are not individuals, but wards. It is very likely that the individuals who are materially deprived are also the individuals who suffer poor health, but this is an assumption, not a necessary consequence of the design of the study. It is conceivable, again, that there could be some third factor impelling people who suffer poor health to live in materially deprived areas even if they are not themselves materially deprived. This danger in making inferences from data about areas to conclusions about people is called *the ecological fallacy*. It would be a case of the ecological fallacy, for example, if we concluded from the fact that there are more escapes from Category D ('open') prisons than Category A ('maximum security') ones, and that there are more 'respectable' criminals (e.g. people in for embezzlement from their firms) in Category D prisons than Category A ones, that embezzlers are a category highly likely to escape. There are indeed more escapes from prisons housing embezzlers than from other kinds of prisons, but it is quite simply not the embezzlers who escape. The term 'ecological fallacy' was coined to describe research in the United States into the correlation of 'race' and intelligence. Using states as the 'unit of analysis', there appeared to be a substantial negative correlation between 'being black' and 'scoring high on intelligence tests': those states with the highest proportion of black population also had the lowest mean IQ score. It was found, however, that if the research was replicated using smaller areas — e.g. counties, or parts of counties — the correlation decreased, and when researchers compared *individuals'* intelligence scores with whether they were black or not the correlation disappeared entirely. In other words, there is no observable correlation between 'race' and intelligence. (The mediating variable was poverty. There is an observable correlation between the poverty of parents and the measured intelligence of their children; the tests are not independent of the effects of schooling, and poor children tend to get less schooling and to fit less well into the school system. Those states with the highest proportion of black population also had the highest incidence of poverty.)

The second comparison in the study — between rural and urban areas — is a *between groups* comparison. That is, the rural wards as a group were compared with the urban wards as a group, and it was discovered that material deprivation predicted poor health status in the latter but not the former, suggesting that the causal relationship did not hold in rural areas. As we saw, however, this conclusion was not tenable: there were at least two extraneous factors, confounding differences between the groups, that could have produced the result.

3.1   THE CONNECTICUT CRACKDOWN

The classic and most often quoted 'between groups' study, capitalizing on changes in the 'real world' rather than changes introduced by a researcher, was 'The Connecticut Crackdown', a drastic public programme reinforcing police action on excessively fast driving, on which a secondary analysis of published figures was carried out by Donald Campbell (Campbell, 1969; Campbell and Ross, 1968). After an unprecedentedly bad year for traffic fatalities, the governor of Connecticut introduced a programme of administrative orders which made it more certain that drivers who drove excessively fast would be caught and, if caught, punished. The net result compared with the year before was roughly a 12 per cent decrease in traffic fatalities in the state. This action as it stands has many of the qualities of the

Pre-test ⟶ Treatment ⟶ Post-test

Figure 2 *A diagrammatic representation of simple action research*

simplest kind of *action research*, where the researchers/practitioners introduce some kind of change and monitor its effects (except that in this case it was the governor of Connecticut, not the researchers, who introduced the change). Figure 2 represents this type of research diagrammatically. In this case, there were 324 traffic fatalities in the year before the Crackdown, and 284 in the year after it.

Do you see any problems with this line of argument? Stop and think about alternative explanations for the results.

Several problems occurred to Campbell, but most of them were answerable by further analysis.

1   There could have been a *trend effect* — the figures could have been going down over the years in any case — coupled with a *regression effect*. (*Regression to the mean* is the technical term for what happens when you look at figures which fluctuate a long way from an underlying mean or trend. Because there *is* a mean or trend, it is very likely that any other figure from the series with which you compare the extreme one will depart *less* extremely from the mean. You will remember that the Crackdown was instituted because of unprecedented levels of death.) To explore this we need to compare figures over a longer period of time than just two years, which is what Campbell did (Figure 3). As you can see from Figure 3, there is no obvious overall trend which would explain the decrease in 1956: the figures tend upwards to 1955, and consistently downwards since 1956.

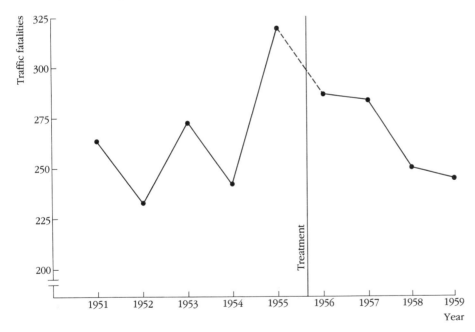

Figure 3 *Connecticut traffic fatalities, 1951–1959*
(Source: Campbell, 1969, Figure 2)

Note further that:

2   There was a possibility that recording practices had changed — e.g. by police being less willing to attribute road deaths to speeding. The mere fact of introducing a public programme could have an effect on the record-keeping as well as the driving. (This would be the human equivalent of unreliability in a measuring instrument.) Such an effect may well have occurred, and the research design is powerless to guard against it.

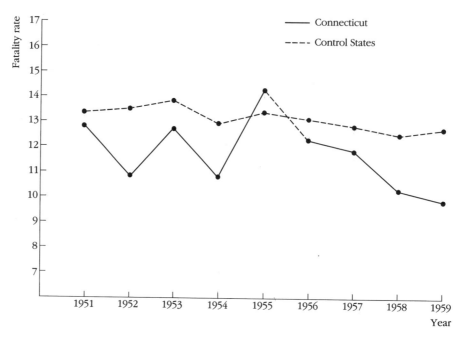

Figure 4 *Control series design comparing Connecticut fatalities with those of four comparable states*

(Source: Campbell, 1969, Figure 11)

3   This is a special case of an *alternative explanation* for results — attributing the effects not to the posited cause, but to some other factor which was active over the same period. Many other factors could have explained a drop in deaths: changed weather, changes in petrol prices, changes in drinking behaviour — anything, in fact, which might change driving behaviour. The design of the study was elaborated to cover this possibility, however, by the introduction of a *control condition* — a set of figures from four comparable states, over the same period, where the Crackdown had *not* taken place. Traffic fatalities in these states failed to show the downward trend visible in Connecticut (Figure 4), and therefore it is unlikely that any of these factors were responsible for the decrease.

This use of comparisons between a 'treated group' and a 'control group' is a regular feature of studies which attempt to show the causal force of treatments, and it is a very strong one. To the extent that the control and treatment groups are alike before treatment, and only the treatment group is treated, if they differ after the treatment the difference must logically be attributable to the treatment. Diagrammatically, this kind of design may be represented by Figure 5.

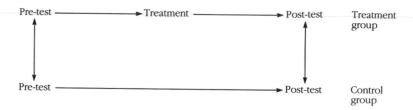

Figure 5 *Diagrammatic representation of comparative research between a treated group and a control group*

The measurements for the two groups will seldom be identical before the treatment, but what we are really interested in is the difference between pre-test and post-test measurements. In Figure 4, for example, the treatment group shows a marked decline from the point of the treatment while the control group does not.

Can this design cope with the problem of changes in recording practice listed in point 2 above?

The use of a control group does not eliminate factors confounded with the treatment. If there were changes in recording practice in the Connecticut case, for example, these would be specific to the treatment group and could not affect the control group, so the presence of a control group does not eliminate them. What it does make less likely is that a factor *independent of the treatment* was the cause of the decrease in fatalities.

We might usefully distinguish, at this point, between *design control* and *statistical control* as means of trying for the same validity of argument. Controlling for alternative explanations in terms of factors independent of the supposed explanatory variable by means of control or comparison groups is an example of *design control*. Figures are collected in such a way that observed differences between treatment and control groups must be due to some characteristic of the treatment group, not something that might be characteristic of both. (If the design is entirely successful, that characteristic must be the treatment itself, not something else which might simultaneously be characteristic of the treatment group.) In *statistical control*, on the other hand, control is effected at the analysis stage, by how the figures are handled. If there were big differences in social class composition between Connecticut and the states used as a comparison group, for example, we could have controlled for them at the analysis stage by adding both groups together, looking for a correlation of social class with traffic fatalities irrespective of state, and seeing whether it appeared to provide a better explanation than 'being in Connecticut' (where the Crackdown took place).

ACTIVITY 2

Think again about the health and deprivation study which we outlined in Section 2.1. What kinds of control form part of the argument? (Look back at this section again if you need to.)

The major design control in the paper is the 'same subject' design, comparing health status in wards with material deprivation in the same wards. This necessarily constitutes a comparison of like with like: it is the same places that are being compared on the two variables.

The examination of the differences in predictability between rural and urban areas is an example of *statistical control*. Having established a relationship between material deprivation and health status, we wanted to see if type of location made a marked difference to it. One of the things we found was that health status was much less predictable from our measures of material deprivation in rural than in urban areas. So we controlled for rural/urban location by examining the results for each type of location separately, and we found that our conclusions held up unambiguously only for the urban wards.

The extensive use of standardization techniques in the paper — standardized mortality ratios, normalized figures — shows features of both kinds of control. It proceeds by statistical means, eliminating the effects of extraneous variables, such as population size and/or composition, by adjusting the figures. On the other hand, the control is built into the original design of the project, not imposed after the event because it is demanded by the argument. In general, statistical control proceeds by (a) collecting information, for all cases, about possible alternative explanations for the expected causal effect, and (b) looking at the analysis stage to see if one of these plausible alternatives has a larger effect than the posited main cause, or interacts with the main cause to determine the pattern of results. Studies of 'natural differences' (differences not created by the researchers), which you will come across in the literature, are often weaker than you might expect in this respect, leaving you asking why a particular form of control was not attempted.

The limitations that we noted for standardization to control for inequalities on extraneous variables hold also for statistical control: we can only control for variables which we collect and which are believed to be important. Some group comparisons suffer from the same limitation: if the groups are explicitly matched on 'important variables', we cannot tell what other variables might have been important (except to the extent that we can anticipate them, collect them, and control for them statistically).

ACTIVITY 3

You should now refresh your memory by looking again at 'Health visitors' and social workers' perceptions of child care', by Robert Dingwall and Susan Fox, reproduced in Offprints Booklet 2. Look at the way that naturally occurring groups are compared, and at the application in the study of the principles outlined above. Note also what has been done in the way of statistical control.

The paper makes a straightforward 'between groups' comparison of health visitors and social workers. These two groups differ in a range of ways, of course, not just in the profession to which they belong, and not much is said about statistical control in the paper. Control analyses *were* carried out. The report of them is hidden at the end of the 'Respondents' section:

> Details about age, sex, child-rearing experience, and data of professional qualification were collected. The social workers were younger ..., more likely to be male ... and to have child-rearing experience. ... None of these showed any significant association with the ratings.
>
> (Dingwall and Fox, 1986, p.126)

However, there is no control for social class of origin, which might have been interesting given research suggesting that child-rearing practices and attitudes of child-rearing differ between the social classes.

4   EXPERIMENTAL RESEARCH

READING

You should now read 'Treatment of depressed women by nurses in Britain and the USA', by Verona Gordon, reproduced in Offprints Booklet 2. Look to see to what extent the design principles outlined above are present in the paper. Look also to see what important *differences* in design you detect between this paper and the other studies in this unit.

Gordon's paper follows the clean lines of the comparative design which we examined above and represented by means of Figure 5. One group of subjects received the treatment; the other, picked to be similar to the first, did not; both were tested before and after treatment was applied to one.

The study differs, however, from those we have already looked at in this unit in two important respects:

1   The researcher had control of the treatment. In the study by Abbott *et al.* (1992) of health and deprivation, and in the analysis of data about the Connecticut Crackdown, the researchers were studying 'naturally occurring' variation. In the one study a legal/administrative change was instituted by a State

Governor. In the other, areas differed in their material state and the authors sought to correlate this difference with their health status. In Gordon's paper, on the other hand, the treatment is initiated by the researcher: it is she who determines what it shall be and how it shall run. You might want to argue that Dingwall and Fox also had control over the research procedures — they administered a questionnaire of their own devising. However, the important 'treatment' — the difference between the groups — was that one consisted of health visitors and the other of social workers, and this was a naturally occurring difference.

2   The similarity of the groups can to a large extent be guaranteed. In all the other papers, the researchers had to 'make do' with naturally occurring dimensions of difference, putting up with whatever alternative explanations might be confounded with the dimension of difference. Campbell and his colleagues had to argue quite carefully and extensively for the validity of the comparison of Connecticut with the four 'control states' — the extent to which the states used for the comparison were really comparable with the state where the 'treatment' occurred. Dingwall and Fox compare groups which differ not only in their profession and professional socialization, but also in gender balance, education, probably social class, remuneration, and a whole range of other plausible alternative explanations.

In the paper by Gordon (1986), however, a sample is assembled and people are assigned at random to treatment and control groups. This maximizes the chances that anything of importance will be equally distributed in the two groups and that they will therefore be comparable in all respects.

(Random allocation is the preferred means for allocating informants to treatment and control groups because it maximizes the chance that *everything* — even characteristics which the researcher has not thought to measure — will be equally distributed between the two groups. If the groups are small, however, randomization does not always have the desired effect. In a sample which is equally split between men and women, for example, if you allocated people at random to one of two groups of 10, the chances of getting many more of one gender than the other in a given group are calculable and surprisingly large. Here, where groups are small and a given characteristic is known to be important, we might well use a *matching* procedure for allocation — selecting pairs who did not differ on the desired characteristics and allocating one of each pair at random to the treatment group and the other to the control. This would entail a risk that the groups differed significantly on variables which it did not occur to us to use for matching and which turned out to have important consequences, but at least we would know that our two groups were comparable on the variables which we *had* used for matching — within the limits of measurement error.)

The difference between Gordon's paper (1986) and the others you have read here is that Gordon's study is *experimental* while the others use at best a *quasi-experimental* design (to use Campbell's term). An *experiment* (also called a *controlled trial* in the medical world) is defined as a study in which:

1   the allocation to treatment and control conditions is under the control of the researcher and can be arranged to maximize the likelihood of having comparable groups; and

2   the treatment is under the control of the researcher and can be arranged to minimize the likelihood of other alternative explanatory factors being confounded with its effects.

What do you see as the advantages of experimental over quasi-experimental designs? Are there corresponding disadvantages?

The same logic underlies both kinds of study. The advantage of experimental designs is that the logic is more clearly applied, eliminating a greater number of possible alternative explanations by the *design* of the study. If you measure the state of a group of people, administer a treatment, produce measurable changes *and can guarantee that no factor other than the treatment could have produced the effect*, then you are on strong grounds in arguing that the treatment produced the effect — indeed, logically it *must* have done so. Quasi-experimental studies which capitalize on existing differences between people and/or their circumstances can never quite offer this guarantee: there are always other potential explanatory factors which might have produced the observed effect. The best you can do, by means of statistical controls at the analysis stage, is to explore and eliminate those which occurred to you and on which you therefore collected data.

Five major disadvantages or weaknesses in experimental designs occur to me:

1   It is not possible, even in principle, to *guarantee* that no factor other than the treatment could produce the effect. You can control for what you know to be important, by the design of the study or by statistical control after the event, and you can use randomization techniques to try to even out any other differences between groups, but you can never be *sure* that you have succeeded.

2   The ethical status of manipulations carried out by the researcher can often be in doubt. The extent to which it is permissible to make changes in people's lives for the sake of testing the efficacy of a treatment or the causal force of an environmental condition may often be doubted. The ethics of *withholding* a treatment where it might have improved someone's life, in order to form a control group, are equally dubious.

3   Some factors cannot be manipulated. Studies of gender, class, age, etc. will always have to be at most quasi-experimental, because we cannot allocate people to different conditions of them: we cannot determine that a given subject shall be male or female, middle class or working class, but must accept them as what they are with all the associated baggage of socialization, home background, structural circumstances and public reaction. (We can *simulate* the effects of the naturally occurring variable — dressing up actors as working or middle class, for example — but this is not quite the same.)

4   Even where the explanatory variable under consideration does lend itself to manipulation and to the allocation of people to one condition or another, the same ethical considerations may require us to confine ourselves to a fairly small manipulation, and this may trivialize what we are studying. Research on depression can all too easily finish up looking at what makes people temporarily happy or unhappy, for example.

5   An added factor about experiments is that they are often very obviously 'research', and this could provide an alternative explanation of any results. If people know they are 'being researched', this by itself can change their behaviour or attitudes. 'Being in an experiment' is a social situation — one with different rules from those of 'normal life', and one with whose rules most participants are familiar at least in outline. (Note that this is not a *necessary* disadvantage of experimental designs. It is possible to run an experiment on people without their knowing that it is running — but the ethics of doing so, again, may be seen as debatable. Note also that it is not a disadvantage which is specific to experiments. Although experimental research is most at risk of creating an artificial situation which determines people's response to it, the same problem is faced by all varieties of research.)

4.1   STUDIES OF LEARNED HELPLESSNESS

So much for the single experiment. Quite often in books and research papers you will find descriptions of a whole series of experiments — a programme planned by one research team, or studies by different people — which together add up to a complex conclusion. The ideal experiment may be impossible, even in principle, because not every confounded or alternative explanatory variable can be excluded in a single design, but sometimes a *series* of experiments can get some way towards this ideal. As an example we might take the rather unsavoury 'learned helplessness' experiments of the 1960s and 1970s, the beginnings of which are described in Martin Seligman's book *Helplessness* (1975). Working on a problem in learning theory, Seligman and his colleagues had occasion to run two particular kinds of experiment one after the other, with the same experimental animals (dogs), with intriguing results. In the first experiment, dogs were 'set up' in sets of three. The first, in the 'active' condition, was restrained (in a kind of hammock) and subjected to electric shocks. Panels were lined up close to the dog's nose, and the dog soon learned that pressing one of the panels with the nose turned off the electric shocks. The second dog, in the 'passive' condition, would be similarly restrained, but nothing it did would affect the duration or timing of the shocks; shocks started for it when they started for the 'active' dog and stopped when the 'active' dog turned them off (and it therefore received precisely the same shocks as the active dog). The third or 'control' condition was to control for the experimental procedure of being restrained; dogs in this condition were tied up in a similar manner but received no shocks at all. In the second treatment, all the dogs were placed in a divided field, and a mild electric shock was administered to the half in which they were. Dogs from the 'active' or 'control' condition rapidly learned to avoid this shock by jumping a low barrier. Some dogs from the 'passive' condition, however, never did learn to avoid the shocks. The stimulus was obviously painful, as judged from their behaviour, but they tended to curl up and whimper or whine, rather than seek active remedy.

Seligman's eventual conclusion was that these dogs had learned a higher-order proposition in the face of inescapable aversive stimulation: that they were *not able* to change the unpleasant experience by their own actions. This conclusion was subject to a large range of possible alternative explanations, however, and to a true behaviourist/learning theorist the notion of dogs learning higher-order propositions was inherently implausible for theoretical reasons. Several further experiments were needed to eliminate obvious alternatives. In one, for example, the experimenters distinguished between behavioural intention (emission of nervous impulse) and the actual behaviour, by administering small doses of a drug which did not deaden nervous conduction but made it impossible for the dog actually to move its nose; they simultaneously altered the equipment so that shock was turned off when certain nerves were activated. In another and perhaps more subtle experiment the turning off of shock was made contingent on *not* moving the nose for a predetermined number of seconds — something the dogs in the 'active' condition learned quite quickly (Maier, 1970). The process was shown to generalize to other species of animals, and to hold for true learning skills rather than instinctual or over-learned and reflexive responses (Maier *et al.*, 1972; Seligman *et al.*,1971). Many of the learned helplessness results were shown to hold for the human species as well, using loud noise or unsolvable puzzles as the inescapable aversive 'treatment' (Hiroto, 1974; Glass and Singer, 1972; Geer *et al.*, 1970). It was pointed out that there were parallels between the behaviour of the animals and what humans suffering from clinical depression say about their lives and abilities (Beck, 1967; Melges and Bowlby, 1969), and some experimental evidence for the connection began to emerge (Gatchel *et al.*, 1975; Wener and Rehm, 1975).

Thus the argument rests not on a single experiment, but on a whole series. Some of these experiments eliminate alternative explanations as conceived within the 'paradigm' in which the theory has been cast. Some begin to fish outside it, to translate an interesting side-branch of animal-learning theory into a useful tool for dealing with human depression. In so doing, the theoretical framework and underlying assumptions are changed, and the whole paradigm comes to be cast much more in terms of human beliefs and much less in terms of animal learning (Roth, 1980; Abramson *et al.*, 1978, 1980; Sapsford, 1983).

Another useful and well-known example of an experimental programme is Milgram's work on obedience in the 1960s. In his original study, Milgram (1963) set up a situation in which people would accept the task of 'teacher', administering a 'learning machine' which appeared to give electric shocks to the 'pupils' attached to it. The 'teachers' administered a shock to the 'pupil' whenever a wrong response (or no response) was made in a learning task, on a scale which increased from a setting marked 'slight shock' up to one marked 'danger — severe shock'. Beforehand, a panel of students were asked to predict what the subject would do, and they predicted that very few indeed would progress beyond 'very strong shock'. In fact about two thirds of the subjects, with some encouragement from the experimenter, went up to the highest possible setting, despite signs of extreme agitation and even apparent cessation of response on the part of the 'pupil'. (What the 'teachers' did not know was that the 'pupil' was in fact a confederate of the experimenter, and in reality no shocks at all were being administered.)

By itself, this study does not in fact constitute an experiment. Why not?

The dependent variable, obedience, is measured by the degree of shock that the 'teacher' was prepared to administer. The independent variable is the degree of authority attributable to the experimenter — in this case a research psychologist from a prestigious university, with the experiment happening on the premises of that university. The study fails to satisfy the requirements of an experiment because no comparison is involved: we have no idea, therefore, whether it is the degree of authority or some other aspect of the situation, or something inherent in the particular 'teachers', or in all people, which led the response. We can see that more or greater shocks were administered than had been predicted, but we cannot see much more. In a series of later studies, however, the independent variable was varied systematically (see Milgram, 1974): conducting the study in rented property in the city instead of at the university, letting the experimenter have no apparent connection with the university, and generally weakening the claim to 'authority' on the part of the experimenter. The programme of studies adds up to one large experiment in which the independent variable, authority, is systematically varied, to see the effect on the resulting degree of obedience. The degree of compliance decreased in the ways and to about the extent that was predicted.

ACTIVITY 4

The logic of the experiment appears to have a very clear and indisputable form of research logic: if we have two identical groups, administer a treatment to one and not the other, control all other possible differences, and produce a difference in outcome, then the outcome must have been due to the treatment. There are still problems, however. Think back to what you read in Block 1 and see if you can identify them.

The weakness of 'experimental logic' as outlined here is that it omits to consider part of the context of the argument.

- First, we have tended to describe the procedure here as if experiments provide proof of theories, but we saw in Block 1 that this is not a logically sound way of looking at them. *At best* they can provide *dis*proof of theories, or fail to provide disproof and thereby offer some confirmation. Block 1 suggested that even the notion that they provide irrefutable *dis*proof is suspect.

- Second, the logic of experiments argues from cause to effect via control of other variables. In many cases, however, the argument that other variables have been controlled, or are not related and may be ignored, will itself rest on a body of theoretical assumptions, and these are not tested by a given experiment but taken for granted. Thus, where an apparent disproof is produced, we shall not know whether the fault is in the theory being tested or in one of the assumptions being taken for granted.

- Finally, and perhaps most importantly, what the variables mean is not something measured, but something interpreted on the basis of a whole body of theory. Again, if a negative finding is produced, we shall not know whether the fault is in the theory under test or in the wider body of theories which define the situation and the meaning of what is being measured.

We might then go on, stimulated by these two experimental programmes, to question experimental research from another important angle — that of its ethics. To what extent are we prepared to acquire our knowledge at the expense of dogs to which electric shocks are applied, or human beings who are led to think they have administered dangerous electric shocks to other human beings? If the 'pay-off' were very great, perhaps this might be acceptable, or at least there would be some basis for argument in its favour. This was certainly Milgram's position in defending his own work — that the American public needed to know that such behaviour was not something specific to Nazis in Germany, but could be induced in ordinary Americans by constructing the circumstances that elicited it. The defence of Seligman's work might be its value for learning theory on the one hand and the fact that it has led to a greater understanding of clinical depression on the other. The doubt remains, however. It is a perennial ethical problem of research into medical or psychiatric treatments, for example, or into new and efficient ways of schooling, that their efficacy can best be demonstrated by applying them to one group of people and withholding them from another.

The ethical problems of research which causes pain or distress to its subjects or informants are not confined to experimental research, although they tend to be most obvious there. One may reasonably ask, for example, whether it is justified to cause distress to people who have suffered in the past by opening up the areas of their suffering and exploring them in interview, simply 'to pursue the truth'. External examiners of courses in conventional learning institutions frequently ask whether students who explored areas such as AIDS or sexual abuse for their end-of-year projects had legitimate access to the area — e.g. by already doing counselling work in it — or whether they were just trading on human misery in order to do an exciting third-year project. The whole question of the use of people and their experiences as 'research fodder' — the treatment of people as objects by researchers — has been opened up in recent years by, for example, feminist theorists (as you will remember from the extract by Mies (1983), which you read in Block 1).

5   USING COMPARISONS TO DRAW BOUNDARIES

So far we have looked at 'quantitative' studies — research which yields data in the form of numbers to be analysed by means of comparison. The logic of comparison also has a large part to play, however, in 'qualitative' studies — ones where the data are in the form of people's words or the researcher's descriptions of what he or she has observed and experienced. When we are analysing interviews or texts for what is said in them, for instance, rather than reducing them in some way to numbers for statistical analysis, we proceed by making comparisons between segments of material — within interviews or observation sessions, and between them. Comparison may also be an underlying element of the *design* of such a study.

For example, in 'Leaving it to Mum', by Pamela Abbott and Roger Sapsford (1987), which you read in Unit 5, an essential feature of the design is the comparison between mothers whose children were labelled 'mentally handicapped' (as the terminology was at the time) and others whose children were not so labelled. To the extent that the two groups of informants were similar so that like was being compared with like (and some pains were taken to make them so, within the resources available), the comparison between them was an important part of the 'logic of argument' of the study. If you describe the lives of *mothers who have children with learning difficulties*, you are necessarily at the same time describing *mothers with children*; the two are inevitably confounded. It is only by having a group of mothers whose children do *not* have learning difficulties that you can draw more specific conclusions with any degree of validity. What the two groups have in common will be what is true of 'having children', but the areas in which they differ will be aspects specific to 'having children with learning difficulties'. The presence of a comparison group acts to draw a boundary around the conclusions, enabling the researcher to say what is true of the larger group and what holds only for the target group.

ACTIVITY 5

If you do not remember how the comparison group functioned in 'Leaving it to Mum', by Abbott and Sapsford, you should quickly re-read that article now (see Offprints Booklet 2).

This kind of use of a comparison group is a special case of a more general principle of qualitative design. For clarification, let us look at a fictional example. (Fictional studies are generally better designed than real ones, being unconstrained by time, fatigue, money and the problems of access.) Suppose we had an interest in why girls tend not to go into science and mathematics at school, except for biology, and to be over-represented in the arts and humanities subjects. We have done our reading and have as 'foreshadowed ideas' the notion that the reason is something to do with the attitudes and behaviour of teachers, or of parents, or of boys in mixed classes, or of the girls themselves. Vague as our initial foreshadowed ideas are, we put them to one side and spend some time exploring the field in a relatively unfocused way, watching and listening to classes, attending to what goes on in the playground and the canteen, visiting homes, hanging around places where young people go in the evenings, and so on. (Already we have used a form of sampling — sampling of the range of contexts in which young people are active and express and learn their ideas.) Gathering data, we progressively focus our original vague question down into something more concrete and explorable. We find, let us say, that among working-class girls it is difficult to say what puts them off the sciences and mathematics, because everything seems to push in the same direction — teachers, parents, friends and boyfriends all seem to express surprise or distaste for a girl becoming involved in the sciences. Among middle-class girls, however, we might find that the parents and the teachers are positively supportive of any interests they might have in the sciences. Their friends, however, and particularly their male friends, seem to treat them as something strange if they opt for the sciences. We have a tentative model of what is going on, therefore: something in the 'boy/girl culture' is having the effect of making some curriculum choices more attractive than others.

The example we are considering is cast in terms of 'open' or 'relatively unstructured' techniques — participant observation, relatively unstructured interviewing, etc. The same principles hold for any kind of study, however, and we might well have gone through the same *kinds* of stages if we had adopted a structured survey approach asking predetermined questions or observing and counting predetermined behaviours, and even in a programme of experimentation. Indeed, there would be great merit in *combining* the relatively unstructured techniques with something more structured. At minimum we would want to collect demographic variables systematically — age, gender, background, educational history, etc. We might have wanted to go further and use early results to construct a structured list of questions which could feasibly be administered to a much larger population than we could afford to reach by relatively unstructured methods, or to identify key phrases or ways of behaving and count them systematically in widely sampled settings. As we have seen, a programme of experiments may also focus itself progressively from one theoretical position to a much sharper and more plausible one (with more evidence that alternative explanations have no force), or even transmute itself into the ambit of a different theoretical paradigm.

A first stage of drawing boundaries would be to sample classes which were very similar to the one we used initially — probably other classes in the same school. If the model fits them as well, then it has at least some generality; if it does not, there was something idiosyncratic about the particular class with which we started. Let us say that it does turn out to have some generality. We should then want to sample more widely, to see *how much* generality it has. Does it hold for other classes in the same city, or is it school-specific? Does it hold for other regions, or is it an expression of a particular regional culture? Does it hold for other English-speaking countries, or is it specific to England? Each of these comparisons is an attempt to see how widely the idea generalizes — to find the boundaries within which an idea is useful, or the conditions under which a theory holds.

Finally, we might want to start testing particular ideas and assumptions by careful sampling of unlikely milieux. Our tentative model is beginning to be cast in terms of a Western, English-speaking 'culture of femininity', let us say. Does it hold, therefore, in schools where the predominant 'culture of femininity' has a potentially different origin? We could test this by finding schools where the majority of the students are of West Indian or Asian origin and seeing whether the same model holds. Above all, our tentative model is about the interaction of the genders, so a very interesting 'crucial case' would be to see what goes on at single-sex schools. If the matter is determined simply by the interaction of the genders, then the model should not be useful in single-sex schools. Suppose, however, that we found that girls who went into science and mathematics were seen differently from others even within single-sex girls' schools. Suppose we found that the way that they are seen is similar to how boys in single-sex boys' schools are seen when they choose these subjects, and that the 'arts-and-humanities' crowd carried its own stereotype in both mixed and single-sex schools. This might be a reason for major revision of the tentative model. It *could* still be gender-related: there could still be 'masculine' and 'feminine' stereotypes, with the cross-gender roles taken by people of inappropriate gender if no one more appropriate was available. In that case we might expect wider stereotyping — that these people acquired inappropriate sex-linked stereotypes outside the field of their academic choices. It might be that we were quite mistaken, and gender is not the determining variable that we were inclined to assume it was. It could be that the influence of parents or boyfriends outside the school is greater than we had supposed. Whatever the case, we would have further research to do before we could come to a satisfactory model of what was going on.

In other words, without a carefully constructed basis of comparison we should not be able to say precisely what it is that has been found out. We cannot say what is specific to girls in schools without contrasting them with boys, nor say whether it is specific to the mixing of boys and girls without contrasting mixed schools with single-sex ones. In the paper by Abbott and Sapsford (1987), which you read earlier, the authors specify what is specific to mothers of children with learning difficulties by contrasting them with other mothers (at the time, a surprisingly rare thing to do in this kind of research). In Milgram's work we cannot tell what is due to 'authority' until we have varied the degree of authority systematically. We could almost say that without a basis of comparison there can be very little understanding of what has been found out.

Thus, in conclusion, we can see that the act of comparison is a central logical device for establishing the validity of a line of argument within research. We use comparison to say why a group is interesting, what about it is interesting, and by how much it differs from expectation. Planned comparisons are a central element of research design — they are what enables us to draw conclusions and to determine the range over which our conclusions hold true. Unplanned or *ad hoc* comparisons in the course of a research programme may also shape the initial idea into a firm conclusion and allow it to be put forward as a finding supported by evidence as well as argument. We know very little about anything, except in comparison with something else.

REFERENCES

Abbott, P. (ed.) (1988) *Material Deprivation and Health Status in the Plymouth Health District*, Plymouth, Polytechnic South West, Department of Applied Social Science.

Abbott, P., Bernie, J., Payne, G. and Sapsford, R. (1992) 'Health and material deprivation in Plymouth', in Abbott, P. and Sapsford, R. (eds) *Research into Practice: A Reader for Nurses and the Caring Professions*, Buckingham, Open University Press.

Abbott, P. and Sapsford, R. (1987) 'Leaving it to Mum', in *Community Care for Mentally Handicapped Children*, Milton Keynes, Open University Press (reproduced in Offprints Booklet 2).

Abramson, L., Garber, J. and Seligman, M.E.P. (1980) 'Learned helplessness in humans: an attributional analysis', in Garber, J. and Seligman, M.E.P. (eds) *Human Helplessness: Theory and Applications*, New York, Academic Press.

Abramson, L., Seligman, M.E.P. and Teasdale, J.D. (1978) 'Learned helplessness in humans: critique and reformulation', *Journal of Abnormal Psychology*, vol. 87, pp.49–74.

Atkinson, P., Shone, D. and Rees, T. (1985) 'Labouring to learn: industrial training for slow learners', in Barton, L. and Tomlinson, S. (eds) *Special Education: Policy, Practice and Social Issues*, London, Harper Row.

Beck, A.T. (1967) *Depression: Causes and Treatment*, Philadelphia, University of Pennsylvania Press.

Campbell, D. (1969) 'Reforms as experiments' *American Psychologist*, vol. 24, pp.409–29.

Campbell, D. and Ross, H.L. (1968) 'The Connecticut Crack-down on speeding: time-series data in quasi-experimental analysis', *Law and Society Review*, vol. 3, pp.33–53.

Dingwall, R. and Fox, S. (1986) 'Health visitors' and social workers' perceptions of child care problems', in While, A. (ed.) *Research in Preventive Community Nursing: Fifteen Studies in Health Visiting*, Chichester, Wiley (reproduced in Offprints Booklet 2).

Gatchel, R.J., Paulus, P.B. and Maples, C.W. (1975) 'Learned helplessness and self-reported affect', *Journal of Abnormal Psychology*, vol. 16, pp.732–4.

Geer, J.H., Davison, G.C. and Gatchel, R.J. (1970) 'Reduction of stress in humans through nonveridical perceived control of aversive stimulation', *Journal of Personality and Social Psychology*, vol. 16, pp.731–8.

Glass, D.C. and Singer, J.E. (1972) *Urban Stress: Experiments on Noise and Social Stress*, New York, Academic Press.

Gordon, V. (1986) 'Treatment of depressed women by nurses in Britain and the USA', in Brooking, J. (ed.) *Psychiatric Nursing Research*, Chichester, Wiley (reproduced in Offprints Booklet 2).

Hammersley, M. (ed.) (1992) *Social Research: Philosophy, Politics and Practice*, London, Sage (DEH313 Reader).

Hiroto, D.S. (1974) 'Locus of control and learned helplessness', *Journal of Experimental Psychology*, vol. 102, pp.187–93.

Maier, S.F. (1970) 'Failure to escape traumatic shock: skeletal motor responses or learned helplessness', *Learning and Motivation*, vol. 1, pp.157–70.

Maier, S.F., Anderson, C. and Liberman, D.A. (1972) 'Influence of shock on subsequent shock-elicited aggression', *Journal of Comparative and Physiological Psychology*, vol. 81, pp.94–100.

Melges, F.T. and Bowlby, J. (1969) 'Types of hopelessness in psychopathological process', *Archives of General Psychiatry*, vol. 20, pp.690–9.

Mies, M. (1983) 'Towards a methodology for feminist research', in Hammersley, M. (1992) (DEH313 Reader).

Milgram, S. (1963) 'Behavioural study of obedience', *Journal of Abnormal and Social Psychology*, vol. 67, pp.371–8.

Milgram, S. (1974) *Obedience to Authority*, London, Tavistock.

Roth, S. (1980) 'A revised model of learned helplessness in humans', *Journal of Personality*, vol. 48, pp.103–33.

Sapsford, R.J. (1983) *Life-Sentence Prisoners: Reaction, Response and Change*, Milton Keynes, Open University Press.

Seligman, M.E.P. (1975) *Helplessness*, San Francisco, W.H. Freeman.

Seligman, M.E.P., Maier, S.F. and Solomon, R.L. (1971) 'Unpredictable and uncontrollable aversive events', in Brush, F.R. (ed.) *Aversive Conditioning and Learning*, New York, Academic Press.

Townsend, P., Phillimore, P. and Beattie, A. (1986) *Inequalities in Health in the Northern Region: An Interim Report*, Northern Regional Health Authority.

Wener, A.E. and Rehm, L.P. (1975) 'Depressive affect: a test of a behavioural hypothesis', *Journal of Abnormal Psychology*, vol. 84, pp.221–7.

ACKNOWLEDGEMENTS

Grateful acknowledgement is made to the following sources for permission to reproduce material in this unit:

MAPS

Maps 1 to 4: Abbott, P., Bernie, J., Payne, G. and Sapsford, R. (1992) 'Health and material deprivation in Plymouth', in Abbott, P. and Sapsford, R. (eds) *Research into Practice: A Reader for Nurses and the Caring Professions*, Open University Press, Buckingham.

FIGURES

Figures 3 and 4: Campbell, D. (1969) 'Reforms as experiments', *American Psychologist*, vol. 24, copyright 1969 by the American Psychological Association. Reprinted by permission.

UNIT 7 CASE STUDY

Prepared for the Course Team by Martyn Hammersley

CONTENTS

ASSOCIATED STUDY MATERIALS

Reader, Chapter 16, 'Increasing the generalizability of qualitative research', by Janet Schofield.

1   INTRODUCTION

The term 'case study' is used in various ways in discussions about social research methodology. Very often, though, it signifies an approach to social research that rejects and offers an alternative to quantitative method. The term 'case study' was used in this way in US sociology in the 1920s and 1930s, when the methods of data collection and statistical analysis characteristic of quantitative research today were only in the early stages of development. It referred then to detailed investigation of particular situations, events or people. It was modelled initially on the way that doctors produce medical histories of their patients, and social workers investigate the circumstances of their clients. Also influential were the examples of investigative journalism and of historical research, and the methodological guidelines developed by historians, notably Langlois and Seignobos in their classic study of 1898 (1966).

This notion of case study as the detailed investigation of particular phenomena was put into practice by Chicago sociologists at that time. They carried out a series of studies of aspects and areas of life in Chicago, from the world of the rich in the 'Gold Coast' hotels to the taxi dance halls, where men (many of them newly arrived migrants) paid women for dances. In the early part of this century, survey research as we know it today did not exist, but in the 1930s and 1940s there was a growing movement towards the use of rudimentary statistical techniques on national and local data of a quantitative kind, especially census data. Initially, case study and statistical work were generally regarded as complementary, on the model of Charles Booth's investigation of the lives of the London poor, published in the last decade of the nineteenth century, which employed a wealth of both sorts of data (Booth, 1889–1902). However, over time, at Chicago and in US sociology generally, quantitative research increasingly came to be presented by its practitioners as more scientific — i.e. closer to the methods of natural science — than case-study research. At the same time, some advocates of case study argued for *its* superiority, on the grounds that statistical method was not scientific because it could produce only probabilistic generalizations, not universal laws (Hammersley, 1989, ch. 4). Such debates about the relative value of qualitative and quantitative methods have continued ever since.

As a result of this history, the term 'case study' tends today to be associated with qualitative approaches to social research like ethnography and life history. And it has acquired an additional burden of meaning from this association which we need to consider.

Ethnography originated in anthropology and is still central to that discipline, but is now widely used in sociology and in various applied areas. Ethnographic work usually has the following features:

1   Investigation of one (or at least a very small number) of cases in depth. These could be residential communities, occupations or organizations, deviant groups or networks, particular settings (public and private), etc.

2   The cases studied are 'naturally occurring' ones, rather than specially created by the researcher as in the case of experimental research.

3   The adoption of a wide initial focus to the research, rather than the testing of narrowly pre-defined hypotheses. Ethnographers tend to begin with only a rather general interest in some types of social phenomena or some issue. Only over the course of the research do they adopt a more specific research focus and engage in hypothesis testing.

4   A range of data collection techniques is employed, not just one. Observation and/or interviewing are usually the main sources of information employed by ethnographers, but use is also often made of documentary sources, and sometimes of questionnaires.

5   There is minimal pre-structuring of the data collected. When observing events ethnographers usually write fieldnotes: they try to describe what they see in whatever terms seem appropriate at the time, rather than, for instance, going into the situation with a list of categories and ticking off events falling into these categories. They may also use audio- and even video-recording. Categories for structuring and analysing the data will be developed in the course of collecting it rather than beforehand. It is for this reason that the observation and interviewing used by ethnographers are sometimes referred to as 'unstructured'.

6   The analysis carried out by ethnographers generally takes the form of verbal descriptions and explanations, with quantification and statistical analysis taking a subordinate role at most.

Life history research involves many of the same features as ethnography, except that it is based primarily, if not exclusively, on in-depth interviews with one or a small number of people, the aim being to reconstruct the pattern of their lives, often giving particular attention to life-cycle and generational factors. In some respects, this approach is analogous to historians' use of biography to study individuals who have played a key role in historical events, a well-known example being Bullock's biography of Hitler (Bullock, 1962). Often, though, even historians are interested in more general issues, as in the same author's more recent comparative study of the lives of Hitler and Stalin as a basis for investigating the nature of totalitarian leadership (Bullock, 1991). In social science disciplines, the aim is also usually to derive more general conclusions about particular social types of individuals, rather than simply to characterize the life of an individual for its own sake. (This is the distinction between a nomothetic and an ideographic focus that we discussed in Unit 1/2.) Thus, within sociology, much life history work has focused on practitioners of deviant occupations, treating them as exemplars of those occupations: for example Shaw's famous study of a 'jack roller' or mugger (Shaw, 1930; see also Snodgrass, 1982) and Klockars' life history of a professional fence (Klockars, 1975). At the same time, some life history work has involved the study of larger numbers of informants, for instance Oscar Lewis's anthropological studies of Mexican families (Lewis, 1961, 1964, and 1970), the work of Bertaux and Bertaux-Wiame (1981) on bakeries in France, and Thompson's investigation of fishing communities in Scotland (Thompson, 1983). Even here, though, the number of cases studied has been relatively small compared with the samples studied by survey researchers.

The term 'case study' is often used, then, to refer to the sort of qualitative research characteristic of ethnographic and life history work (see, for example, Becker, 1971). Such work is also often treated as exemplifying a paradigmatic approach to social research based on philosophical assumptions that are at odds with those that motivate most quantitative research (for example, Plummer, 1983). However, this is not the way that we shall use the term 'case study' in this course. As I argued in Unit 3/4, the conceptualization of social research methodology in terms of competing, comprehensive paradigms oversimplifies the range of choices that are available to the researcher. Distinctions between paradigms do not capture the variety of strategies that one finds deployed in social research. Nor are they reasonable philosophically. Epistemological debate among philosophers has not been, and is not today, a dialogue between only two positions. The arguments are more diverse and complex. What this means is that in doing research one is not faced with a choice between two well-defined routes that go off in opposite directions. Instead, the research process is more like finding one's way through a maze. And it is a rather badly kept and complex maze, where paths are not always distinct, where they wind back on one another, and where one can never be entirely certain that one has reached the centre.

Given this, we shall use the term 'case study' in a narrower sense than is common in the methodological literature today: to refer to a strategy for dealing with one aspect of the research process, the task of case selection. In this sense, the term carries no implications for the sort of data that might be employed, or for which forms of analysis should be used. Case studies, in our terms, may be quantitative as well as qualitative. They do not even necessarily involve the collection of primary data; the data employed may be secondary.

Case selection is a problem that all research faces. What I mean by the term 'case' here is the phenomenon (located in space/time) about which data are collected and/or analysed, and that corresponds to the type of phenomena to which the main claims of a study relate. (This was the way we used the term in Activity 6 in Unit 1/2.) Examples of cases can range from micro to macro, all the way from individual people or particular events, social situations, organizations or institutions, to national societies or international social systems.

We define 'case study', then, in terms of only one of the central features commonly associated with ethnographic and life history research: the investigation of a single case or a small number of cases. As I noted in the discussion of life history work, research may be aimed at drawing conclusions about a particular case that is of interest in itself. For example, occupational practitioners sometimes study their own work situations with a view to solving problems they face, their interest in this investigation not extending much beyond that situation. However, even where studies are aimed at more general conclusions, a single case or a small number of particular cases may reasonably be studied rather than a large sample. Where this occurs a case study strategy has been employed.

In order to clarify further the concept of case study, let me compare it with the two other main case selection strategies discussed in this Block: experiment and survey.[1] What is distinctive about an experiment is that the researcher constructs the cases to be studied: through the establishment of the research situation, the manipulation of the variables that are the focus of the research, and the control of at least some of the relevant extraneous variables. The distinctiveness of surveys, on the other hand, is that they involve the simultaneous selection for study of a relatively large number of naturally occurring (rather than experimentally created) cases. Case study combines some features of these other two strategies, involving the investigation of a relatively small number of naturally occurring (rather than researcher-created) cases.[2] The three strategies differ, then, in how many cases are studied and how these are selected.

Each of the case selection strategies may be usable to investigate any particular research topic, though their strengths and weaknesses will have varying significance, depending on the purposes and circumstances of the research. It is not uncommon to find in the literature discussions of case study that either treat it as inherently superior to other approaches, or dismiss it as inferior. Neither of these is the attitude we adopt in this course. In our view, in selecting one case selection strategy rather than another, we are usually faced with trade-offs. Each strategy has its advantages and disadvantages. We can never have everything we want, and usually we can get more of one thing only at the expense of getting less of something else. In other words, a researcher can usually gain the benefits of one strategy only at the expense of costs that could be avoided by using another strategy, but whose use would carry other costs. The choice of case selection strategy ought to be determined, then, by judgment of the likely resulting gains and losses in the light of the particular goals and circumstances of the research, including the resources available.

---

[1] Our interpretation of the terms 'survey' and 'experiment', like that of 'case study', is narrower than in most common usage.

[2] It may involve the study of only one case, but where more than one is studied these may be selected consecutively rather than simultaneously, so that analysis of data from the first case influences the choice of subsequent cases for investigation. This is what Glaser and Strauss (1967) refer to as 'theoretical sampling', which is discussed below.

2 CASE STUDIES AND SURVEYS

ACTIVITY 1

What do you think the respective advantages and disadvantages of case studies and surveys are? Jot down your answer before you read on.

Let me begin, then, by comparing the case study with the survey. The great strength of case study in this comparison is that research employing this strategy usually provides more detailed information about the case(s) studied, and information that is more likely to be valid. This is because, given finite resources (including time), more of these resources can be spent on the investigation of each case than is possible in a survey. Of course, this does not guarantee that in any particular instance case study data will be more accurate than survey data; this is simply the likelihood, other things being equal. Furthermore, this advantage is bought at the cost of being less able to make effective generalizations to a larger population of cases. By 'generalization', I mean the extent to which, assuming valid information about the cases studied, the conclusions of the research can be legitimately inferred to be true for other cases in a larger population that have not been studied. In general, the more cases from a population we study, the more likely our findings are to be representative of that population. Here the survey usually has a clear advantage over the case study.

I can illustrate the relationship between the strengths and weaknesses of the case study and the survey by means of a diagram (see Figure 1). It is worth noting two things about this diagram. First, the difference between case studies and surveys is a matter of degree. We have a gradient or dimension here, not a dichotomy. As the number of cases investigated is reduced, the amount of detail that can be collected on each case is increased, and the chances of there being error in the

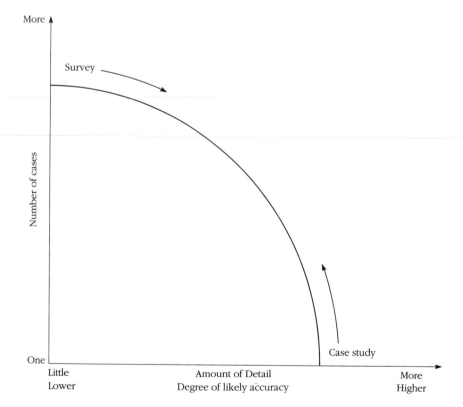

Figure 1 *The relationship between the survey and the case study*

information probably reduces too. As this happens, we shift imperceptibly from survey to case study.

Of course, this trade-off is relative to the relationship between resource demands and the resources available. An investigation focusing on relatively small and easily accessible cases, and/or having a relatively high level of resources (more researchers, more time, etc.), would be able to study more cases in more detail than one focusing on geographically and/or temporally large cases and/or having fewer resources. The effect of these factors in terms of the diagram is to move the curve outwards or inwards, but not to change its shape. The trade-off remains whatever the levels of resource demands and resource availability.

This leads me to the second point I want to make. It might be thought that with lavish resources we would be able to maximize both the number of cases studied and the detail and accuracy of the information provided. This would be true, however, only if there were finite end-points to the two dimensions in the diagram. As we shall see, this is, at best, likely to be true only under certain conditions.

Let me deal with the possibility of a maximum amount of detail first. It is sometimes thought that case study involves the representation of a case in unique and concrete terms; perhaps involving its reproduction or evocation. Thus, in an otherwise instructive book about case-study research, Bromley (1986, p.288) talks of case studies as preserving 'the wholeness of the phenomenon studied'. But this is misleading. All description is selective. Descriptions never reproduce the phenomena described. We can always in principle provide more or different detail. Of course, practically speaking, we can usually resolve the problem of what and how much detail is required with little trouble. Our purposes generally dictate fairly clearly the degree of detail that is necessary. But given different purposes the descriptions produced would vary.

The same sort of argument applies to accuracy. The accuracy of information can always be subjected to further checks, in principle at least. It is sometimes argued that studies should be replicated several times before we take their conclusions to be sound; and further replications can always be called for. Similarly, faced with research making a particular claim, we may ask not just for evidence in support of that claim, but also for evidence of the validity of the evidence provided, and so on *ad infinitum*. There is no absolute foundation for us to reach that would necessarily stop this process, as we saw in Unit 1/2. Practically speaking, though, we usually soon reach a point at which we decide that it is not reasonable to demand further replications, or search or ask for further evidence. The appropriate point at which to stop is impossible to specify in the abstract: it will depend considerably on the nature of the claim and evidence involved; in particular, on their plausibility and credibility and on the purpose which the information is intended to serve. However, wherever we do stop, we could, in principle, always have gone further in checking the validity of the findings.

Let me turn now to the other dimension highlighted in the diagram: number of cases. Here, there is an obvious possible end-point. If we were trying to represent a population, the maximum number of cases would be reached if we decided to study every case in the population. But this assumes that the population of cases in which we are interested is finite. Sometimes this is true. But there are situations where the population of interest is not finite. This is the case, for example, where we are interested in testing a theory, where the term 'theory' implies universal or probabilistic relationships among categories of phenomena. Such theories refer to all possible instances that meet their conditions: those that have occurred in the past and those that could occur in the future. While even here (other things being equal) the more cases we study the better, there is no possibility of us studying all of them.

It is worth emphasizing that not only are there often no end-points to these two dimensions in principle, for most practical purposes the dimensions are likely to extend beyond the trade-off point the researcher chooses; so that in most studies the researcher could always have pursued more detail or done more checking for accuracy, or collected information on more cases.

So, the distinction between case study and survey is a matter of degree, and it usually involves a trade-off between the likely generalizability of the information obtained on the one hand, and the detail and likely accuracy of data about particular cases on the other. This is not always recognized, as I noted earlier. Often case studies and surveys are regarded as quite different sorts of research. Thus it is sometimes denied that case studies are intended to be representative or typical in the sense that is true of the findings of surveys. For example, Yin (1984) distinguishes between the logic of 'statistical' and 'analytical' generalization, arguing that only the latter is relevant to case studies. Similarly, Mitchell (1983) claims that case-study research involves 'logical' but not 'statistical' inference. Both these authors define generalization from sample to population as statistical and as irrelevant to case-study research.

This is quite wrong. As I pointed out earlier, it is true that where we are concerned with the development and testing of theory, the issue is not generalization to a finite population. And where the population is infinite, cannot be assumed to be homogeneous in the relevant respects, and its members are not all accessible to study, statistical techniques do not offer a solution to the problem of generalizing from sample to population. Random selection of a sample from the population is not possible under these circumstances, and so the relationship between the characteristics of any sample and those of the population remains uncertain in statistical terms. It is also true, as mentioned earlier, that sometimes we are not interested in any larger population, but only in the case(s) studied. For instance, a study of the National Front, such as that by Nigel Fielding (1981), may be concerned simply with describing that organization; so that the issue of generalizabilty across cases does not arise.[3] However, often the issue of generalizability to a relatively large, finite population *is* relevant to case-study work. It is quite common for research employing this strategy to make such claims. For instance, in his book *Policing the Inner City* (1979), Maurice Punch bases general statements about policing the inner-city areas of modern Western societies on an investigation of police officers in the Warmoestraat area of Amsterdam. Similarly, Peter Woods treats the option system at the secondary school he studied as typical of those at other English secondary schools (Woods, 1979). Moreover, such empirical generalization is just as legitimate a goal for case-study research as is the development and testing of theories, and in some respects it is more straightforward.

Where empirical generalization is the goal, there is no doubt that, whatever its advantages in terms of detail and accuracy, case study is usually weaker than the survey in the generalizability of its findings. But to say this is not to say that case study provides no basis for such generalization, or that the generalizability of its findings cannot be improved or assessed. It is very important not to think of generalizability as synonymous with the use of statistical sampling techniques. The latter are one useful way of providing for generalizability to a finite and accessible population; but they are neither perfect nor the only way. If they cannot be used, as is usually the position in case-study research because the number of cases investigated is too small, we should not assume that the findings are therefore not generalizable, or that we cannot make reasonable judgments about whether they are representative or not.

A variety of strategies for improving and/or checking the generalizability of the findings of case-study research is available:

1 It may be possible to draw on relevant information in published statistics about the population to which generalization is being made. So, for example, in their study of two juvenile courts, Parker *et al.* used statistics about the proportions of different sorts of disposal in such courts in England and Wales and in the Merseyside area to show the atypicality of one of the courts they studied (Parker *et al.*, 1981, p.79). Figure 2 suggests that the County Juvenile Court had a distinctive pattern of outcomes compared to others.

---

[3]The problem of generalization within the case may still arise, but not that of generalization across cases, which is my concern here.

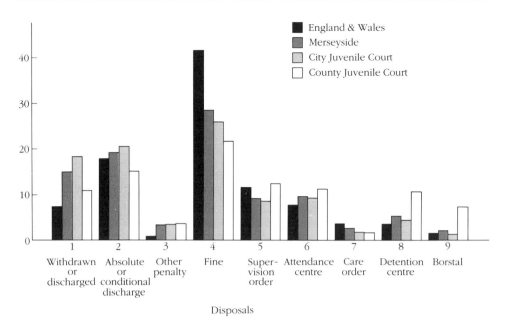

Figure 2 *Means of disposal of all juveniles (10–17 years) proceeded against as percentages of all cases dealt with for indictable and non-indictable offences (1978–79)*
(Source: Hammersley, 1991, p.92)

There may, of course, be problems in obtaining the information necessary to make such comparisons. For instance, in studying longshoremen in Portland, Oregon, USA (the equivalent of dockers in the British context), Pilcher wanted to document their income. Unfortunately, this information was not available. However, he *was* able to obtain official statistics about the average earnings from waterfront work of longshoremen in Oregon as a whole. This information obscured variations in earnings between workers in different ports in Oregon. Even more important, it omitted income from other forms of work (the uncertain nature of waterfront work makes other sources of income a necessity for many) and fringe benefits, official and unofficial (Pilcher, 1972, pp.15–17). However, despite its limitations, such information is better than nothing. It can often be used to get a general sense of whether or not the case studied is atypical.

2 Another possibility is increased collaboration between ethnographers and survey researchers, or the combination of case study and survey strategies in the same investigation. (The advantage of this over reliance on already available statistics is, of course, that information that is not provided in those statistics can be collected.) Thus, survey researchers have sometimes complemented their work with more detailed case studies; and ethnographers sometimes use questionnaires to provide information from a broader sample (though often this is generalization within, rather than across, cases). An example of the latter would be Olesen and Whittaker's study (1968) of the socialization of nurses, in which they used a questionnaire to collect background information about the nurses they studied, and those in preceding and succeeding years. In much the same way, Rock (1973) employed a small social survey of public knowledge and opinion to complement his ethnographic study of the process of debt collection in London in the 1960s. There are also some investigations that represent a more even balance between case study and survey, including much of the work of the Institute of Community Studies (see Platt, 1971) and, more recently, the study by Millham *et al.* (1986) of children in care and their families. There have long been calls for a more systematic combination of case studies and surveys, but there has been only limited progress towards this (see Zelditch, 1962; Sieber, 1973; and Bryman, 1988).

3 It may also be possible for those adopting a case-study approach to select for investigation cases that cover some of the main dimensions of suspected heterogeneity in the population to which they wish to generalize. For instance, in investigating the degree of choice given to pupils by option-choice schemes in secondary schools, if we were to study more than one school we might select

them to cover dimensions which could be expected to affect this issue: such as large/small number of pupils, predominantly working-class/middle-class catchment areas, and so on. This sort of 'cross-site' investigation is usually only possible on a significant scale where a team of researchers is involved, and even then very often the time that can be spent investigating each case may be much less than where a smaller number of cases is investigated. Here, as elsewhere, a trade-off is involved. (On such multisite qualitative studies, see for example Firestone and Herriot, 1984.) However, even where an intensive study of only one case is being carried out, it may be possible to make brief investigations of one or more other cases in order to assess the ways in which the primary case is or is not representative of the larger population that is of concern. Skolnick's study (1966) of law enforcement processes in US cities is an example of this strategy. The bulk of his research took place in one city, but he made a brief investigation of another to assess the likely generalizability of his findings.

4 Similarly, where studies have been carried out by others on other cases in the same population, comparison may allow some judgment of typicality to be made. This strategy is illustrated by Strong's study (1979) of paediatric consultations. He seeks to generalize from the cases he studied to a larger population by comparing his data with those from other studies in the sociology of medicine. He argues that the bureaucratic format he identified as characteristic of those consultations is not typical only of them. With minor modifications, it predominates in all medical consultations in the British health service. In order to establish this, he first considers the extent to which the fact that children were the patients in the paediatric consultations he studied shaped the pattern of interaction characteristic of them, arguing that it made little difference. Secondly, he draws on other studies of medical consultation involving adults as patients, to assess how far these conformed to the bureaucratic mode.

It is worth noting that where the case-study strategy is adopted, cases are sometimes selected for investigation on the basis of their *atypicality.* In the early 1960s, Cicourel and Kitsuse investigated Lakeside High, a school which they pointed out was unrepresentative of US high schools at the time, particularly in having a professional counselling service (Cicourel and Kitsuse, 1963). But the authors argued that in this respect the school was in advance of changes that were taking place among US high schools generally, so that more and more schools would become similar to Lakeside High in the future. On this basis, Cicourel and Kitsuse claimed that their findings would be generalizable to many US high schools of the future. This sort of generalization requires different kinds of support compared to the more conventional process of generalization to an already existing population of cases. In assessing Cicourel's and Kitsuse's claims, we need to be sure that their assumptions about the trend in the development of US high schools are accurate. In fact, they do not provide much evidence for this; though we are in a better position now to assess whether they were right.

I am not suggesting that these various strategies are always able to give case-study researchers a very sound basis for generalization, but they can provide some evidence, and we should not scorn that evidence simply because it is not statistical. By means of these strategies a researcher can moderate the relative weakness of case study in providing for the generalizability of findings to a large, finite population of cases. And often this is necessary if the findings of research using a case-study strategy are to be of value.

READING

You should now read 'Increasing the generalizability of qualitative research', by Janet Schofield, reproduced in the Course Reader.

In this article, Schofield examines the problem of generalizability as it arises in the context of applied qualitative research in the field of education. As you read the article, take particular note of how Schofield conceptualizes generalizability, and also of what she identifies as the main targets of generalization and the strategies that can be used to achieve it.

So, the first implication of my definition of case study is that in relation to the survey it involves a trade-off between empirical generalizability on the one hand and accuracy and detail of information on the other. However, I have emphasized that these are tendencies, not inevitabilities, and that generalizability to large, finite populations is not always the goal of research. Furthermore, as outlined above, there are ways in which case-study researchers can improve their methods and assess the representativeness of the cases they study.

3 CASE STUDIES AND EXPERIMENTS

ACTIVITY 2

What do you think the respective advantages and disadvantages of case studies and experiments are? Jot down your answer before reading on.

If we turn now to the distinction between case study and experiment, we will see highlighted a complementary dimension of strength and weakness on the part of case studies. This is one that is primarily relevant to theory development and testing. Here the trade-off is between more and less researcher control of variables on the one hand, and the level of likely reactivity on the other. What is meant by the term 'reactivity' here is the effects on the phenomena studied of the research process itself. One of the most common criticisms of experiments is that their results are not generalizable to situations outside the laboratory because the behaviour they study is an artefact of the experimental situation. In particular, when people know that they are taking part in an experiment, what they do may be affected by that knowledge, and this could shape the results. This would reduce the ecological validity of the study: the extent to which its findings can be generalized to non-experimental cases.

It is precisely in this respect that the case study has an advantage over the experiment. Because it involves the investigation of naturally occurring cases (rather than cases created by the researcher in the laboratory), the case study provides us with information that is less likely to be affected by reactivity and is therefore more likely to be ecologically valid. Of course, case-study research may involve some reactivity, for instance where the researcher plays an influential role within the setting, either intentionally (as in action research) or inadvertently (as in the, probably apocryphal, story of the ethnographer who investigated a delinquent gang and ended up as its leader! Ball, 1972, pp.163-4). Furthermore, reactivity is not the only source of ecological invalidity: natural cases can be unrepresentative in relevant respects of other cases falling under the same theoretical category, simply because there is variability within that set of cases. In general, however, reactivity is likely to be lower and ecological validity higher in case study as compared with experimental research.

This potentially higher ecological validity in the case study is bought, though, at the cost of making it more difficult to come to convincing conclusions about the existence of causal relationships. By constructing cases for investigation, experimenters can vary theoretical and extraneous variables fairly easily. This enables them to maximize the chances of coming to sound conclusions about whether the causal relationship they are investigating does or does not hold, other things being equal; though we must remember that experiments do not guarantee the control of all relevant extraneous variables.

Once again, then, we are not faced with a contrast between a superior and an inferior case-selection strategy, but rather with strategies that have related advantages and disadvantages. Furthermore, while it might seem that the difference between case studies and experiments is one of kind rather than one of degree — we either create cases or we study existing ones — this is not so. The difference here is quantitative too. Quasi- and field experiments involve less control over variables than do true experiments, but more than case studies, and therefore constitute mid-points on a scale. What is involved here is variation in the degree of control exercised by the researcher over theoretical and extraneous variables. Once again, I can illustrate the relationship by means of a diagram (see Figure 3).

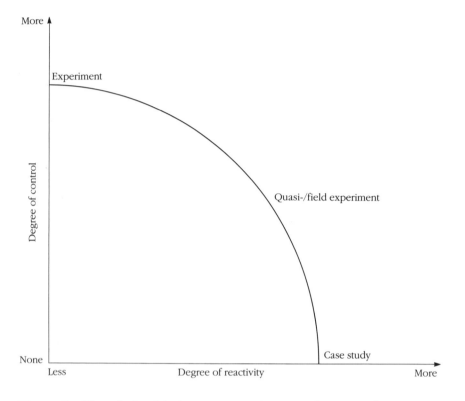

Figure 3 *The relationship between experiment and case study*

The weakness of case-study research as a basis for identifying causal relationships has not always been recognized by advocates of this sort of research. It is sometimes argued that case studies can identify causal relationships in a relatively direct manner. This argument has quite a long history. It occurs in an article from the 1930s by Willard Waller, a Chicago-trained sociologist and advocate of case study. He draws on Gestalt psychology to claim that 'there is in some cases a direct perception of the causal interdependence of events'; though later he recognizes that such insight can be mistaken (Waller, 1934, pp.285, 297). More recently, Glaser and Strauss in an influential text on qualitative research claimed that 'in field work ... general relations are often discovered in vivo, that is, the field worker literally sees them occur' (Glaser and Strauss, 1967, p.40). Something of this kind also seems to be implicit in Mitchell's defence of case study (Mitchell, 1983; Hammersley, 1992a; ch. 10). Yet, this is not convincing. As the Scottish philosopher David Hume argued long ago, we do not see causal relationships in some immediate fashion; the ascription of causal power always relies on assumptions. Indeed, it is widely accepted by philosophers today that we cannot see anything directly or immediately. All perception and observation involve presuppositions, even though most of the time we are not aware of those presuppositions (Hanson, 1958; Gregory, 1970).

Does this mean that we must simply accept that research employing case study is unable to identify causal relationships? This does not follow at all. For one thing, the generation and development of causal hypotheses is as important as the testing of them; and that is a task where it is widely accepted that case study can be of great value. The detail and accuracy of information it can provide about particular cases sometimes enables researchers to identify likely causal relationships in a way that is not possible in either survey or experimental research.

An important technique for such theory development is the 'grounded theorizing' of Glaser and Strauss (1967). They criticize the idea that research should simply be concerned with testing hypotheses derived from what they refer to as 'armchair' theorizing. They insist that the generation and development of theory can be done most effectively through the collection and analysis of empirical data. And what they refer to as 'theoretical sampling' is a central element of this. It involves the selection of cases in such a way as to facilitate the development of fruitful theoretical ideas. This may involve both comparison among cases where differences are known to be minimal and among those where the differences are greater, in an attempt to clarify and elaborate the theoretical categories with which the researcher is working. Here is an example from Glaser's and Strauss's own research on 'the awareness of dying' in hospitals and its effects on relationships between staff and patients:

> Visits to the various medical services were scheduled as follows: I wished first to look at services that minimized patient awareness (and so first looked at a premature baby service and then a neurosurgical service where patients were frequently comatose). I wished next to look at dying in a situation where expectancy of staff and often of patients was great and dying was quick, so I observed on an Intensive Care Unit. Then I wished to observe on a service where staff expectations of terminality were great but where the patients' might or might not be, and where dying tended to be slow. So I looked next at a cancer service. I wished then to look at conditions where death was unexpected and rapid, and so looked at an emergency service. While we were looking at some different types of services, we also observed the above types of service at other types of hospitals. So our scheduling of types of service was directed by a general conceptual scheme — which included hypotheses about awareness, expectedness and rate of dying — as well as by a developing conceptual structure including matters not at first envisioned. Sometimes we returned to services after the initial two or three or four weeks of continuous observation, in order to check upon items which needed checking or had been missed in the initial period.

> (Glaser and Strauss, 1967, p.59)

While Glaser and Strauss present grounded theorizing primarily as a strategy for developing rather than testing theory, they sometimes suggest that it also serves to *test* theoretical hypotheses. Indeed, in a later publication, Strauss claims that in grounded theorizing 'the theory is not just discovered but *verified*' (Strauss, 1987, p.17). And he argues that built into grounded theorizing is the same logic as governs experimental research: the hypothetico-deductive method. However, while grounded theorizing conforms to this method in some respects, it deviates in others: notably in that while the selection of cases it recommends is systematic, it is not designed in such a way as to test theoretical hypotheses rigorously.

Another strategy sometimes used to guide case-study research with a view to developing and testing theory is analytic induction. Cressey provides a classic account of this approach:

> First, a rough definition of the phenomenon to be explained is formulated. Second, an hypothetical explanation of that phenomenon is formulated. Third, one case is studied in light of the hypothesis with the object of determining whether the hypothesis fits the facts in that case. Fourth, if the hypothesis does not fit the facts, either the hypothesis is

re-formulated or the phenomenon to be explained is re-defined, so that the case is excluded. This definition must be more precise than the first one. Fifth, practical certainty may be attained after a small number of cases [have] been examined, but the discovery by the investigator or any other investigator of a single negative case disproves the explanation and requires a re-formulation. Sixth, this procedure of examining cases, re-defining the phenomenon and re-formulating the hypothesis is continued until a universal relationship is established, each negative case calling for a re-definition or a re-formulation.

(Cressey, 1953, p.16)

The process of analytic induction is summarized in Figure 4.

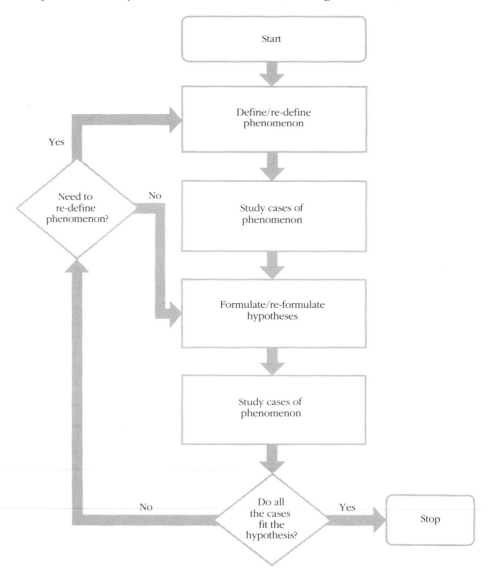

Figure 4 *A formalization of the process of analytic induction*
(Source: Hammersley, 1989)

In the case of Cressey's own research into embezzlement, he reports how he began from a legal definition of embezzlement but found that the term was not used consistently. He therefore formulated his own definition of what he came to refer to as 'financial trust violation'. This was held to have occurred where a person had accepted a position of financial trust in good faith and later exploited that position. Cressey notes that, 'These criteria permit the inclusion of almost all persons convicted for embezzlement and, in addition, a proportion of those convicted for larceny by bailee, forgery, and confidence game'. For data, he relied on interviews with 'all the prisoners whose behavior met the criteria and who were confined at the Illinois State Penitentiaries at Joliet' (Cressey, 1950, p.740).

In setting out to explain financial trust violation, Cressey began with a first hypothesis that,

> ... positions of financial trust are violated when the incumbent has learned, in connection with the business or profession in which he is employed, that some forms of trust violation are merely 'technical violations' and are not really 'illegal' or 'wrong'.
>
> (Cressey, 1950, p.741)

However, this explanation was soon abandoned because it was found that many financial trust violators stated 'that they knew the behavior to be illegal and wrong at all times and that they merely "kidded themselves" into thinking that it was not illegal' (Cressey, 1950, p.741).

An alternative hypothesis was developed that 'positions of trust are violated when the incumbent structures a real or supposed need for extra funds or extended use of property as an "emergency" that cannot be met by legal means' (Cressey, 1950, p.741). This hypothesis was also soon rejected in the face of counter evidence, for example: 'persons were found who claimed that while an emergency had been present at the time they violated the trust, other, perhaps even more extreme, emergencies had been present in earlier periods and they did not violate it' (Cressey, 1950, p.741).

The fourth hypothesis was that people violate financial trust when they incur 'financial obligations that are considered as nonsocially sanctionable and which, consequently, must be satisfied by private or secret means' (Cressey, 1950 p.741). However, Cressey reports that,

> ... when the cases were re-examined in light of this hypothesis it was found that in a few of them there was nothing which could be considered as financial *obligation*; that is, as a debt which had been incurred in the past and for which the person at present felt responsible. Also, in some cases there had been nonsanctionable obligations at a prior time, and these obligations had not been alleviated by means of trust violation. It became increasingly apparent at this point that trust violation could not be attributed to a single event, but that its explanation could be made only in terms of a sequence of events, a process.
>
> (Cressey, 1950, pp.741–2)

After further revisions and developments, Cressey arrived at his final formulation:

> Trusted persons become trust violators when they conceive of themselves as having a financial problem which is non-shareable, have the knowledge or awareness that this problem can be secretly resolved by violation of the position of financial trust, and are able to apply to their own conduct in that situation verbalizations that enable them to adjust their conceptions of themselves as trusted persons with their conceptions of themselves as users of the entrusted funds or property.
>
> (Cressey, 1950, p.742)

Cressey reports that this explanation fitted all the cases that he had investigated and that no new cases emerged that challenged it.

Like grounded theorizing, analytic induction is often presented as being concerned with testing as well as developing theoretical hypotheses. But once again it deviates from the hypothetico-deductive method, this time in being concerned only with the identification of necessary rather than sufficient conditions for the causal production of the type of phenomena being studied. It does this because the cases selected for investigation are only those in which the *phenomenon* to be explained occurs. In order to identify sufficient conditions, the researcher must also investigate cases where the *conditions* specified by the theory are known to hold in order to find out whether or not the phenomenon occurs there (Robinson,

1951; Hammersley, 1989, chs 7–8). Cressey does this to some degree by looking at relevant experiences in the lives of the people he interviewed before they became trust violators. But to study sufficient conditions systematically, he would have had to study some cases where people not yet identified as trust violators saw themselves as having financial problems which were non-shareable, realized that these could be secretly resolved by violation of financial trust and had rationalizations available to them that would preserve their trustworthiness in their own eyes. This involves modifying the process of analytic induction as indicated by Figure 5.

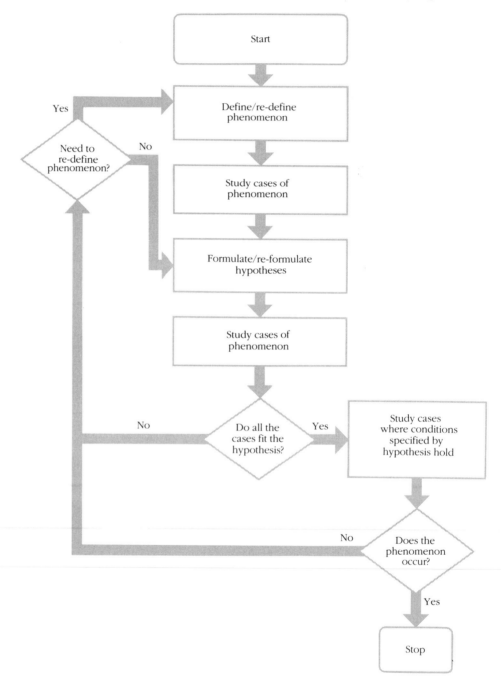

Figure 5 *A modified formalization of the analytic induction process (Source: Hammersley, 1989)*

In the case of Cressey's work, it would have been very difficult to find the sort of cases demanded by this modified version of analytic induction. However, there are examples of case-study research that come close to the hypothetico-deductive ideal. One is a sequence of investigations in the sociology of education by David Hargreaves, Colin Lacey, and Stephen Ball, each involving a lengthy study of a single secondary school. This research was concerned with the development and testing of differentiation-polarization theory: the claim that differentiation of pupils on academic-behavioural grounds (in the form of streaming or banding in secondary schools) produces polarization in their attitudes towards school, with high-status (i.e. top stream/band) pupils becoming pro-school, and low-status (i.e. bottom stream/band) pupils becoming anti-school.

The first of these studies to be published was an investigation of a streamed, secondary modern school, where the researcher can have had little doubt that polarization of attitudes would be found since it was a well-known feature of such schools (Hargreaves, 1967). What Hargreaves' study amounted to was the description of a case where differentiation was high and so too was polarization.

ACTIVITY 3

On the basis of the very limited information I have supplied, can you see any problems in concluding that differentiation causes polarization on the basis of Hargreaves' study? Answer this question before you read on.

Useful though Hargreaves' evidence is, it is rather weak support for the validity of the theory. After all, many other factors were likely to have been operative in the situation, some of which may well have produced the high level of polarization. For instance, perhaps the streaming system in the school Hargreaves studied sorted pupils on the basis of their attitudes to school, these being largely a product of extra-school factors. This could have occurred both directly, because pupils' attitudes were judged by teachers to be an important consideration, and indirectly, because these attitudes affected the pupils' academic performance. Differences in pupil attitude produced by factors outside the school could therefore explain the correlation between stream and orientation to school that Hargreaves found.

If we turn now to Lacey's study of Hightown Grammar School, we can see how it contributes to the process of testing the theory (Lacey, 1970). Not only does he document much the same correlation between stream and attitude as Hargreaves, but:

1   The case he studied involved some comparative control over the factor of differences in pupils' attitudes on entering the school. This is because Hightown was a selective school and most of the pupils who were recruited to it had been successful in their primary schools, and were highly motivated to continue their academic success.

2   He shows that the polarization in attitude increased over time from the point of initial differentiation in the first year through to the fourth year of secondary schooling.

In my judgment, these features add considerably to the plausibility of the theory, even if they do not render it absolutely convincing.

ACTIVITY 4

On the basis of the information I have provided, can you see any ways in which differentiation-polarization theory may still be false despite the evidence Lacey provides?

There are always potential doubts. For instance, in relation to point 1 above, we must remember that differences in attitude are a matter of degree. Despite relative homogeneity by comparison with differences in attitude across the whole age group, there will still have been differences in attitude among the new recruits to Hightown Grammar, and the streaming system may simply have allocated pupils to streams on that basis, hence reflecting, rather than generating, attitude polarization. Similarly, we could explain the growing polarization over time, not as the product of differentiation, but as the result of external factors operating on existing differences in attitude. After all, a lot of things happen to children outside of school during their secondary school careers — e.g. changes in relationships at home and in peer groups — and some of these are likely to be systematically related to attitude towards school.[4]

In the third of this sequence of studies, Stephen Ball (1981) investigated a comprehensive school. As a result of this choice of school type, he was not able to control for pupils' attitudes on entry in the way that Lacey had. However, he did look at change in pupils' attitudes over time, and confirmed Lacey's findings. Furthermore, he documented a change in the level of differentiation in the institution (the abandonment of banding in favour of mixed ability grouping), looking at the effects of this on the level of polarization. Given that this involved a change within a single institution over a relatively short period of time, we can assume that much (though not everything) remained the same between the two situations, before and after. Ball shows that the level of polarization was lower after mixed ability grouping had been introduced.

This is further important evidence in support of differentiation-polarization theory, increasing the confidence we can reasonably have in it. Of course, it does not place it beyond all doubt. The selection of cases studied does not rule out all other relevant possibilities. For example, the data produced by these studies could be explained by a kind of imitation theory whereby the attitudes of members of a school class are affected by the initial balance of pro- and anti-school pupils to be found within it, a theory that some teachers hold. This would explain the reduction of polarization following the abolition of banding, independently of the level of differentiation. But, as we saw earlier, even experimental research cannot establish causal relationships beyond all possible doubt. And what this series of investigations illustrates is that while case studies do not involve manipulation of variables, it is sometimes possible to use the comparison of existing cases to make reasonable judgments about causal relationships.[5]

Case studies may of course be combined with experiments in order to test hypotheses about causal relationships. A classic example is *When Prophecy Fails* (Festinger *et al.*, 1956), a social-psychological study that was designed to test cognitive-dissonance theory — a theory about the conditions of attitude change. It involved an ethnographic investigation of a small religious sect whose leader had prophesied the end of the world on a particular date. Festinger and his colleagues had tested cognitive-dissonance theory under experimental conditions but recognized the opportunity offered by the sect: 'we were understandably eager to undertake a study that could test our theoretical ideas under natural conditions' (Festinger *et al.*, 1956, p.1). They set out to investigate what would happen when the prophecy failed to be fulfilled. The theory predicted that rather than leading the sect's members to abandon their religious ideas, prophetic failure would result in their engaging in increased proselytising; and that is indeed what happened!

4   CONCLUSION

In this unit I have tried to clarify the concept of case study, treating it as one case-selection strategy amongst others. I started out from the position that it is not fruitful to think of social research methods in terms of contrasting paradigms. The methodological decisions faced by social researchers are more complex than this, allowing for more variation than such dichotomous models assume.

I defined case study as one means of tackling the problem of case selection. I contrasted it with two other case-selection strategies: surveys and experiments;

---

[4] Lacey was aware of these factors and incorporated them into his account, but as subordinate factors to differentiation. His analysis of differentiation *within* school classes, which I have not discussed here, adds further support to his general argument.

[5] For a more detailed discussion of the work of Hargreaves, Lacey and Ball from this point of view, see Hammersley, 1985. See also the recent development of this work by Abraham 1989.

and I emphasized the trade-offs involved in selecting one rather than another of these strategies. Compared with the survey, case study involves a potential trade-off between generalizability of findings to finite populations on the one hand, and the likely detail and accuracy of information on the other. Compared with the experiment, case study involves a trade-off between control of variables and level of reactivity. I noted that the significance of these trade-offs varies according to the goals and circumstances of the research. In both respects, case studies have considerable strengths. I also argued that there are various supplementary strategies which can be used to at least partially overcome their weaknesses.

When we broaden our focus from single studies to looking at the development of research in particular fields, we can see that it may be possible to maximize the advantages of two or more case-selection strategies by combining them. Succeeding units will provide more detail about other strategies and will also explore the possibilities of combining case-selection strategies in order to capitalize on their respective strengths and overcome their relative weaknesses.

REFERENCES

Abraham, J. (1989) 'Testing Hargreaves' and Lacey's differentiation-polarization theory in a setted comprehensive', *British Journal of Sociology*, vol. 40, no. 1, pp.46–81.

Ball, D.W. (1972) 'Self and identity in the context of deviance: the case of criminal abortion', in Scott, R.A. and Douglas, T. D. (eds) *Theoretical Perspectives on Deviance*, New York, Basic Books.

Ball, S.J. (1981) *Beachside Comprehensive*, Cambridge, Cambridge University Press.

Becker, H.S. (1971) *Sociological Work: Method and Substance*, London, Allen Lane.

Bertaux, D. and Bertaux-Wiame, I. (1981) 'Life stories in the bakers' trade', in Bertaux, D. (ed.) *Biography and Society: The Life History Approach in the Social Sciences*, London, Sage.

Booth, C. (ed.) (1889–1902) *Life and Labour of the People of London*, 17 vols, London, Macmillan.

Bromley, D. (1986) *The Case Study Method in Psychology and Related Disciplines*, Chichester, Wiley.

Bryman, A. (1988) *Quality and Quantity in Social Research*, London, Unwin Hyman.

Bullock, A. (1962) *Hitler: A Study in Tyranny*, Harmondsworth, Penguin.

Bullock, A. (1991) *Hitler and Stalin: Parallel Lives*, London, Harper Collins.

Cicourel, A. V. and Kitsuse, J.I. (1963) *The Educational Decision-Makers*, New York, Bobbs-Merrill.

Cressey, D. (1950) 'The criminal violation of financial trust', *American Sociological Review*, vol. 15, pp.738–43.

Cressey, D. (1953) *Other People's Money*, Glencoe Ill., Free Press.

Festinger, L., Riecken, H., and Schachter, S. (1956) *When Prophecy Fails: A Social and Psychological Study of a Modern Group that Predicts the Destruction of the World*, Minnesota, University of Minnesota Press.

Fielding, N. (1981) *The National Front*, London, Routledge and Kegan Paul.

Firestone, W.A. and Herriot, R.E. (1984) 'Multisite qualitative policy research: some design and implementation issues', in Fetterman, D.M. (ed.) *Ethnography in Educational Evaluation*, Beverly Hills, Sage.

Glaser, B.G. and Strauss, A.L. (1967) *The Discovery of Grounded Theory*, Chicago, Aldine.

Gregory, R.L. (1970) *The Intelligent Eye*, London, Weidenfeld and Nicolson.

Hammersley, M. (1985) 'From ethnography to theory', *Sociology*, vol. 19, pp.244–59.

Hammersley, M. (1989) *The Dilemma of Qualitative Method: Herbert Blumer and the Chicago Tradition*, London, Routledge.

Hammersley, M. (1991) *Reading Ethnographic Research*, London, Longman.

Hammersley, M. (1992a) *What's Wrong with Ethnography?*, London, Routledge.

Hammersley, M. (ed.) (1992b) *Social Research: Philosophy, Politics and Practice*, London, Sage (DEH313 Reader).

Hanson, N. (1958) *Patterns of Discovery*, Cambridge, Cambridge University Press.

Hargreaves, D.H. (1967) *Social Relations in a Secondary School*, London, Routledge and Kegan Paul.

Klockars, C. (1975) *The Professional Fence*, London, Tavistock.

Lacey, C. (1970) *Hightown Grammar*, Manchester, Manchester University Press.

Langlois, C.V. and Seignobos, C. (1966) *Introduction to the Study of History*, London, Duckworth.

Lewis, O. (1961) *The Children of Sanchez: Autobiography of a Mexican Family*, London, Secker and Warburg.

Lewis, O. (1964) *Pedro Martinez*, London, Secker and Warburg.

Lewis, O. (1970) *A Death in the Sanchez Family*, London, Secker and Warburg.

Millham, S., Bullock, R., Hosie, K. and Haak, M. (1986) *Lost in Care: The Problem of Maintaining Links between Children in Care and their Families*, Aldershot, Gower.

Mitchell, J.C. (1983) 'Case study and situational analysis', *Sociological Review*, vol. 31, no. 2, pp.187–211.

Olesen, V.L. and Whittaker, E.W. (1968) *The Silent Dialogue: A Study in the Social Psychology of Professional Socialization*, San Francisco, Jossey Bass.

Parker, H., Casburn, M. and Turnbull, D. (1981) *Receiving Juvenile Justice*, Oxford, Blackwell.

Pilcher, W. (1972) *The Portland Longshoreman: A Dispersed Urban Community*, New York, Holt, Rinehart and Winston.

Platt, J. (1971) *Social Research in Bethnal Green: An Evaluation of the Work of the Institute of Community Studies*, London, Macmillan.

Plummer, K. (1983) *Documents of Life: An Introduction to the Problems and Literature of a Humanistic Method*, London, Allen and Unwin.

Punch, M. (1979) *Policing the Inner City*, London, Macmillan.

Robinson, W.S. (1951) 'The logical structure of analytic induction', *American Sociological Review*, vol. 16, no. 6, pp.812–18.

Rock, P. (1973) *Making People Pay*, London, Routledge & Kegan Paul.

Schofield, J.W. (1990) 'Increasing the generalizability of qualitative research', in Hammersley, M. (1992b) (DEH313 Reader).

Shaw, C. (1930) *The Jack Roller*, Chicago, University of Chicago Press.

Sieber, S.D. (1973) 'The integration of fieldwork and survey methods', *American Journal of Sociology*, vol. 78, pp.1335–59.

Skolnick, J.P. (1966) *Justice without Trial*, New York, Wiley.

Snodgrass, J. (1982) *The Jack Roller at Seventy: A Fifty Year Follow-up*, Lexington, Mass., Lexington Press.

Strauss, A. (1987) *Qualitative Analysis for Social Sciences*, Cambridge, Cambridge University Press.

Strong, P. (1979) *The Ceremonial Order of the Clinic*, London, Routlege and Kegan Paul.

Thompson, P. (1983) *Living with the Fishing*, London, Routlege and Kegan Paul.

Waller, W. (1934) 'Insight and scientific method', *American Journal of Sociology*, vol. 40, no. 3, pp.285–97.

Woods, P. (1979) *The Divided School*, London, Routlege and Kegan Paul.

Yin, R. (1984) *Case Study Research*, Beverley Hills, Sage.

Zelditch, M. (1962) 'Some methodological problems of field studies', *American Journal of Sociology*, vol. 67, pp.566–76.

ACKNOWLEDGEMENTS

Grateful acknowledgement is made to the following sources for permission to reproduce material in this unit:

FIGURES

Figure 2: Hammersley, M. (1991) *Reading Ethnographic Research*, Longman Group UK Ltd. Adapted from Parker *et al.* (1981) *Receiving Juvenile Justice*, Basil Blackwell Ltd; Figures 4 and 5: Hammersley, M. (1989) *The Dilemma of Qualitative Method: Herbert Blumer and the Chicago Tradition*, Routledge, © Martyn Hammersley, 1989.

UNIT 8 SAMPLE SURVEYS

Prepared for the Course Team by W.N. Schofield

CONTENTS

ASSOCIATED STUDY MATERIALS

There is no set reading associated with this unit, but the use of the NUMERACY computer-assisted learning disc is recommended.

1 INTRODUCTION

In much behavioural and social science research measurements are made on a sample taken from a population and these measurements are then used to make inferences about the whole population. This is usually the case for all quantified methods, whether the design is that of an experiment, a straightforward descriptive sample survey, or a complex survey intended to supply data for constructing quasi-experimental models of supposed causal processes. This unit is about the methods and problems of designing and undertaking sample surveys. The contents are relevant to other quantified research methods, however, since inferences about population values from sample measurements will be at the heart of all of them.

Sample surveys are a feature of modern, everyday life, in business and commerce, politics and government policy, consumer marketing and entertainment, as well as in scientific research. It would be hard to find some aspect of living nowadays which was not influenced by sample survey findings. These might range from something as apparently trivial as the design of a package used to retail a commodity, or the evaluation of a television commercial, to findings used to advise policy-makers on matters which could affect the living conditions of a nation.

Consequently, it is not surprising that many individuals take survey findings for granted, at face value, and assume that those who conduct the surveys will have found and reported the true facts. This unit will show that the contrary must, at least to some extent, always be the case, although a well designed and well conducted survey can provide close estimates of the desired true values. You might have noted above, the word 'inference' and paused to wonder how 'inference' is involved in the matter of describing population characteristics. Surely this is purely descriptive, and inference is for experiments, not sample surveys? You will find as you study the material which follows, that the answer to this question is a decisive 'No'. Even at the simple level of a survey conducted on one occasion, possibly by questionnaire, or structured interview, or planned selective observation, inference is involved. What is being inferred is a characteristic, or characteristics, of the population, and this is inferred from the subset of measurements obtained from the sample. Behind this process are mathematical models and theorems which underpin the validity of the inferences so made.

This unit is not concerned with mathematical statistics but with understanding the basic methodology and how and why the various procedures work. It assumes no previous knowledge of statistics, and no more mathematics than simple arithmetic. In much descriptive research and commercial use, sample surveying is seen as an end in itself. Whatever is being investigated is described, and estimates are made of the likely range of error in this description. But, as has been mentioned, this same methodology is also a component of more complex social and behavioural research. Experiments from which inferences are to be made about populations, whether they are undertaken in the laboratory or in the field, are equally dependent on the extent to which the sample represents the intended population. The first problem of a sample survey is representation, and in dealing with this in the simplest surveys we have to employ methods equally applicable to more complex research designs.

Already in this introduction a number of technical terms have been used, and you will probably be uncertain of their meaning. This is nothing to be concerned about. A specialist topic such as sampling methodology is bound to need a specialized terminology, and the first objective of the sections which follow is to explain this terminology and to give examples. The overall aims of the unit can be summarized in two sentences:

1   It will introduce methods for obtaining representative samples of appropriate size from a population, and for providing estimates of how accurate any such sample is likely to be.

2   It will present and discuss problems in applied survey sampling, for example non-response, unreliable or invalid measurement, sample loss, incomplete data, and ways of reducing the effect of these on the final results.

How you study this material will depend on your own custom and preference, but one way would be to begin by skimming through each section to get a general idea of what the overall contents are. The next step could be to work through the sections in order, completing the activities, paying particular attention to sampling terminology and making sure that you understand the technical meaning of such apparently harmless words as 'population', 'random' and 'quota'. This unit also briefly explains such descriptive statistics as the mean and standard deviation, and how the probability of the occurrence of a value in a data set can be estimated by expressing its distance from the mean in terms of standard deviation units (z-scores). It is important that you do understand these ideas, not only for this unit but because of their relevance to statistical tests and hypothesis testing in general.

2   SAMPLING

A *sample* is a set of elements selected in some way from a population. The aim of sampling is to save time and effort, but also to obtain consistent and unbiased estimates of the population status in terms of whatever is being researched. The important point to note here is the very restricted meaning given to the term *population* in statistics, which is quite different from everyday usage. Thus a population could be all the children in some group of interest, perhaps all the children in one school, or all the children in a specified age range in a certain district, or city, or in the UK overall. A population consists of individuals, or *elements*, and these could be persons, or events, or cabbages, nuts or bolts, cities, lakes, patients, hospitals or thunderstorms: anything at all of research interest, including observations, judgements, abstract qualities, etc.

Previously you will have learnt how data can be used to calculate descriptive statistics such as the mean and the standard deviation. These provide meaningful description of the samples for which they are calculated — in this case central tendency and dispersion, respectively — but usually, in survey research, we will be interested not just in the characteristics of a sample, but in those of the population from which the sample has been drawn. Descriptive statistics for a population are called *population parameters* to contrast them with *sample statistics*. Usually the aim of a research project is not exact measurement of population parameters, such as is undertaken in a general census, but the collection of sample data to be used both to calculate sample statistics and to estimate how close these are to the unknown population parameters, i.e. to estimate the extent of *sampling error*, a concept which will be explained fully in this unit.

Thus matters of interest in applied sampling include:

- What methods are available and what are the advantages and disadvantages of each of them, theoretically, in practical terms, and in terms of cost?

- How close will statistics calculated from samples be to the unknown population parameters?

- How much will sample size influence this?

- Which will be the most effective methods of drawing representative samples — i.e. minimizing sampling error as much as possible — and in which circumstances?

- Given that a sample has been appropriately drawn, how can the effects of non-response, or sample loss in any form, be estimated?

Researchers and statisticians have developed techniques for dealing with matters such as these, and they have also developed a specialized terminology so that they can be defined and discussed. The objective of this section is to introduce you to the essential basics of this terminology.

ACTIVITY I

In this introduction to Section 2 a restricted meaning has been given to the word 'population' so that it can be used as an unambiguous technical term. Write a brief glossary entry defining this term, and give examples.

Restricted meanings are also given, or implied, for other words used in this section — those which have been italicized. List a further three of these, noting any information which would help define each of them. Complete this activity now, but do not check your answer until you have also completed Activity 2.

2.1 DEFINING THE POPULATION TO BE SAMPLED

The first step in sampling is to define the population of interest clearly and accurately. Such definition may seem obvious to a novice, but it is where survey design can all too easily be defective. For example, the intended population might be housebound single parents of young children, but if these were found *via* the records of a social or health service agency then a substantial bias might be introduced by the exclusion of parents not using, or not known to, such agencies. A further obvious example is using the telephone to contact respondents; this limits representativeness to persons meeting selection criteria, but only if they also are available by telephone. Such individuals might differ in very relevant ways from the intended population of interest. Problems such as these can be avoided by defining a population as the total collection of elements actually available for sampling rather than in some more general way. The words 'group' and 'aggregate' get close to what statisticians mean by a population (Kendall, 1952). A useful discipline for the researcher, therefore, is to bear firmly in mind precisely which elements were available in the intended population and which were not, and to use this information to limit the extent of the claims he or she makes about the generalizability of the results.

2.2 SAMPLING UNITS

For the purposes of sampling, populations can be thought of as consisting of *sampling units*. These are collections of elements which do not overlap and which exhaust the entire population. For example, if the elements were fingers, and the population all the fingers in the UK, then the sampling units could be geographical regions, provided they covered the whole of the UK and did not overlap. Or the sampling units could be families, or individual persons, or hands. Another example would be if the elements under study were persons over 60 who lived alone but who were currently receiving nursing care in hospital immediately following major surgery, and the population were all such individuals in the UK. The sampling units could be geographical regions, or hospitals, but not cities because these might not exhaust the population of interest — sampling cities might, for example, exclude rural cases.

2.3 THE SAMPLING FRAME

When a survey is being set up, the data units are organized by the researcher into a sampling frame. A *sampling frame* is whatever is being used to identify the elements in each sampling unit. Remember that each sampling unit could contain many elements, in the case of geographical regions, or just one, in the case of simple random sampling from the voting register. Whatever the circumstances, the sampling frame provides access to the individual elements of the population under study, either via sampling units, or directly when these and the population elements are identical (e.g. where we are sampling people from a finite population and we have a complete list of the names of the population).

The sampling frame could be anything at all provided that it exhausts the total population. For example, it could be company employment records, or school class lists, or hospital files, or the voting register. Such lists and records will always contain mistakes, but they may be the only method of finding the sample elements so that they can be surveyed. The survey itself will give some information on the extent of inaccuracy of this sort, for example by providing a count of voters no longer resident at the address given in the register, and it will be possible to see whether or not these inaccuracies are fairly evenly spread across the sampling frame. It is possible that greater housing mobility will be more typical of certain sample elements than others, leading to bias in the survey results. [Incidentally, the term *bias* has a precise meaning in statistics. In this unit it refers to an effect on the sample data from anything which moves the value of a statistic calculated from that sample (such as a mean) further from the true population value than would have been the case if that effect were not present.]

Much more dangerous and invidious errors originate through faulty selection of the sampling frame itself. In the real world of survey research a sample is not really a random set of elements drawn from those which define the population being researched; we can only strive to make it as close to this as possible. In practice a sample can only be a collection of elements from sampling units drawn from a sampling frame, and if that *sampling frame* is not fully representative of the population which we want to describe, then the sample will also be unrepresentative. For this reason great care should be taken in deciding just what sources will provide the sampling frame for a survey, before the frame is set up and the sample drawn.

ACTIVITY 2

The preceding paragraphs have introduced some further technical terms essential for the methods to be explained in the paragraphs which follow. Add these to your list commenced for the items in Activity 1 and add to, or amend, the answers you gave then if this seems necessary. Also say why precise definition of these terms is important.

Check your answers to both Activities 1 and 2 against those given at the end of this unit.

The classic example in the sampling literature of error due in part to choice of sampling frame was a newspaper survey which attempted to forecast the outcome of the 1936 American Presidential election. This predicted that the Republican candidate would defeat the Democratic candidate decisively by obtaining 57 per cent versus 43 per cent of the votes. In the event the result was in the opposite direction. The Democratic candidate (Roosevelt) achieved 62.5 per cent of the vote, and the Republican only 37.5 per cent. One probable reason for this was that the response rate was low in an initial sample claimed to include 10,000,000 persons, although well over 2,300,000 persons did respond. Another was that literacy was assumed, in that a postcard questionnaire had to be read, and posted back. But the most obvious design mistake was that the sampling frame did not truly represent the population of voters in the election. This was because it was compiled from lists of subscribers to the publication concerned, from lists of car owners, and from telephone directories. This introduced bias which would not have been overcome even if all 10,000,000 persons had returned their postcards — poorer people did not subscribe to the publication and were not on the telephone.

If a sampling frame is a biased representation of the population to be studied, increasing sample size will not help; the bias remains. Even an up-to-date Electoral Register might not provide an accurate frame for selecting a sample from the population of *voters* in an approaching election. This is because it will include persons who did not, in the event, vote, although they may have intended to do so when surveyed, and these individuals might differ in relevant ways from those who did vote. It will also include those who have moved away, or died, and will not include those who have actively avoided registration for some reason — for example to avoid jury service or the Community Charge.

These points have been stressed because, until one is faced with the task of accounting for an unexpected or even improbable result in survey research, locating the elements of a population might seem to involve only the practical issues of gaining access to records or lists. Clearly there is much more to it than this.

3   SELECTING A SAMPLE

Having identified the population to be researched, and arranged access to it via an accurate sampling frame, the next step will be to decide how the sample itself is to be selected. The objective will be to obtain estimates of population parameters, and some methods will do this more accurately than others. The choice of method will be a question of balancing accuracy against cost and feasibility. The methods available fall into two main categories: probabilistic sampling and non-probabilistic sampling. The former includes simple random sampling, stratified random sampling, and, if selection is at least in part random, cluster sampling. The most widely used method of non-probabilistic sampling is quota sampling. Each of these methods will be described in the sections which follow.

Often sampling will be the only feasible method of obtaining data, quite apart from questions of time and cost. But do not assume that extending a sample to include all elements in a population — i.e. conducting a census — would necessarily give better information. In some circumstances a sample will be more accurate than a census, as well as cheaper, quicker and less invasive of the community. Some sources of discrepancy between the estimated (measured) and true population value, which will hereafter be referred to as *error*, are more likely in a large-scale census than in a small and tightly managed sampling survey.

ACTIVITY 3

Write a brief account (100–120 words) of what you think might be greater problems for a census than for a sampling survey — assuming a fairly large, and dispersed, population (as in the national census).

Answers to activities are given at the end of the unit.

You will have concluded, when reading the previous paragraph, from the italics, that error is another word with a restricted meaning in sampling theory, as in statistics in general, and that it should be added to the list commenced for Activity 1. It is not synonymous with 'mistake', and does not mean 'wrong', although a mistake by an interviewer or a wrong answer to a question would each contribute to error in a survey, whether a sample survey or a census. In addition to this, for many things measured there will be variation from many sources, including individual variation, and looking at this from the perspective of a summary statistic such as the mean, this will also be error. By the time you have finished this unit, you should have a good understanding of what is meant by error, and you will also have learnt that there are various sources of error, each with different implications for survey methodology.

In your answer to Activity 3 you probably mentioned some factors such as field-work problems, interviewer-induced bias, the nature or insensitivity of the measuring instrument, or clerical problems in managing large amounts of data. Bias from sources such as these will be present irrespective of whether a sample is drawn, or a census taken. For that reason it is known as *non-sampling* error. It will be present in sample survey results, but will not be attributable to the sampling method itself. This is an important distinction.

Error which *is* attributable to sampling, and which therefore is not present in census-gathered information, is called *sampling error.* Since a sample has both kinds of error, whereas a census only has the former you might conclude that an advantage really does stay with the census. The point from Activity 3 was, however, that the scale of census-taking makes it difficult to reduce the risk of non-sampling error, and that this can be easier to do in a well-planned sample survey. Also, as you will see later, sampling error can be controlled (or at least the extent of it can be estimated, which amounts to the same thing). Thus there are occasions when a survey could produce less error overall than a full census.

As has been mentioned above, there are two basic methods of sampling: *probability sampling* and *non-probability sampling.* The former includes simple random sampling, stratified random sampling and some forms of cluster sampling. The latter, sometimes called purposive, includes (at its most sophisticated) quota sampling and (at its *least* sophisticated) what is sometimes called 'opportunity' sampling — the simple expedient of using as a sample whoever is available and willing (e.g. a 'captive' school class). A practical approach to each of these will be given in the paragraphs which follow. First, however, some further comments will be made on the contrast between probability and non-probability sampling, because (as you have guessed) these are further important technical terms. The distinction between them is closely related to the problem of dealing with error, and to a process called 'randomization'.

Probability samples have considerable advantages over all other forms of sampling. All samples will differ to some extent from the population parameters, i.e. will be subject to sampling error. Thus, suppose we sampled 100 children, and the average height of the 100 children was 1.2 metres. If the average for all the children in the population from which the sample was drawn was 1.1 metres, then the error attributable to drawing the sample rather than measuring the whole population would be 0.1 metres. For probability samples very accurate estimates can be given of the likely range of this error, even though, obviously the population value will not be known. This involves a fundamental statistical process, the randomization of error variation. Just what this means will be explained in Section 3.1 on simple random sampling.

Often in the social and behavioural sciences methodological compromise is necessary and the researcher will have little or no choice at all as to the individual subjects available for a study. A small survey might be limited to one or two hospital wards, and even then the nursing officer in charge might insist that certain patients are not included. On the day of testing there might be further loss due to ward staff decisions, or patient circumstances. Similarly, at a centre for the elderly, local staff may have arranged that certain 'difficult' individuals are not available when the survey is being taken. In such context, if a researcher is overly persistent in her or his attempt to preserve sample integrity, there could be increases in procedural and/or personal reactivity, biasing results even more than the sample loss, or at worst the researcher might simply be thrown out.

Generalizability, as you will remember from Unit 5, is an aspect of external validity. It is the extent to which research findings are true for subjects other than the ones the researcher used. The generalizability of findings from small non-random samples in circumstances such as those in the preceding paragraph might be limited but all is not lost. Firstly, any randomization which *can* be introduced into a study will help. For example, in a study of management regimes the intention may be to contrast various groups managed in different ways. Even if these groups have been preselected, they can at least be randomly allocated to 'treatment' and 'control' conditions.

Further, survey findings based on small opportunity samples will have the advantage of having little cost. There will be the risk that the population is not truly represented. But replication in a second cheap opportunity sample in which there were likely to be further, but different, sources of bias, would imply that the replicated effect was robust. Paradoxically there are circumstances in which more weight might be given to findings from two such studies than from one adequately sampled (and more expensive) study, which could have more error from some other source than sampling. There is more to evaluating research findings than deciding whether or not the rules have been followed, although these do provide yardsticks against which evaluation can be made.

3.1 SIMPLE RANDOM SAMPLING

The fundamental method of probability sampling is simple random sampling. Random sampling means that every element in the population of interest has an *equal and independent* chance of being chosen. Here the word 'independent' means that the selection of any one element in no way influences the selection of any other. 'Simple' does not mean that random sampling is easier to carry out than other methods, but that steps are taken to ensure that nothing influences selection each time a choice is made, other than chance. In theory this requires selection with replacement — any element sampled should be replaced in the sampling frame so that it has a chance of being chosen again — or else the probability of being selected would change each time an element was removed from the sampling frame and placed in the sample. In practice, however, samples in survey research will generally be comparatively small in contrast with the number of elements potentially available for sampling, and the effect of non-replacement will be trivial and need not concern us further.

Beginner researchers sometimes think that if they do nothing, but simply take what comes, then that will somehow amount to 'chance' selection. But in sampling practice the chance of selection applies to the probability of particular elements of the population being selected, and not to whether or not a random sample has been achieved. That certainly cannot be left to chance. Random sampling does not mean 'haphazard' — i.e. following no thought-out plan to obtain sample elements. Possibly worse than the beginner who does nothing is the experienced scientist who believes that he or she can select randomly, near enough. There is much literature showing that this is not the case. Even for something as matter-of-fact as selecting wheat plants from a field for the study of growth characteristics, experienced researchers trying to choose randomly were shown to have introduced strong bias. For samples taken when the plants were young there was over-selection of those which were tallest, whereas a month later when ears had formed, there was strong bias towards middle-sized, sturdier plants (Yates, 1935).

Simple random sampling might not be at all simple to achieve, depending on circumstances. For example it might be very difficult to achieve a random sample of serving seamen in the merchant navy, even if an accurate sampling frame could be compiled. Random sampling does not just mean stopping individuals in the street. Which individuals? Which street? Obviously, there would be a risk of stopping only individuals who looked as if they would be helpful. Or of choosing a well lit, safe street. The flow of passers-by might be influenced by some biasing event: a store sale, an office or bureau somewhere in the not too immediate vicinity, etc.

Random sampling is similar to tossing a coin, throwing a dice or drawing names from a hat, and in some circumstances procedures such as these might be adequate, but usually random number tables or computerized random number generators will be used. The first step is to number in order the individual elements in the population, as listed in the sampling frame. Sometimes this numbering will already be present, or will be implied. If tables are to be used the next step is to enter them at some random place, e.g. by dropping a small item onto the page and selecting the number nearest to it. This then will provide the first random number. From this start the required set of random numbers is then achieved by stepping forwards or backwards or sideways through the tables in any systematic way. Until recently, statistical texts usually contained tables of random numbers, and we have supplied one in the Statistics Handbook, but nowadays most researchers use computer programs to generate a list of random numbers containing whatever number of items is required.

Many survey reports will not have used true random sampling (from random number tables or a computer-generated list), but something called *systematic sampling*. If, for example, you have a list of a hundred names from which to sample ten, an easy way to obtain a sample is to start from a randomly chosen point on the list and take every tenth item (treating the list as circular and starting again at the beginning when the end is reached). The great advantage of systematic sampling over simple random sampling is that it is easier to perform and it provides more information per unit cost than does simple random sampling. Also because it is simpler, fieldworkers are less likely to make selection errors. For example, constructing a simple random sample of shoppers leaving a certain supermarket might be very difficult to achieve in practice, but selecting one at random, and then subsequently stopping every twentieth shopper would be less so. A systematic sample is more evenly spread across a population than a simple random sample, and in some circumstances this could be advantageous, for example in monitoring items on a production line, or for choosing a sample of accounts for detailed auditing. Mostly systematic sampling will be adequate as a form of random sampling, but only to the extent to which there is no 'pattern' in the sampling frame and the placing of any item in it really *is* independent of the placing of other items. This is by no means always the case. If we were using the Electoral Register, for example, we would expect the members of each household to be listed together and, as there are seldom as many as ten people in a household, the selection of a given household member would guarantee the exclusion of all other household members if we were to take every tenth name. Worse, systematic sampling can occasionally introduce a *systematic bias*: for example, if the names in a school class were listed systematically as 'boy, girl, boy, girl … ' and we sampled every second name, we should obtain a sample made up of a single gender from a class made up of the two genders in equal proportions. When such risks are known they can be avoided by choosing a suitable sampling interval, or else after a set number of elements have been sampled a fresh random start can be made.

3.2   STRATIFIED RANDOM SAMPLING

One problem with simple random sampling is that sample size may need to be disproportionately large to ensure that all subgroups (or *strata*) in the population are adequately represented. For example, a researcher who intends surveying the attitudes of school leavers to further training might see age at leaving school as an important relevant factor. A simple random sample would need to be large enough to remove the risk of inadequate representation of the ages of leaving with least frequency in the population. This could be avoided by dividing the population into age strata, and randomly sampling from each of these. The objective would be adequate representation at reduced cost.

To draw a stratified random sample the elements of a population are divided into non-overlapping groups — *strata*. Simple random samples are drawn from each of these, and together they form the total sample. If the proportion of the sample taken from each stratum is the same as in the population, then the procedure is called *proportionate* random sampling, and the total sample will match the population. In some cases, however, this might result in small strata of interest not being represented adequately in the final sample. This can be avoided by increasing sample size in all such strata, but not for other strata, and still with random selection. The result would be *disproportionate* stratified random sampling. Here the sample will not match the population, but it will differ from it in known ways which can be corrected arithmetically. (An unbiased estimator of the population mean will be a weighted average of the sample means for the strata, i.e. the contribution of each subset of data to the population estimates will be in proportion to its size. Estimates of variance and of sampling error can also be weighted.)

You may well wonder, why not always stratify, and thus reduce cost? One problem is that stratification is not always a simple matter. In any reasonably sized survey a number of variables will be possible candidates for governing stratification. Deciding which can be no easy matter. Decisions which seem clear-cut when the sample is being selected are sometimes reassessed as unfortunate when the survey results are interpreted.

Further, although the purpose of stratification is to increase precision by reducing sampling error without increasing cost, it can, in some circumstances, lead to less precision than simple random sampling. For example, in a national educational survey stratification could be made in terms of Education Authorities, on the grounds that these vary greatly in size and character, and also for administrative convenience, but there could be other units unequally distributed within authorities, such as type of school district or level of institution, with greater variability than between authorities. Unfortunately this might remain unknown until the survey results are analysed, when it would become clear that a simple random sample of the same size would have provided better population estimates.

Even so, for many surveys an advantage is seen for stratification, and it is possibly the most popular procedure in survey research. Money is saved by reduction in sample size for the required degree of statistical precision. Fieldwork costs, such as time, travel, interviewer and administration fees, and the printing and processing of questionnaires, are reduced.

Table 1 illustrates proportionate and disproportionate random sampling from a population of 6,000 school leavers in a provincial city. The objective of the survey was to find what proportion of the school leavers were in full-time education or employment 18 months after leaving school. The researchers were asked to provide a breakdown of the findings by sex and any other factor found to be relevant when the sample data were analysed. For the purpose of the example it will be assumed that sample size was limited to 400.

Table 1 Proportionate and disproportionate random sampling from 6,000 school leavers

School leaving age	Population size	Percentage total in each stratum	Proportionate		Disproportionate	
			sample size	sampling fraction	sample size	sampling fraction[a]
16	2,730	45.5		1/15		1/20
17	1,950	32.5		1/15		1/15
18 and over	1,320	22.0		1/15		1/10
Total	6,000	100.0	400	1/15	402	1/15

[a] The denominators for the disproportionate sampling fractions have been rounded to give whole numbers.

ACTIVITY 4

The columns in Table I for proportionate and disproportionate sample size for the separate strata have been left blank. Calculate and enter on the table the missing figures. Before reading further make a note of which method of sampling you think ought to have been used on this occasion and, very briefly, why. Check your calculations against the completed table given at the end of this unit.

The decision as to whether proportionate or disproportionate stratified random sampling should be used in this case cannot be made on statistical grounds. If the overall population parameters are the main interest then proportionate sampling will give the best estimates of these. But is this likely to be the case? A breakdown by sex has been requested, and assuming that the school leavers are about half female and half male, the oldest leavers will be represented by about 44 boys and 44 girls. Considering that the researcher will break these down into those who are employed, unemployed, or in further education, then group size will be getting very small. And what about other groups of potential interest, such as race, or new immigrant categories: is it likely that the client will want information on sex differences within these as well?

When making decisions on sampling the researcher will have to balance these various potential needs, and there will have to be compromise. In general, if there is a risk that subgroups of interest will be insufficiently represented in some strata of the sample, then sample size will need to be increased, and the cost of this will be less if the increase is made only in the strata where it is thought to be needed. This could then compromise some other aspect of the findings, by reducing sample size in other strata if the same total sample size needs to be maintained, and mostly there will be no completely satisfactory answer to problems of this kind in practice.

For the present example the preferred method would be simple random sampling, with a sample size big enough to provide adequate numbers in the smallest groups of interest. As an adequate size for the smallest subgroup could mean 40 or more children, this would be unrealistic. Consequently, disproportionate random sampling would be used. This would cost more per element sampled, because of the need to include age strata as a sampling criterion, but overall it would be cheaper because fewer elements would be required. In the full sample, however, there would be over-representation of minority groups and the sample would not accurately reflect population characteristics, although this could be taken into account in calculating and interpreting statistics.

3.3   CLUSTER SAMPLING

Cluster sampling improves on stratified random sampling by further reducing costs, but with a risk of increasing sampling error. A *cluster sample* is a probability sample in which the elements are all the members of randomly selected sampling units, each of which is a collection or cluster of elements from the population sampled. Cluster sampling is advantageous when a sampling frame listing population elements is not available, or is not easily obtained, or is likely to be very inaccurate, and also when the cost of conducting the survey will be unduly increased by the distance separating the elements. This distance is usually in the geographical sense, but it could also be in time — for example when supermarket customers, or the persons brought into a police station, or casualty clinic, are sampled at designated time periods during a week. For a genuine probability sample both the time periods, or any other form of cluster, and the individuals surveyed should be chosen at random. Simply accepting all the individuals who turn up or pass by at some specified time or times until the required number has been obtained would not constitute cluster sampling which is a probability method.

Cluster sampling can be proportionate, or disproportionate as described above for stratified random sampling. Further, in many contexts there will be another level of selection within clusters, either by random selection, or by additional clustering. The following paragraphs will make this clearer.

In a study of teacher/parent relationships within one large Local Education Authority, interest centred on the final two years of infant education and the first two years of junior school. This is an age range when there is an emphasis on learning to read, and on improving reading skill and vocabulary. Some infant and junior classes were within one school, under one head, but in other cases infant and junior schools were separately housed and administered, although intake at the junior school was always from its related infant school. Further, the schools were of different sizes, ranging from one to three parallel classes.

For sampling purposes children attending school in the authority in the four relevant school years were the population, and clustering was in non-overlapping blocks of all classes within the two infant and two junior years at the same school or schools related by intake. The survey was in fact to be conducted four times, at yearly intervals, so that children in the first infant year at the beginning of the study could be followed in subsequent years and compared with parallel previous and future year groups, both within and between schools. The study thus matched a design to be dealt with in Unit 9, but it is important to understand that the sampling plan for a repeated (longitudinal) survey, or for an intervention project, could be basically the same as for a once-only survey.

For the purpose of this example assume that six of these clusters were chosen at random for the survey. This would give clusters containing disproportionate numbers of classes, i.e. ranging from a total of four to twelve depending on school size. A random sample of children could have been chosen from each of these clusters, or if intact classes were required one class could have been chosen by lottery from each school year within each cluster.

As mentioned above, cluster sampling is cheaper than other methods because the cost of data collection can be greatly reduced. In the example a sample size of between 600 and 700 children would be expected in the first year. Clearly interviewing or testing would have been more time consuming and costly if these had been randomly selected from all the authority's schools, instead of being concentrated in just a few. The task of following and individually testing these children as they progressed across the four school years would also have been considerable.

In this hypothetical research (modified from Tizard *et al.*, 1982) there would be the risk that the clusters had unfortunately fallen by chance on a small group of schools that were unrepresentative, either totally or to some significant extent, of the other schools under the authority's care. There is no way that this risk could be ruled out without taking into account information from outside the survey findings, since these would only include material on the selected schools. Clearly any such information could be taken into account in the first place and used to formulate selection criteria. These criteria could then be used to select clusters larger than needed and from which random selection could take place. Sometimes cluster samples are non-probability samples at every level, except that if there are treatment and control groups then these are allocated to those conditions randomly. It is essential that this one element of randomization is preserved, and even then the sampling is not strictly cluster sampling but is of the non-probabilistic, opportunity, variety.

ACTIVITY 5

Assume that you have been called on to advise the research team for the example given above.

The study was in fact an intervention project, because treatment and control groups are mentioned, i.e. outcomes are to be measured for some children who have received an intervention, and some who have not. If it had been a straightforward survey, what advice would you give if you were asked whether or not simple random sampling would be appropriate? (Your answer should be approximately 100 words in length.)

Assuming that there was to be an intervention, i.e. some children were to receive a treatment not given to others, and that six clusters each of four classes had been chosen, what (sampling) advice would you give to a researcher who proposed randomly sampling 30 children from the four classes in each cluster, i.e. total sample size $n = 180$, if the intervention was (a) a daily multivitamin pill or (b) a classroom learning method using a new computer provided for that purpose. (Approx. 100 words.)

Sometimes cluster sampling is the only alternative realistically available, e.g. for surveying the unemployed and homeless, when compilation of a sampling frame would in practice be impossible. Or in cases where lists of the elements in a population may exist, but are unavailable to the survey researcher, or are known to be unredeemably defective.

Much policy-related survey research is undertaken in developing countries and can influence the funding policy of aid agencies. Sample findings which did not generalize to the population in need of aid could have disastrous consequences, yet random or stratified sampling from population lists is not likely to be possible. Cluster sampling will usually include at least some element of randomization, which in contrast with a totally haphazard method will permit qualified estimation of the extent of sampling error. Common sense and professional judgement are likely to be needed even more than usual when evaluating research results in such circumstances.

For example, in a study of children moderately to severely ill with malnutrition in overcrowded and economically disadvantaged areas of a tropical city, it was arranged that all 200 central public health clinics (clusters, the first level of support in the community) would refer all cases on to the Outpatient Department of a hospital where the research team was based. At this stage information from clinical examination, questionnaires to parents or caretakers, and treatment information provided survey-type data. Severity of illness then determined which children were admitted for hospital treatment, and which were allocated to a home treatment programme supervised by health workers. So far, sampling was in all ways non-probabilistic, and could not ethically have been otherwise.

Three separate studies were developed from this basis, and randomization was introduced into these. The children admitted to hospital were randomly allocated to a group discharged for community-based care when they had recovered from their initial illness, and to a group given this additional care in hospital. The children not admitted were randomly allocated to different nutritional and antibiotic treatments (Heikens et al., 1989). In evaluating this research clinicians and health policy-makers will take into account the sampling procedure, and also the results of door to door surveying in the same community (Fletcher et al., 1990), as well as other related research. Obviously, the matter of prime interest is how far the findings can be generalized, not only to other nutritionally ill children in the same community, but to similarly ill children elsewhere, and information on sampling is obviously highly relevant to decisions on this.

3.4   QUOTA SAMPLING

In the most widely used method of non-probability sampling the population is split up into non-overlapping subgroups, as for stratified sampling. Quotas of the desired number of sample cases are then calculated proportionally to the number of elements in these subgroups. These quotas are then divided up among the interviewers, who simply set out to find individuals who fit the required quota criteria. They continue doing this until they have filled their quota. A given interviewer, for example, might have to find five middle-class and five working-class women over the age of 30, with no other control over who these people are or how they are located, as long as they fill the criteria. This method is called *quota sampling*.

One reason for using quota samples is, again, to reduce costs, but another is that this method seems to have intuitive appeal to some survey practitioners. For example, quota sampling is widely used in market research. Thus, if a population is known to have 60 per cent females and 40 per cent males it might require a comparatively large sample to reflect this proportion exactly. It might, however, seem important to the researcher that it should be so reflected, whatever the sample size. This can be achieved, for the present example even in a sample of ten, by selecting quotas of six females and four males.

The major problem with quota sampling is that attempts to deal with one known source of bias may well make matters worse for others not known, or at least not known until after the data have been collected and it is too late. Further, as there is no element of randomization, the extent of sampling error cannot be estimated. For example, in an earlier Open University research methods course students undertook a research project on class attitudes in the UK. A questionnaire designed and piloted by the course team was administered by each student to a small group of respondents. The student then collated the data for her or his small subsample, and sent them off to the university to be merged with the data from all other students. For 1991 this produced a national sample of well over 900 respondents, as did the preceding year. Questions were included on class consciousness, class awareness, and aspects of class structure. There were questions intended to identify class stereotypes, and questions seeking biographical information on such matters as sex, age, educational attainment, housing, and previous voting behaviour. The intended population was all adults in the UK.

ACTIVITY 6

Write a very brief note saying which sampling method would, in an ideal world, have been best for this study, and what the main advantage of this would be. (Approx. 75 words.)

In fact the method chosen, for practical reasons, was quota sampling. Each student was asked to collect data from four respondents in an interlocking quota design which took into account three criteria: social class, sex and age. This design is shown in Figure 1. Thus a student with an even OU student number (right-hand side of the figure) found one respondent for each of the following categories:

> male/working class/18–34 years,
>
> male/middle class/35+ years,
>
> female/middle class/18–34 years,
>
> female/working class/35+ years.

As you can see from Figure 1, a student with an odd student number also chose four respondents, but with the position of the social class categories reversed.

		Odd student number:		Even student number:	
		Age		Age	
		18–34	35+	18–34	35+
Sex	Male	middle	working	working	middle
	Female	working	middle	middle	working

Figure 1 *Interlocking quota sampling design for a survey project. Social classes ABC1 are shown as 'middle', and social classes C2DE as 'working'*

When the course was being developed a pilot study was undertaken using this quota design. The results revealed what appeared to be a strong bias in the sample. For example, there was an unexpectedly high number of respondents in social class A or B who appeared to have 'left-wing' attitudes. Further, the pilot study did not find some of the differences between the social classes expected from other research. The pilot interviewers had correctly followed the quota procedure but had selected middle-class individuals who were not representative of the national population. The same may well have applied to the selection of working-class respondents. It is easy to think of many possible sources of bias when respondents are selected by interviewers solely to fill sampling quotas.

Although the bias in the pilot study was noted when the results were analysed, it was decided that in a large sample collected by OU students across all parts of the

UK there would be no such problem. In the event, as the years went by, successive waves of students collected and analysed the pooled data, both regionally and nationally. Invariably it was found that although students had selected individuals to fill their quotas according to the set criteria, the working-class individuals sampled by OU students differed in material ways from what was expected for that social class in the population at large, and the same was true for the middle-class component of the sample. Random sampling, if it had been possible, would have avoided this persistent and pervasive selection bias, whereas increasing sample size did not. In general, selection bias will never be overcome by increasing sample size, which will in the circumstances merely inflate costs to no avail.

At a number of previous places in the text of this unit other non-probability methods such as 'opportunity' sampling — the simple expedient of including as subjects whoever happens to be available from the population of interest — have been mentioned. These methods, or lack of methods, are sometimes referred to as 'haphazard' sampling, but the term 'opportunity' is preferred because it implies usually what is the case, i.e. the necessity of accepting whatever is available, with no realistic alternative. Thus in a study of new admissions of the elderly to institutional care, the sample might be all admissions until adequate sample size has been achieved at the only institution, or institutions, available to the researcher. Alternatively, data collection could be continued until certain predetermined quotas were achieved. For example, a quota could be set for the minimum number of persons diagnosed as suffering from senile dementia. Note that this differs from regular quota sampling, where there is an element of choice in that the fieldworker selects individuals to fill the quotas. It also is not *sequential sampling*, which is a method assuming both independence and random selection, but in which sample size is not predetermined. Instead random sampling continues sequentially until a pre-established criterion has been met, e.g. that the sample includes 30 individuals diagnosed as having senile dementia. The purpose of sequential sampling is to find out what sample size will be needed to reach the set criterion in the population under study.

Introducing quotas to an opportunity sample might increase the usefulness of the data obtained but would probably render the sample even less representative of admissions to the institutions concerned than would otherwise have been the case. A decision as to which method would be most appropriate would take into account the specific interests and needs of the researcher and her or his clients, as it would be likely to influence results in some significant way.

4 ESTIMATION OF POPULATION PARAMETERS

To follow this section you need to understand in principle the main measure of central tendency — the mean — and measures of dispersion such as the variance and standard deviation. You will also need to understand how probability can be defined as relative frequency of occurrence, and that it can be represented by the area under a curve — by a frequency distribution.

ACTIVITY 7

If you are not familiar with any of these concepts, work through Topic 2 ('Making sense of measured data') on the NUMERACY computer-assisted learning disc, and the sections of Topic 3 ('Looking for differences') on means and standard deviations, before continuing.

Figures 2, 3 and 4 are intended to refresh your memory. Figure 2 is a histogram showing the heights for a sample of 1,052 mothers. The central column of this

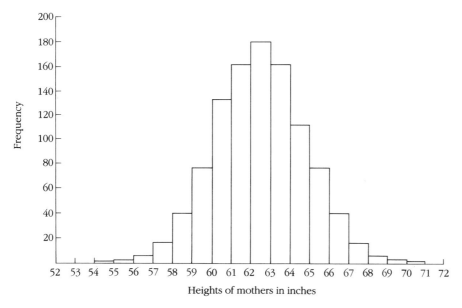

Figure 2 *Distribution of heights in a sample of 1,052 mothers*
(Source: data originally from Pearson and Lee, 1902)

histogram tells us that about 180 mothers in the sample were between 62 and 63 inches high. From the column furthest to the right we can see that almost none were over 70 inches high. Histograms are simple graphical devices for showing frequency of occurrence. You will be familiar with this idea from the 'Making sense of measured data' topic on the computer-assisted learning disc, but study Figure 2 carefully before reading further so that you can relate what you have learnt previously to the present context.

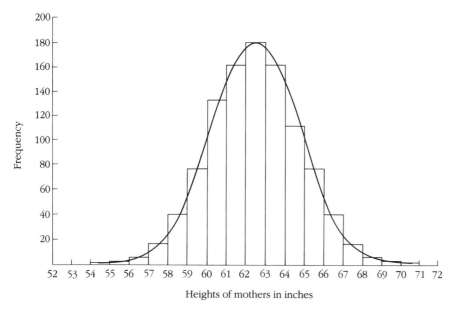

Figure 3 *Mothers' heights: histogram and superimposed normal curve*

Figure 3 shows another way of representing this same information, this time by a continuous curve — but the histogram has been left in as well, so that you can see that the curve does fit, and that either method provides a graphical representation of the same information. Mothers' heights are a continuous measure, and in a way the curve seems more appropriate than the histogram. But the histogram makes it clear that what is represented by the area within the figure, or under the curve, is frequency of occurrence. Thus the greatest frequency, i.e. the most common height for the mothers is the 62 to 63 inch interval. Reading from the curve, we can more accurately place this at 62.5 inches. Check this for yourself.

Now look at Figure 4. Here only the curve is shown, together with the scale on the axis, plus some additional scales and markings. Take your time, and study

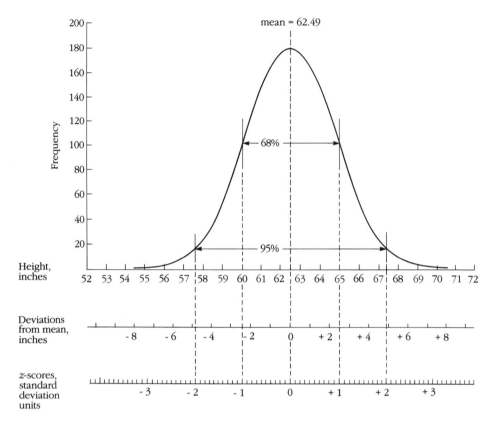

Figure 4 *Mothers' heights expressed in deviation and z-score units*

these carefully. Note first of all that the total area under the curve from its left extreme to its right extreme represents the variation in height of all 1,052 mothers. It is important to understand the idea of the area representing, in the sense of being proportional to, the variation in the mothers' heights. Some other matters need revision before the additional scales shown on this figure are explained, and we will also, for the moment, defer explanation of the areas on the figure marked off as 68 per cent and 95 per cent of the total area under the curve.

You will recall that the *mean* is simply the total height of all mothers, added up and divided by the number of mothers, i.e. the arithmetical average. The mean is at the centre of the distribution shown in Figure 4. Half of the mother's heights (50 per cent or 0.5 as a proportion) are above the mean and half are below it. The *standard deviation* is also an average, but not an average representing where the centre of the distribution is but how it is spread out, i.e. an average of the dispersion. The standard deviation of a population is found by calculating the mean; finding the difference between each value and the mean; squaring each of the differences (deviations) so obtained; adding them all up; dividing by the number of values averaged, and finding the square root of the final answer to get back to the original scale of measurement. If you read through the preceding sentence quickly it might seem complicated, and standard deviations may remain a mystery. If you are still unsure on this idea of averaging the dispersion then re-read slowly, and perhaps use a pencil to re-express the procedures described in your own words.

ACTIVITY 8

Better still, using only the information given in the preceding two paragraphs calculate the mean and the standard deviation of the following numbers:

{1, 2, 3, 4, 5}

and also for

{1, 1, 0, 1, 12}

Compare the two means and the two standard deviations, and make a note of any way in which they are similar, or different. Check your results against those given at the end of the unit.

In the preceding paragraphs to provide a clear account of what the mean and the standard deviation (SD) represent it has been assumed that the simple set of numbers

{1, 2, 3, 4, 5}

form a complete population. If, however, they represent a sample from a population then an adjustment would be needed to allow for the fact that the standard deviation is a biased estimator of the population standard deviation. It does seem intuitively obvious that the dispersion in a sample drawn from a population must on average be less than the dispersion in the total population. Also, that the smaller a sample is, then the greater the comparative effect of this bias will be. For that reason when the SD of a sample is calculated, rather than that of a population, the divisor in forming the average of the squared deviations from the mean is not the sample size n, but $n - 1$.

Now, to return to Figure 4: the point about this curve is that it follows a well-known mathematical model, the normal distribution, and is completely described by its mean and standard deviation. Once you know the mean and SD of any normally distributed variable, then you can say precisely what shape the distribution will be, and whereabouts within this shape any particular value will fall. This will be a statement about probability of occurrence.

Thus if you had the height of just one mother there would be a 100 per cent (near enough) probability that it would fall somewhere under the curve shown. There would be a high probability that its actual value would be somewhere between 1 standard deviation above and 1 standard deviation below the mean, since 68 per cent of the area of the curve in *any* normal distribution is in this range. There would be a low probability of it being greater than 2 standard deviations above the mean, because less than 2.5 per cent of the area under the curve is that far above the mean. You can see this in Figure 4 where the proportions of area within the ranges of 1 and 2 standard deviations above and below the mean are shown.

Before moving on let us consider one further example using different data. Suppose the mean IQ of a sample is 100 and the SD is 15. Then one individual with an IQ of 145 would be 3 standard deviations above the mean. This person's IQ would be located at the extreme right-hand side of the curve. This far out the area under the curve is a very small proportion of the total area. Finding an IQ this high in a sample with mean 100 and SD 15 is a rare event. The probability for the occurrence of this event is very low, and can be calculated precisely.

Finally, Figure 4 includes two new scales drawn beneath the horizontal axis. The first simply replaces each value by its deviation from the mean. These are *deviation scores*. If you summed them, they would add to zero. They are expressed in inches, as that is the scale of the variable represented, i.e. height. Negative values give inches below the mean, positive values are inches above the mean. Do not read on until you have looked back at the figure to check the deviation score scale.

Below the deviation scores is a further scale for the horizontal axis. This is marked out in *z-scores*. These have been obtained by dividing each deviation score on the line above by the standard deviation, i.e. the deviations from the mean are no longer expressed in inches, but in standard deviation units. (You met these in Unit 6, where they were used to 'normalize' data on health and material deprivation.)

The crucial point to grasp is that, whatever units are used on the horizontal axis, the frequency distribution above the axis remains unchanged. All we have is three different ways of representing the same thing. These are mothers' height in inches, mothers' height in deviation scores, and mothers' height in z-scores (sometimes called standard scores). You can read off that the average mother is 62.5 inches tall, or that her height as a deviation from the mean is zero, or that her height on a scale of standard deviations from the mean is zero.

These three different scales for reporting mothers' height go beyond just a matter of convenience, such as changing from inches to centimetres. To say that a mother is 62.5 inches high tells us just that. But to say that a mother's height expressed as a z-score is 0 tells us that in this sample the mother is precisely of average height. A mother with a height of +2.5 on this scale is a very tall woman, and we could say what the probability would be of finding someone that tall by working out what proportion of the total area under the curve is 2.5 SD above the mean. Similarly a mother with a z-score of −2.5 would have a low probability of occurrence. In practice we will not need to calculate these probabilities because they will be the same for any normal curve and can be found in a table, for example in the Statistics Handbook. This is an advantageous characteristic of z-scores, not present when the measurements were expressed in the original scale of inches. Another advantage of z-scores is that they provide a common scale for measurements initially made on different scales. (It was for this purpose, among others, that they were used in the health and material deprivation study in Unit 6.)

To conclude this revision, consider that Figure 4 represents a random sample drawn from all mothers in the UK early in this century. We have calculated the sample mean, and by using the standard deviation and a mathematical model — the normal distribution — we have found a method of calculating the probability for the occurrence of any individual data item in that sample, which at the same time provides a common scale of measurement for any normally distributed variable, i.e. standard deviation units, or z-scores.

4.1 HOW SAMPLE MEANS ARE DISTRIBUTED

In the previous subsections a method was developed for calculating the probability for the occurrence of any individual data item in a sample for which the mean and the SD were known. This involved the simple expedient of re-expressing the scale of measurement as one of z-scores. We have seen what z-scores are in SD units. A z-score of +1.96 is 1.96 standard deviation units above the mean. A z-score of −1.96 is 1.96 standard deviation units below the mean. For *any* normal distribution these values mark off the lower and upper 2.5 per cent of the area under the curve. Thus a value which is outside the range of + or −1.96 SD from the mean has a probability of occurring less than five times in every 100 trials. This is usually written as $p < 0.05$.

ACTIVITY 9

If you are still having difficulty with the idea of the normal distribution, look again at the section on it in Topic 2 of the NUMERACY computer-assisted learning disc ('Making sense of measured data').

The important point to keep in mind for the remainder of Section 4 is that we will no longer be considering individual items of data, from which one mean value is to be calculated, but just *mean values* themselves. We are concerned with mean values because we want to know how confident we can be that they are accurate estimates of population parameters.

Can we use the method of the previous subsection for finding the probability not of encountering one individual data element of a particular value, e.g. one woman 62.5 inches high, but for finding the probability for the occurrence of a *sample mean* of that, or any other, size? Well obviously what would be needed to do this is not a frequency distribution of data values, but a frequency distribution of sample means. Using a statistical package called Minitab I have generated just such a distribution (Minitab, 1985). I have used a random number generator to draw 100

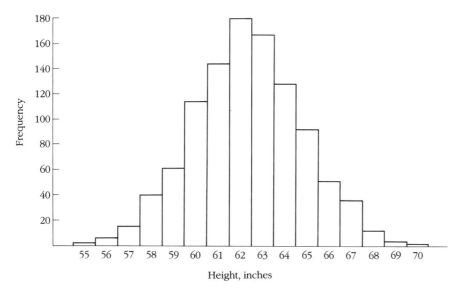

Figure 5 *Distribution of simulated mothers' heights in a single random sample, mean = 62.49, SD = 2.45*

samples, each with n = 1,052, from a population with the same mean and standard deviation as shown in Figure 2, i.e. mean = 62.49 and SD = 2.435. This is as if I had measured the heights of 105,200 mothers, 1,052 at a time. Just one of these samples is illustrated in Figure 5. It has a mean of 62.49 and SD is 2.45. Both are close to the population values. A histogram including this mean and means for the other 99 samples can be seen in Figure 6 with the horizontal scale (inches) the same as for Figure 5, but with the vertical scale (frequency) reduced so that the columns fit on the page.

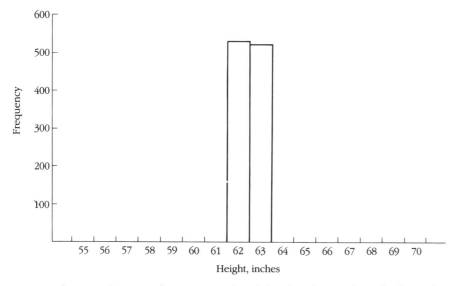

Figure 6 *Distribution of mean simulated heights from a hundred random samples, mean = 62.498, SD = 0.074*

The mean of the means given in Figure 6 is 62.498 much the same as for the full sample, but the SD is dramatically reduced to only 0.074. Clearly a distribution of sample means is more closely grouped around the central value, than is a distribution of data values. So that you can see that within this narrower range the individual means do follow a normal distribution, Figure 6 has been redrawn as Figure 7 with more bars. Note that the range of mean values in Figure 7 is from a minimum of 62.25 to a maximum of 62.75, in contrast to the sample data in Figure 5 where it is from 55.0 to 70.0 — a range of less than 1 inch, compared to a range of 15 inches.

Armed with the information in Figure 7, we can now put a probability on different means, i.e. determine their relative frequency. We can see, for example, that a mean of 62.75 is in the top extreme of the distribution. This mean would have a

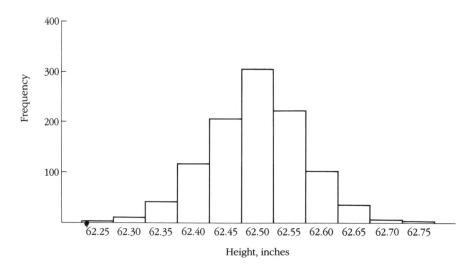

Figure 7 *Distribution of mean simulated heights from a hundred random samples (same results as in Figure 6, but scaled for more detailed display)*

z-score of +3.62, and from statistical tables I have found that the probability of obtaining a z-score with this value is only $p < 0.0001$, i.e. only 1 in 10,000. A sample from the present population with this mean would indeed be an exceptionally rare event.

This is all very well, but if a researcher has undertaken a sample survey, and has calculated a mean value for a variable of interest, what would be the good of knowing that if many more samples were randomly selected and a mean calculated for each of them to give a distribution of sample means, then probabilities could be calculated? Fortunately these are just the kinds of problems where statisticians have come to the aid of researchers, and have provided a simple but accurate method of estimating from just one sample of data — provided it has been randomly sampled — what the standard deviation (which we will refer to as *standard error*, SE, which is represented by a capital S as indicated in the Statistics Handbook) would be for a distribution of sample means from the same population. The formula for doing this, together with an example of the calculations, is:

$$SE = SD/\sqrt{n}$$

i.e.

$$S_{mean} = s/\sqrt{n}$$

where s is standard deviation and n is sample size. We can make these calculations for the data given in Figure 5 where the mean is 62.49 and the SD is 2.45:

$$S_{mean} = 2.45/\sqrt{(1,052)}$$

$$= 2.45/32.4346$$

$$= 0.076.$$

Hopefully you will be amazed at just how simple this procedure is. The standard deviation which we have just calculated is given the special name of standard error because it is used to estimate the sampling error associated with one specific sample mean. The standard error of a mean is an estimate of the standard deviation of the distribution of sample means.

Now since the standard error is the standard deviation of a distribution of sample means and these are normally distributed, then 95 per cent of the values in that distribution are within the range of ± 1.96 standard deviations from the mean, i.e. approximately ± 2 standard deviations from the mean. In the present example that gives a range from approximately 0.15 below to 0.15 above the mean (2 × 0.076), i.e. from 62.34 to 62.64. We can be 95 per cent confident that the true population mean will be somewhere within this range.

Notice how close the value we have just calculated by weighting the SD of one sample by the square root of the sample size, i.e. 0.076, is to the true SD of the distribution of sample means, which we do have in this case, i.e. 0.074.

4.2   THE STANDARD ERROR OF A PROPORTION

Often survey findings are expressed not as mean values, but as proportions or percentages. For example, a finding might be that 36 per cent of all households use brand X to wash the dishes. Assuming that this assertion is based on a sample survey for which 1,000 households were sampled, what would the likely margin of error be? Provided sampling was by a probability method, e.g. simple random sampling, then an unbiased standard error can be calculated.

The theory behind calculating descriptive statistics and standard errors for proportions is harder to follow than is the case for means. This is because it involves using what is known as the *binomial distribution*. This distribution is appropriate when a proportion p of the members of a population possess some attribute. The proportion which does not possess this attribute will be $1 - p$. This is written as q. Thus for the example above:

$p = 0.36$

and

$q = 0.64.$

It is often not realized that a proportion is itself a mean. For example, suppose that we had a sample representing the possession, or the lack of, an attribute. The sample is $n = 10$ and possession is coded as 1 and non-possession as 0. If six individuals in this sample possessed the attribute then the data would be

{1 1 1 1 1 1 0 0 0 0}

and this would give

$p = 0.6.$

But if we average the ten numbers we will get exactly the same value:

mean = 6/10

= 0.6.

If the variable coded by these data were gender, then it would seem strange to say that the mean maleness (or femaleness, depending on what the code of 1 represented) was 0.6, but if we did, it would amount to the same as saying that the proportion of the sample who were male was 0.6, or 60 per cent.

With this in mind it will not surprise you to learn that the formula for the approximate standard error of a proportion looks much the same as that for the standard error of the mean provided sample size is large, i.e. the term which makes the division is the square root of the sample size. As the SD of a proportion is $\sqrt{pq}$ then the standard error is calculated as:

$$S_{\text{proportion}} = \sqrt{(pq/n)} \ .$$

For the example given above where 36 per cent of the households in a sample of $n = 1,000$ were found to use brand X to wash the dishes, the approximate standard error can be calculated as follows:

$$S_{\text{proportion}} = \sqrt{(0.36 \times 0.64/1,000)}$$

$$= \sqrt{0.00023}$$

$$= 0.015.$$

Thus, the 95 per cent confidence limits will be:

$\pm 1.96 \times 0.015$

which is close to 0.03 or 3 per cent. Accordingly, we can be 95 per cent certain that if we drew another sample of 1,000 from the same population, and tested them exactly the same way as for the first sample, then the proportion of households found to be using brand X would be within the range of 33 per cent to 39 per cent (36 per cent plus or minus twice the standard error, approximately). This range is referred to as the 95 per cent confidence limits for the proportion found in the survey to use brand X. A common way of writing this result is 36% ± 3%.

ACTIVITY 10

Table 2, below, contains the mean, sample standard deviation, and sample size for four variables. Calculate the standard error and 95 per cent confidence interval for each of these.

Table 2

Variable	Mean	SD	n
Age, years	1.17	0.61	36
Birth weight, kg	2.65	0.54	36
Weight, kg	6.53	1.58	36
Mother's age, years	23.84	5.63	25

Every sample statistic — the mean, median, mode, the standard deviation itself, a total, or a proportion — has a standard error which can be estimated from just one random sample when it is needed. As we have seen, knowledge of standard error enables statements about probabilities. For example, comparing how far apart two means are in terms of standard errors provides a test of whether the two means differ by more than chance; this is discussed in Block 4.

Formerly a lot of time could be spent learning formulae and calculating confidence limits and significance levels using standard errors. However, in research, calculations are now done by computer. Thus the details of statistical formulae are not important to survey researchers. What is important is that the method being used and its assumptions are fully understood. In this case you need to understand thoroughly what is meant by a *distribution of sample means*, and how the standard deviation of this distribution can be estimated from one sample. Further, you need to understand the use to which this SD is put in its role as standard error of just one sample mean. Working through the simple calculations above will help develop this understanding.

A final important point should be mentioned, although space does not permit it to be developed in any way. Very often in social and behavioural science, data distributions do not look at all normal, and it might seem that procedures which assume a normal distribution cannot be used. However, firstly, various things can be done about this, including transformation of the scale to one which is normal for the measure concerned. Secondly, the relevant mathematical models require that the *underlying* variable which is being measured is normally distributed, and it is to be expected that individual samples (especially small samples) will look rather different. Thirdly, and this is the most fortunate point of all, even if the population distribution is far from normal, as sample size increases the distribution of sample means from that population will move closer and closer to the desired normal form, thus permitting valid statistical inferences to be made about those means. This statement rests on a fundamental theorem in statistics (the central limits theorem). This theorem justifies much of the data analysis undertaken when quantifying and estimating the reliability of survey research findings (Stuart and Ord, 1987).

5 ERROR, SAMPLE SIZE AND NON-RESPONSE

As has been mentioned in the discussion of Activity 3, there are two categories of error in survey research: sampling error and non-sampling error. Conceptually the terms sampling error and non-sampling error refer to different entities, and it is theoretically important to consider them as such, but in practice we can never have a true measure of sampling error, but only an estimate of it, and the influence of non-sampling error is hopelessly confounded within that estimate. Both researcher and research evaluator have to ensure that non-sampling error is avoided as far as possible, or is evenly balanced (non-systematic) and thus cancels in the calculation of population estimates, or else is brought under statistical control. As has been shown, the difference between sampling error and non-sampling error is that the extent of the former can be estimated from the sample variation, whereas the latter cannot. Further, we have seen that sampling error can only be reliably estimated if the selection of respondents has been random. At best, random sampling will allow unbiased estimates of sampling error; at worst, quota and opportunity sampling will provide little or none.

In practice researchers often overlook or are unaware of these difficulties and quote standard errors, i.e. estimates of sampling error, even for samples where their use is not justified in theory. For example, a research project testing the effect of an innovation in method on the progress of children might use one school class for the innovation, and one other for control. Assume that these were the only classes available to the researcher, but that a coin had been tossed to decide which of the two classes received the innovation and which would be the control. Means could be calculated for the outcome measure and then standard errors could be calculated for these means. These standard errors could be used in a test to determine whether or not there was a significant difference between the means (as explained in Block 4), and the results could legitimately be reported. If you were evaluating this study you would note the positive finding, but also that the method used was 'purposive' or 'opportunity' sampling, and consequently that the standard errors would not be based on random components with a beneficial cancelling of bias. You would further note that for this reason the finding might not stand up to replication — that generalizability would be suspect. You would look for other information to take into account. You would be pleased if it were said, or shown from school progress records, that the two classes were comparable before the research began. You would be equally pleased to know that allocation to treatment and control groups had been at random.

ACTIVITY 11

Write a brief note of possible sources of error in this study if the school head had insisted on which class should receive the innovation and which should be the control. Say if this would contribute to sampling error or non-sampling error, or both.

Assume, on the other hand, that only two pre-selected classes were available and that treatment and control children were randomly sampled from these. How far would this improve the possibility of obtaining good estimates of sampling error, if at all? What about non-sampling error? (Approx. 150 words.)

In presenting standard errors in circumstances such as this, researchers are in effect saying:

> OK, I know I haven't got a random sample, and so can't estimate sampling error. But this is the best I could do. It could be the case that it hasn't mattered very much, and thus I have calculated the standard

errors and have used them in further tests. My finding has support from the literature, and looks useful. It's up to you dear reader, to decide how much reliance you will place on it. Perhaps you'll think that the result is important, and will be able to replicate it without the sampling difficulties which I have had, *and have reported.*

At least sampling error *can* be calculated, whether appropriately or not. The various sources of error grouped together as non-sampling errors are another matter — not because they will be necessarily greater in extent, although this could well be the case, but because they are difficult to control, or even detect. The great virtue of randomization is that it takes care of potential sources of bias both known and unknown. If it can be assumed that error, whatever its source, will be randomly spread across a sample, and will cancel when statistics are computed, then one does not even need to know what it is that is cancelled. The problem is systematic, non-random error, which will not cancel.

Non-sampling error is often overlooked when survey findings are evaluated, and if an estimate of sampling error is given, then it is often wrongly assumed that this shows the likelihood of total error. For example in the 1992 general election in the UK one survey predicted a Labour Party vote of 42 per cent ± 3 per cent. The figure of 3 per cent here will be derived from the estimated sampling error for the percentage of 42 per cent and the number of respondents sampled. Presumably it represents approximately twice the standard error, and thus the 95 per cent confidence range for this result would be from 39 per cent to 45 per cent. This says that if the same pollsters drew sample elements in exactly the same way, and questioned and recorded in exactly the same way, from the same population, a sample of the same size, then they could expect to obtain a value in that range 95 times for every 100 samples so drawn and tested.

This statement about error tells us nothing whatsoever about whether the sampling frame truly represented the voters of the UK overall, let alone the more restricted set of those who actually did vote. It tells us nothing about interviewer bias, or procedural reactivity, or untruthfulness on the part of respondents. If one took a guess and allowed another 3 per cent for all of these, then the predicted range would increase to 36–48 per cent, which would greatly decrease the usefulness of the survey finding, since in a moderately close election it would be very unlikely to predict successfully which way the outcome would go, because the estimates for the two major parties would always overlap. An advantage the pollsters do have, however, is replication. Many polls are taken, and by different organizations. Taking all into account might give some possibility of balancing some sources of non-sampling error — but not all. It could, of course, be the case that all the polls suffered from similar defects in which case pooling would not cancel the bias and prediction would be highly unreliable.

Major sources of non-sampling error related to the sampling process itself include: sampling-frame defects, non-response, inaccurate or incomplete response, defective measuring instruments (e.g. questionnaires or interview schedules), and defective data collection or management. Some of these are the subject of other units in this course, but their relevance here should also be kept in mind. Many of these effects are, or can be, controlled by proper randomization in sampling. For example, in a large survey the error related to small differences in technique on the part of interviewers (perhaps consequent on personality differences) will be randomly spread across the data, and will cancel out. Any residual effect should be small and would be lost in the estimates of standard errors, possibly here balancing with other small residual effects.

5.1 SAMPLE SIZE

Often selecting an appropriate sample size has been a hit and miss business of choosing a size which can be managed within the resources available, or a size similar to that used in earlier published work. There is a misconception that sample size should be related to the size of the population under study. As has been shown above, the precision of sample estimates depends very much on sample size (the sample SD is divided by the square root of the sample n) and no reference is made to the size of the population sampled.

Assuming that for a sample survey the 95 per cent level of confidence is required ($p < 0.05$), and the maximum error is set to 5 units on the scale of measurement, then the following formula will provide the estimated sample size:

sample size $= 2 \times 1.96(SD)^2/5^2$.

If the estimated SD is 10 then the required sample size would be approximately 16. If the limit for the difference of interest was reduced from 5 to 2 points, then estimated sample size would increase to close to 100 assuming that the SD remains unchanged. Note that the researcher had to provide an estimate of the SD, although the actual value will not be known until the research is concluded.

This is a very simple account of what might appear to be a simple subject, but which in fact is a complex one. Just how big a sample should be is a matter of balancing cost against the level of precision required. True, as sample size increases the size of the standard error of any estimate of a statistic does decrease. But this needs to be qualified by knowledge that large samples may introduce more non-sampling error (as mentioned in the answer to Activity 3) than smaller ones, where measurements and management problems may be smaller. Also the power of the statistical test to be used must be taken into account and tables have been published for doing this (Cohen, 1969; Lipsey, 1990). But, in theory at least, the precision with which a sample statistic, such as the mean, has been estimated will depend on anything which makes the standard error smaller.

5.2 NON-RESPONSE

Estimating the required sample size needed for a stated level of precision has been discussed. There is, however, little point in reporting that sample size was formally determined to achieve maximum precision, if a sizable proportion of the sample were subsequently lost through non-response, or because items of data were missing. This is a major source of error in many surveys.

Procedures for dealing with non-response and missing data have to be established when the research is being planned, and not left to desperate *post hoc* remedy. In establishing such procedures total non-response should be distinguished from failure to respond to individual items in a questionnaire, and both should be distinguished from data which are simply missing, i.e. lost or inadequately recorded. Preliminary data analysis will also lead to further data loss, usually due to the dropping of elements (individuals or cases) found to have been included in the sampling frame by mistake, but which do not belong to the population studied, or because inconsistent or highly improbable values have been found on crucial variables for the elements dropped.

Final reports should contain information on the extent of sample loss and missing data, which amounts at least in part, and sometimes completely, to the same thing. Non-response rates as high as 50 per cent or more have frequently been reported. Some elements of the sample simply will not be found, others will refuse to participate either completely or in part. In addition data, and sometimes whole subjects, will be lost due to clerical inaccuracy. The extent of data lost for this reason alone is seldom reported, but is usually surprisingly high, e.g. as much as 8 per cent (Schofield *et al.*, 1992). Response rate is influenced by such design matters as the appearance of a questionnaire, its layout, length and readability. The details of these topics are dealt with elsewhere in this course, but they are introduced briefly here because of the important influence on error in sample survey research. Information on such matters will be sought in pilot studies, in which different versions of a survey instrument can be tested. Sample loss for these reasons is likely to introduce bias, because it might increase the proportion of more persistent or better educated respondents.

If the survey involves home interviews, non-response might be related to time of day at which the interview was sought. From Table 3 it can be seen that a higher proportion of persons over 14 years of age are at home in the early hours of the evening on Sunday, Monday and Tuesday than at any other time. This, however, is also evening meal time, and a busy time for families with young children. Again sample loss could be systematic, and it could introduce bias.

Table 3 Proportion of households with at least one person over 14 years of age at home

Time of day	Proportion by day of week						
	Sun.	Mon.	Tue.	Wed.	Thur.	Fri.	Sat.
8.00–8.59 am	(B)	(B)	(B)	(B)	(B)	(B)	(B)
9.00–9.59 am	(B)	(B)	(B)	0.55	0.28	0.45	(B)
10.00–10.59 am	(B)	0.47	0.42	0.38	0.45	0.40	0.55
11.00–11.59 am	0.35	0.41	0.49	0.46	0.43	0.50	0.62
12.00–12.59 pm	0.42	0.53	0.49	0.56	0.45	0.55	0.60
1.00–1.59 pm	0.49	0.44	0.50	0.48	0.43	0.51	0.63
2.00–2.59 pm	0.49	0.50	0.52	0.47	0.45	0.45	0.59
3.00–3.59 pm	0.54	0.47	0.49	0.54	0.50	0.50	0.65
4.00–4.59 pm	0.52	0.58	0.55	0.57	0.57	0.56	0.53
5.00–5.59 pm	0.61	0.67	0.65	0.67	0.59	0.57	0.56
6.00–6.59 pm	0.75	0.73	0.72	0.68	0.65	0.64	0.59
7.00–7.59 pm	0.73	0.74	0.75	0.64	0.61	0.57	0.66
8.00–8.59 pm	(B)	0.51	0.51	0.59	0.74	0.52	(B)
9.00–9.59 pm	(B)	(B)	(B)	0.64	(B)	(B)	(B)

(B) = base less than 20.

(Source: Weeks et al., 1980)

If, when a survey is being planned, it seems likely that response rate will be low due to the nature of the information sought, or the accuracy of the sampling frame, or the method used to contact respondents, then sample size could be increased. This might seem to be an obvious and easy solution, but will be costly in terms of management and material, and in any case, would be unlikely to solve the problem.

ACTIVITY 12

In the planning of a sample survey by questionnaire sent by post it has been calculated that a sample of $n = 200$ will give the required level of precision for estimating population means at the 95 per cent confidence level or better for most items of interest. But only about 40 per cent to 50 per cent of those sent questionnaires are expected to return them. The researchers propose simple random sampling with sample size increased to $n = 400$.

Comment on this proposal. If you were an adviser, what advice would you give? (Approx. 75 words.)

Increasing sample size to cover expected non-response would, in fact, be more likely to increase than to decrease bias. More money would be spent, to no avail. Studies have shown that non-responders tend to be: the elderly; those who are withdrawn; urban rather than suburban, or rural, dwellers; individuals who fear they will not give the information adequately in comparison to others, or who fear that they might expose themselves, and be judged in some way by the responses they make. To lose such individuals selectively would very likely reduce the representativeness of a survey sample. To increase sample size whilst continuing to lose such individuals would in no way help, and could lead to comparatively stronger influence from, perhaps, initially small biasing groups.

Whether information is collected by questionnaire or by interview, positive effort should be made to follow up non-responders. Even when second copies of a questionnaire are sent out, or repeat interviews arranged, response rates above about 80 per cent are seldom achieved. The task for the researcher, who wants sample results which truly represent the population studied, plus information which will help evaluate how far this objective has been achieved, is to get as much information as possible on those individuals who are still missing when all possible action has been taken to maximize response rate.

For this reason the records of individuals who have made only partial, or even nil, response should never be dropped from a data set. Usually information will be available on some variables, for example geographical region, home address, perhaps age or sex. Analyses can be made to see if the missing individuals are at least randomly distributed throughout the sample in terms of these measures, or grouped in some way which might help identify the possible direction and extent of bias on other measures for which there is no data.

Even better would be a small follow-up survey of a random sample of non-responders possibly involving home visits and/or the offer of incentives, so that reliable predictions can be made about the likely characteristics of all non-responders. In some circumstances this could be counter-productive in that interviewer/respondent reactivity might be increased. One way or another, however, the problem of non-response has to be tackled. Vagueness or, worse, total lack of information on this topic, is no longer permissible.

6   CONCLUDING REMARKS

This unit has dealt with methods and problems of designing sample surveys, and has related these to the wider research context where ultimately the validity of findings will rest on how well the sample represents the population being researched. We have seen that the quality of the inferences being made from a sample will be related to both sample size and sampling method. We have seen that provided a probabilistic method has been used then a reliable estimate can be made of the extent to which the sample results will differ from the true population values, and that error of this type is known as sampling error. The methods discussed included both simple and stratified random sampling, systematic sampling, and cluster sampling, and also non-probabilistic methods such as quota sampling. Selecting the best method for any particular research will usually involve compromise, and will be a matter of balancing the level of precision required, in terms of the width of the error estimates, against feasibility and cost.

We have also seen that error from many other sources — non-sampling error — will have to be taken into account when planning survey research and when evaluating results. Major sources of non-sampling error which have been discussed in this unit include faulty selection of the sampling frame, as in the 1936 Presidential election survey, and non-response. There are many others, such as the instruments used for collecting the information, e.g. schedules, questionnaires and observation techniques. The problem for researchers is that however well they plan the technical side of sampling and calculate estimates of sampling error of known precision, non-sampling error will always be present, inflating overall error, i.e. reducing representativeness. Estimating the extent of this is a matter not of mathematical calculation, although statistical procedures can help, but of scientific judgement, based on an awareness of what problems are likely, as well as common sense.

ANSWERS TO ACTIVITIES

ACTIVITIES 1 AND 2

In Sections 1 and 2 of this unit restricted meanings have been given to the following words:

Population: for Activity 1 you probably noted that a population was a collection of elements and gave such examples as those given in the section on sampling, e.g. all the children under 5 years old in the UK. For Activity 2 you possibly amended this to say that a population was a collection of elements about which inferences were to be made, but of course the examples would be unchanged.

Element: an element is the object, quality, process or individual on which a measurement has been taken, e.g. individual children in a population sampled.

Sample: a sample is a set of elements selected in some way from a population, and which is to be used to make inferences about that population. More precisely, a sample is a collection of sampling units (each containing one or more elements) drawn from a sampling frame.

Population parameter: population parameters are statistics, such as the mean, or a proportion, and their standard deviations, calculated using all of the elements of the population, and not just a sample of these. Such parameters are usually unknown.

Sample statistics: a sample statistic is a statistic calculated from the data in a sample, e.g. a mean, or a proportion, or standard deviation, and which is used to estimate the value for the same statistic in the population from which the sample was drawn.

Sampling error: developing the concept of sampling error more fully is a major task in this unit, but at this stage it can be thought of as the error introduced by estimating, for example, a mean from the data in a sample, rather than from measurement of every element in a population.

Sampling units: sampling units are collections of elements which do not overlap, and which exhaust the entire population. For example in a national survey sampling units could be geographical regions.

Sampling frame: a sampling frame is a list of sampling units. It provides access to the individual elements of the population under study, either via sampling units, or directly when the population elements and the sampling units are identical.

Bias: bias in this unit is defined as any effect on data which moves the calculated value of a statistic (such as the mean) further from the population value than would have been the case if that effect were not present such that repeated samples influenced by the same bias would not be centred around the population value.

It is important to learn and understand the technical definition of these words, and many others which follow later in the unit, so that sampling methods and problems in sampling can be established and discussed without ambiguity.

ACTIVITY 3

The main advantages of a sample survey over a full census is that it will be easier and cheaper to set up, manage and analyse than a full census. Although the results based on a sample will, in theory, be less accurate than if the whole population had been included (assuming this to be possible), this might not be the case in practice. Many sources of bias — for example management problems, faulty measurement, lost or corrupted data — will potentially be present whichever method is used, and will be easier to control in a tightly constructed and managed survey than in a full census.

ACTIVITY 4

The table, with the missing entries added, is shown below. The first of these, in the fourth column, is the sample size (*n*) for proportionate sampling. This was found by calculating 45.5 per cent of the total sample of 400. This gave a sample proportion of *n* = 182 for representation of 16-year-old school leavers. Similar calculations were made to find the other sample proportions. For the disproportionate method the total sample was divided into three equal groups, one for each school leaving age, without taking into account the differing incidence in the population of each of these groups.

Table 1 (completed)

School leaving age	Population size	Percentage total in each stratum	Proportionate		Disproportionate	
			sample size	sampling fraction	sample size	sampling fraction[a]
16	2,730	45.5	182	1/15	134	1/20
17	1,950	32.5	130	1/15	134	1/15
18 and over	1,320	22.0	88	1/15	134	1/10
Total	6,000	100.0	400	1/15	402	1/15

[a] The denominators for the disproportionate sampling fractions have been rounded to give whole numbers.

Compare your note on the sampling method you would choose with the explanation given in the three paragraphs following the activity in the text, where several non-statistical reasons are given for balancing the various alternatives. If you have not included the points discussed in your note, it would be a good idea to add a summary of them now to aid your end of course revision.

ACTIVITY 5

Your advice in answer to the first question would probably involve pointing out the difficulty of conducting random sampling across two school years in all the infant and junior schools in a Local Education Authority. You would mention the time and financial cost, and the difficulty of following up those absent from school when the survey was conducted if these were spread across the whole school area. You would probably then suggest cluster sampling, and ask for more information on what the objectives of the survey were to be.

To the researcher proposing a multivitamin intervention you would agree that random sampling within the cluster would be the best procedure from a theoretical point of view, assuming an appropriate research design. But you would advise the researcher intending to introduce a computer into a classroom for some children to use (those randomly sampled), and others not to use, that this would be impracticable, and certain to bias population estimates and to inflate sampling error. You would suggest that cluster sampling should be used throughout, i.e. that the intervention should be given to intact classes, rather than individual children, and that the classes to receive the intervention should be chosen at random.

ACTIVITY 6

Clearly a probabilistic method would be preferable since this would permit a valid estimate of the extent of sampling error. As the population of interest is all the adults in the UK, a simple random sample would be costly and difficult. Precision relative to sample size could be increased by appropriate stratification, and thus you would recommend a stratified random sample.

ACTIVITY 8

The mean of the first set of figures is 3, and the mean of the second is also 3. The two standard deviations are, respectively, 1.414 and 4.517. In other words, the two sets have the same mean but very different standard deviations because they differ greatly in the way the individual values are distributed about the mean. The average of this dispersion (the standard deviation, SD) is much greater for the second set than for the first.

ACTIVITY 10

The standard errors given in Table 4 have been calculated by dividing the standard deviations in Table 2 by the square root of the sample size.

The lower extreme of the 95 per cent confidence interval was found by subtracting 1.96 times the standard error from the sample mean. The upper limit was found by adding the same value to the sample mean. Strictly the multiplier of 1.96 is only accurate for larger samples than those in the table, but small sampling theory is not dealt with in this unit. If to simplify the calculations you rounded 1.96 up to 2.0 then your interval may be slightly wider than those given in Table 4.

Table 4

Variable	Standard error, S	95% confidence interval
Age	0.10 years	0.97 to 1.37 years
Birth weight	0.09 kg	2.47 to 2.83 kg
Weight	0.26 kg	6.02 to 7.04 kg
Mother's age	1.13 years	21.63 to 26.06 years

ACTIVITY 11

As randomization would be totally missing no valid estimate could be made of sampling error. In addition there would be a high risk of non-sampling error from some special feature of the classes, not known to the researcher, but presumably motivating the head teacher's insistence. In these circumstances the study would be better not undertaken at all.

Random sampling from two pre-selected classes would certainly improve the situation in so far as sampling error is concerned, but the sample so obtained would only be representative of those two pre-selected classes. Generalization of findings to a wider context could only be on the basis of judgement outside the research itself. The influence of non-sampling error (which would in turn inflate the estimate of sampling error) would depend, amongst other things, on the nature of the intervention, and would be great if there were reactivity between sampled or non-sampled children or from classroom staff in relation to this.

ACTIVITY 12

You will probably want to accept the decision to use random sampling, provided that an appropriate sample frame is available, and also that there is sufficient finance to cover the cost of obtaining a sample of the size needed for the required precision. You will then point out that with an expected response rate of 40–50 per cent the sample is not likely to be representative of the population of interest as the non-responders are likely to differ in important ways from those who do respond. Merely increasing sample size will be costly, and will not help. You would suggest that the additional money should be spent instead on making a second, and even a third, approach to non-responders; doing analyses on whatever limited data is available for the non-responder to see how they differ from those who do respond; or setting up a small random study of the characteristics of non-responders, perhaps by visiting their homes, or offering an incentive for participation.

FURTHER READING

Moser, C.A. and Kalton, G. (1971) *Survey Methods in Social Investigation*, London, Heinemann.

Although somewhat dated, this remains a standard text for material covered in this unit.

Scheaffer, R.L., Mendenhall, W. and Ott, L. (1990) *Elementary Survey Sampling*, Boston, PWS-Kent.

A further elementary text, recently revised, which includes some of the mathematical derivations of sampling methods, but with many practical examples of surveys and methods. Useful later if you have the task of designing a survey.

Lipsey, M.W. (1990) *Design Sensitivity*, Newbury Park, California, Sage.

A short and fairly readable text on statistical power in social science research. It includes charts for determining sample size, and is mentioned here so that you have a reference to a source of information on this.

REFERENCES

Cohen, J. (1969) *Statistical Power Analysis in the Behavioral Sciences*, New York, Academic Press.

Fletcher, P.L., Grantham-McGregor, S.M. and Powell, C.A. (1990) 'Nutritional states of Jamaican children in an economic depression', *Ecology of Food and Nutrition*, vol. 21, pp.167–72.

Heikens, G.T., Schofield, W.N., Dawson, S. and Grantham-McGregor, S.M. (1989) 'The Kingston project: I. The growth of malnourished children during rehabilitation in the community', *European Journal of Clinical Nutrition*, vol. 44, pp.253–69.

Kendall, M.G. (1952) *The Advanced Theory of Statistics*, London, Griffin.

Lipsey, M.W. (1990) *Design Sensitivity*, Newbury Park, California, Sage.

Minitab (1985) Release 5.1.3, Minitab Inc., State College, Pennsylvania.

Pearson, K. and Lee, A. (1902) 'On the laws of inheritance in man. I Inheritance of physical characters', *Biometrika*, vol. 2, pp.356–462.

Schofield, W.N., Heikens, G.T. and Irons, B. (1992) 'Methodological aspects of medical and nutritional studies in the community', *Journal of Tropical and Geographical Medicine*, in press.

Stuart, I. and Ord, K.J. (1987) *Kendall's Advanced Theory of Statistics* (5th edn), London, Arnold.

Tizard, J., Schofield, W.N. and Hewison, J. (1982) 'Collaboration between teachers and parents in assisting children's reading', *British Journal of Educational Psychology*, vol. 52, pp.1–15.

Weeks, M.F., Jones, B.L., Folsom, R.E. and Benrud, C.H. (1980) 'Optimal times to contact houscholds', *Public Opinion Quarterly*, vol. 44, pp.101–14.

Yates, F. (1935) 'Some examples of biased sampling', *Annals of Eugenics*, vol. 6, p.202.

ACKNOWLEDGEMENT

Grateful acknowledgement is made to the following source for permission to reproduce material in this unit:

TABLE

Table 3: Weeks, M.F., Jones, B.L., Folsom, R.E. Jr. and Benrud, C.H. (1984) 'Optimal times to contact sample households', *Public Opinion Quarterly*, vol. 48, Spring 1984, © 1980 by The Trustees of Columbia University.

UNIT 9 VARIETIES OF SURVEY AND THEIR PROBLEMS

Prepared for the Course Team by Victor Jupp

CONTENTS

ASSOCIATED STUDY MATERIALS

Offprints Booklet 2, 'The origins of crime: the Cambridge Study in Delinquent Development', by D.P. Farrington.

Offprints Booklet 2, 'Criminal careers of those born in 1953, 1958 and 1963', by K. Shaw and D. Lobo.

ASSOCIATED STUDY MATERIALS

1   INTRODUCTION

The preceding unit introduced some of the main features of social surveys, such as quota and random sampling, cluster sampling and stratified sampling. These represent different forms of case selection. The examination of such forms of case selection was carried out against a background of what is sometimes termed 'one-shot designs'. This means that cases are selected at one particular point in time and that data about them are collected at that same point of time. However, one-shot designs are not always used. In this unit we add to our understanding of the variation in case selection in surveys by looking at ways of sampling through time. This is the key aim of the present unit. A secondary aim is to indicate that social surveys do not necessarily involve the selection of individuals as cases but can also extend to surveying other units of analysis: for example, social interactions and documents. These can also be examined in a one-shot fashion or at different points in time.

The data generated by a survey can be thought of as a rectangle (see Figure 1). Typically, this rectangle is made up of rows, with each row representing a case selected to be part of the sample, and columns, with each column representing a variable about which data are collected for each case in the sample. Where a sample comprises 200 cases about which data on 50 variables are collected, the dimensions of the rectangle of data will be 200 by 50. In many respects, this unit's definition of a survey could encompass the concept of case study, as discussed in Unit 7: systematic measurements can be made, especially in quantitative case studies, thereby yielding a rectangle of data. However, what distinguishes the case study from the social survey, especially in relation to the rectangle of data, is that the number of cases (rows) included in surveys tends to be relatively large and the data collected for each variable (columns) tends to be relatively shallow.

In this unit we shall treat the one-shot cross-sectional survey using structured questionnaires and schedules to collect data from individuals, as the benchmark for examining the variety in social survey design. We will begin this examination by looking at some of the limitations of the typical one-shot design.

2   LIMITATIONS OF ONE-SHOT DESIGNS

The limitations to be addressed are as follows:

1 One-shot cross-sectional surveys are, in effect, snapshots taken at a particular time. As a result, such surveys are not useful vehicles for examining social change in society or for mapping social trends over time. For example, Dingwall and Fox's paper (1986), which you read earlier in the block, gives an idea of professional attitudes at the time of the study described, but this should not be used to make claims about professionals in other decades. One way of overcoming this is by taking equivalent samples at different points in time and collecting data on the same variables with a view to examining changes or trends. This is known as a *trend* or *time-series design* and will be discussed in Section 3.

2 One-shot designs sometimes collect retrospective data — about past experiences, for instance — with a view to correlating past experiences with present actions or attitudes. Such correlations subsequently form the basis for causal inferences suggesting, say, that such past experiences cause or produce contemporary attitudes or actions. There are, however, difficulties with this. For example, there are always doubts about the reliability of respondents' memories of past experiences. More crucially, correlations indicating potential relationships between past experiences and current attitudes and actions do not by themselves provide suf-

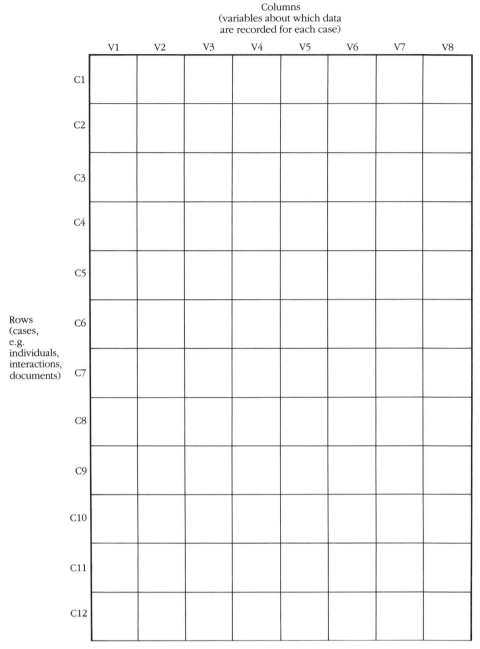

Figure 1 *Rectangle of data*

ficient evidence of causality. What is missing is evidence of time-ordering: namely, that the experiences are not only related to particular attitudes and actions but also preceded them. Where fairly short time-periods are involved, it is often difficult for respondents (and for us!) to disentangle past experiences, current attitudes and current reconstructions of 'how I must have felt then' in the light of current attitudes. When longer time-periods are involved, the last of these three elements becomes very important. None of us, for example, remembers his or her childhood *as it was experienced by the child*; the memories are an adult's memories. One way of getting firmer evidence of time-ordering is by collecting data from the same individuals over a period of time, possibly a lifetime. This is known as a *longitudinal design* and will be discussed in Section 4.

At this point it is appropriate to pause to clarify the terminology used in this text. This is important because the word 'longitudinal' is sometimes used differently by different writers. For example, 'longitudinal' can be used in a general sense to encompass any design which has a time element associated with it and would, therefore, include time-series designs as outlined above. Also, it is sometimes taken to include 'before–after studies' and 'panel studies'. For the purposes of this text, however, we shall not use 'longitudinal' in this general sense. Instead, we can distinguish the following four designs — note that they all possess a time element, but that only the last, 'cohort studies', are what we mean here by the term 'longitudinal design':

1 *Time-series* or *trend designs* take equivalent samples at different points in time with a view to examining social change and social trends. It is highly unlikely that these samples will include the same individual members. We will illustrate the features of this design in the next section by means of the British Crime Survey (BCS).

2 *Before–after studies* are two-stage surveys which involve taking measurements from a sample prior to some event or the introduction of some 'treatment'. The same or equivalent measurements are taken some time afterwards with a view to examining whether any subsequent changes can be attributed to such events or treatments. In some cases, equivalent or matched sub-samples are measured at the first stage, only one of these sub-samples receives the 'treatment' or is exposed to the event, and then both sub-samples are measured again. For example, in research carried out by the author, two matched sub-samples of children and adolescents were measured on a scale relating to attitudes towards the police. During the summer of 1991 one of these groups took part in a range of sporting and recreation activities organized by and including police officers. Both sub-samples were subsequently measured using the same scale, to examine whether those taking part in the sporting and recreational events developed more favourable attitudes towards the police (Jupp, 1992). (For a summary of research using such designs, see Robins, 1990.) Such a design is equivalent to a quasi-experiment and the sub-samples are equivalent to control and experimental groups, as outlined in Unit 6. The key stages in quasi-experimental design are illustrated in Figure 2.

3 *Panel studies* involve two or more waves of data collection using the same sample, and often taking the same or similar measurements at different points, but not explicitly with a view to assessing the impact of an intervening event or treatment. Panel surveys are very common in market research where samples are often purposively recruited to assess a particular product over a period of time or to report on consumer preferences and behaviour over a period of time. For example,

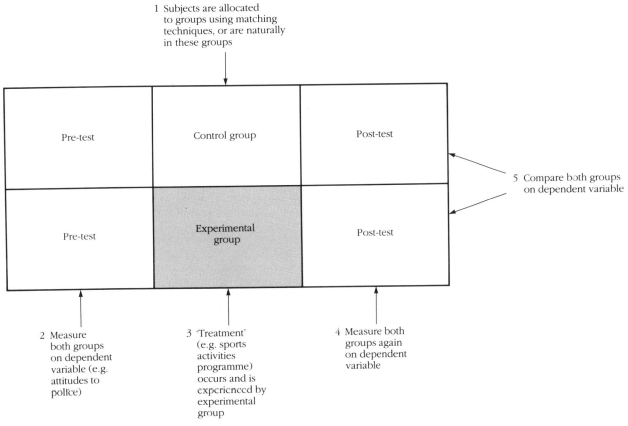

Figure 2 *Features of before–after quasi-experimental design (using two sub-samples)*

panels are recruited by audience researchers to report on television programmes watched by families during the preceding month. They are also common in the study of voting behaviour, where researchers return to a panel of respondents on several occasions prior to and during a general election campaign in order to assess trends in political attitudes and voting preferences.

4 *Cohort studies* also return to the same sample over a period of time. However, they are distinguishable from other designs in the following ways. First, the sample is drawn from a particular 'cohort', which is defined by membership of a particular group or category such as individuals born in a particular week or year, children entering school at the same time, or offenders found guilty of committing crimes at the same time. Second, cohort studies focus on sample members for a much longer period — in some cases a lifetime — than other designs. Third, there is often an emphasis upon describing and explaining personal development, the progression of life events, and the onset of behavioural patterns (such as alcoholism, criminality, mental illness). This is not a necessary feature of cohort studies — they can be used for a variety of purposes — but it does fairly describe the aims of a number of the cohort studies that have been carried out. Fourth, cohort studies seek not only to describe and explain, but also to develop predictions of behavioural or other changes. Section 4 will be concerned with illustrating the use of cohort studies, and within the present text the use of the term 'longitudinal survey' will be restricted to cohort studies.

ACTIVITY 1

To check that you are clear about the terminology used in this unit, pause and consider each of the following studies. To which of the categories described above does each belong?

(a) A survey of people's preferences for instant coffee, asking a large sample of coffee-drinkers what brand(s) they use and what they like or dislike about them.

(b) A quarterly 'audit' of 'consumer durable goods' (cookers, refrigerators, food-mixers, televisions, home computers, etc.). Every three months a large random sample of households is selected, and interviewers record the number and type of appliances in the households.

(c) A survey of television viewing. Devices are attached to the televisions of a large sample of viewers, recording when the television is on and which channel is showing. The sample is also asked to keep a 'diary' of who is in the room when the television is on. The diaries and records from the devices are collected weekly.

(d) A survey of the market impact of a new brand of Vermouth. A sample of drinkers is interviewed before the new brand is marketed to ascertain which of them drink Vermouth and which brand(s) they drink; they are re-interviewed six months after the launch of the new product, to see if their drinking habits have changed.

(e) A sample survey explores people's attitudes to breakfast cereal before a new advertising campaign is launched. After the campaign another sample is interviewed, to see if attitudes have changed.

(f) A random sample of children born in a given month is selected, and they or their parents are interviewed every three years to see what shoes have been bought by or for them in the last six months; the study continues until they are aged 30.

(g) The same study is carried out, but in addition further samples are drawn to match their past ages. In other words, when the informants are 6, a sample of 3-year-olds is also drawn; when they are 9 the research also samples children aged 3 and 6, and so on.

You will find my answers to this activity at the end of the unit.

Although the above discussion distinguishes several different ways of sampling time, this unit will concentrate on only two of these: time-series or trend designs (Section 3), and longitudinal cohort designs (Section 4).

It is often assumed that social surveys inevitably involve the sampling of individuals and the collection of primary data from these individuals. For various reasons, however, this is not necessarily the case and may not even be desirable. For example, with certain kinds of subject matter, questionnaires, schedules or the interview situation in general may be thought to produce excessive reactivity in such a way that responses may be more a reaction to the procedures and techniques of data collection than accurate reflections of respondents' feelings, beliefs, attitudes or actions. In other cases it may not be possible to have access to respondents (perhaps because of over-protective 'gate keepers' or even, in historical research, because the potential respondents are dead!). Further, the individual may not be the relevant unit of analysis. This is the case, for example, with police–public social *interactions*, with crime rates in different *communities*, or decision-making processes in different criminal justice *institutions*. For all of these reasons, researchers may choose to sample units of analysis other than individuals and to use sources of data other than questionnaires and schedules. These can include records of interactional patterns, diaries, letters, essays, newspapers, organizational memoranda, and official statistics. The use of different sources of data will be outlined and illustrated in Sections 5 and 6.

The variety of survey designs to be covered in subsequent sections will be illustrated predominantly by means of case studies of research on crime and criminal justice. However, it should be remembered that the general principles propounded are equally applicable to all areas of educational and social research.

3 THE MEASUREMENT AND ASSESSMENT OF SOCIAL CHANGE

With one-shot cross-sectional designs a sample is selected and data collected from or about each of the units in the sample at a particular point in time. The sample may be selected using random sampling techniques, or it may be chosen purposively, perhaps, using quota controls. Figure 3 represents a one-shot cross-sectional design where a random or purposive sample of individuals is taken at *one* of the points A, B or C. In effect, it is a single and particular slice through time. Thus, there are two aspects of sampling: the sampling of units of analysis and the sampling of time. In this unit the focus is on sampling of time.

With a one-shot design there is the capacity to collect both past and present data, and perhaps to find relationships within and between these. An example of this is the survey of the attitude of Londoners to crime and policing which was commissioned by the Metropolitan Police and conducted by the Policy Studies Institute (Smith and Gray, 1983). Its commissioning followed concern about relations between police and the community, particularly ethnic minority groups in London. A major strand of the survey was a random sample of 2,420 people designed to be representative of all those aged 15 and over in the Metropolitan Police District. This was made up of two sub-samples, one of which was a general sample (of 1,411 people) of the population, and the other a special sample of 1,009 people of Asian and West Indian origin. Each respondent was contacted and interviewed once. In this respect the survey of Londoners is random, cross-sectional and one-shot. It took a sample of Londoners at a particular point in time (August to October 1981) with a view to measuring their attitudes towards the police. Even so, one aspect of the research involved collecting retrospective data about past

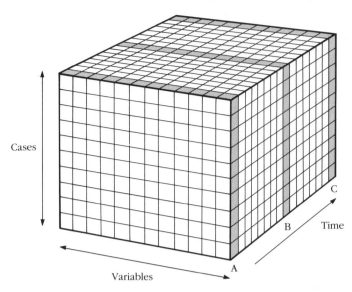

Figure 3   *Sampling through time*

contacts with the police with a view to relating these reported experiences to data collected from the same individuals about present attitudes towards the police. The final report concluded by being critical of the way in which police had related to sections of the community, particularly ethnic minorities, thereby generating anti-police attitudes.

This is not the place to delve into the merits of such arguments or into the extensive literature on police–public interactions and relations. It is sufficient to note here that where one-shot cross-sectional surveys collect retrospective data, with a view to placing such data in a pivotal position in any analysis and conclusion, the validity of such data should be treated with caution. For example, in a detailed analysis of the problems of using retrospective data in studying 'undesirable behaviour', Janson (1990) identified several threats to data validity, including problems of recollection, telescoping (reporting events as being more recent than they were), omission (deliberate or otherwise), and reinterpretation (reinterpreting events in a different way as a result of more recent experiences). Even if one is satisfied with the validity of retrospective data, there is the further problem that one-shot designs are not especially strong in providing direct evidence that particular kinds of experiences (say, types of contact with the police) cause particular kinds of attitudes (say, types of attitudes to the police) to come into existence. To establish causation, it is not enough to argue that the experiences preceded the attitudes. Though the experiences are at least a *necessary* condition of causation of attitudes, they are not a sufficient condition, and one-shot surveys cannot provide good evidence that the attitudes did not exist *before* the experiences. It is to provide firmer evidence about causality that researchers sometimes turn to longitudinal surveys, as we will discover in the next section. For the moment, we shall focus on another problem with one-shot designs, namely their inappropriateness for the measurement and analysis of social changes and social trends. In this analysis we shall use victim surveys as our example.

3.1   VICTIM SURVEYS

Surveys of victims of crime have been influential tools of criminological research, particularly in the 1980s and 1990s. (For a good review of such surveys see Walklate, 1989.) Their popularity has been given impetus by official policies relating to law enforcement and also to communities' taking responsibility for crime prevention. On a methodological front, further impetus was given by the widely held view of social researchers that official statistics on crime, such as appear in the annual Home Office publication *Criminal Statistics*, fail to provide accurate measures of the true level of crime. *Criminal Statistics* includes data on two aspects of crime and criminal activity which provide ways of measuring the extent of crime and the numbers of people committing criminal offences. First, statistics are provided on the number of *notifiable offences* recorded by the police. Second, statistics are provided on *known offenders*. In both cases it is well recognized that there is a gap between, on the one hand, what official statistics show as the amount of crime and the number of offences, and, on the other hand, the true extent of crime and the correct number of offenders. For example, the number of offences recorded by the police is very much dependent on the ability or willingness of individuals or groups of individuals to report crimes, and it has long been suspected — as research has subsequently confirmed — that certain kinds of offences, such as sexual offences, are seriously under-reported. This results in the so-called 'dark' figure of unreported crime. Victim surveys developed as means of estimating this 'dark' figure, thereby providing more valid estimates of the true extent of crime.

Basically, victim surveys involve the selection of a representative sample from the population. Questions are asked of sample members — whether they have been victims of crime within a specified period of time and whether they reported such crimes to the police. A major landmark in the development of victim surveys was their use in the USA by the President's Crime Commission (see Ennis, 1967). A number of victim surveys were commissioned, the largest of which was a representative sample survey of 10,000 households across the country. The surveys reported a high incidence of victimization, much higher than was recorded in official statistics on crime. Closer to home, Sparks and his colleagues carried out a much smaller and more localized victim survey in 1977. The survey found that nearly half of the sample had experienced actual or attempted crime in a twelve-month period (assuming that the informants were reporting correctly — victim surveys also have their methodological problems) and also reported an 11:1 ratio of victim-perceived to police-recorded crime (Sparks *et al.*, 1977). The design involved a representative sample of three areas of inner London and can be described as typically one-shot and cross-sectional. The work of Sparks *et al.* provides a more valid estimate of the true extent of crime in 1977 than is reported in official crime statistics. However, it does not permit us to examine changes and trends in crime over a period of time. This is a major weakness of the typical one-shot cross-sectional design.

ACTIVITY 2

Spend a few minutes thinking of different ways in which this weakness might be overcome. Make a note of your conclusions.

One way around this problem is to examine findings from a succession of one-shot surveys carried out *at different points in time*. Indeed, findings from subsequent surveys have been reported, for example from Merseyside (Kinsey, 1986) and Islington (Jones *et al.*, 1986; Crawford *et al.*, 1990). These show the same general pattern of a gap between crimes reported by victims to surveyors and crimes recorded by the police. At a methodological level, the comparison of results from a succession of one-shot studies provides a means by which variations in the extent and distribution of victimization can be examined between different areas and also between different time periods for the same area. In this way, the secondary analysis of independent surveys of the same subject matter can provide a basis for examining social changes and social trends. Such comparisons should, however, be made with care. For example, surveys may differ in the way in which they define, operationalize and measure social phenomena such as victimization, and in the ways in which the sample is constructed (say, in terms of whether random or purposive sampling is used, whether the sample is stratified, what stratification factors are used, and so on). Such differences can limit the extent to which valid comparisons can be made. A much sounder basis for comparison exists where successive surveys sample the same population, are constructed in the same way and are uniform in their definition, operationalization and measurement of variables. For example, the General Household Survey has asked questions about burglary victimization in several years of its operation, allowing comparison over time for this limited category of crime. Another example of this is provided by the British Crime Survey.

The British Crime Survey, which is carried out under the supervision of researchers within the Home Office Research and Planning Unit (HORPU), represents a significant development relating to victim surveys. The BCS is an example of a *trend* design. This design can be illustrated by Figure 3 which appears at the beginning of this section. Unlike a one-shot cross-sectional design, the trend design samples at points A, B *and* C, and the same or similar items of information are collected at each point. The individuals chosen to be sample members at each of the points are not the same, although the procedures for selection are. The samples, therefore, are equivalent and permit researchers to look for trends in society over time. The first BCS was carried out in 1982, the second in 1984, the third in 1988, and there are plans to continue sampling at 4-year intervals. At each point in time, sample members are asked whether they have recently been the victim of a crime; they are asked to specify the type of crime; and they are asked to indicate whether the crime was reported to the police. The main analysis, therefore, provides data on crimes, of different kinds, reported and not reported to the police. Adjustments are made to the number of crimes reported by sample members to facilitate comparisons with crime officially recorded in *Criminal Statistics* and, as with the other surveys mentioned, there is evidence of sizeable under-reporting of crimes (which, incidentally, can vary according to the type of crime) — assuming that the informants' reports are correct. One important finding to emerge from the earlier surveys is that there is great fear of crime, particularly among women, older people and those living in inner-city areas; this fear, it is suggested, is out of all proportion to the realities of crime as measured by the surveys. The analysis also provides insights into the subjects' reasons for not reporting crimes. Perceived triviality of the offence is by far the most important reason, but perceived uninterest and impotence on the part of the police are important. For all of these items — extent of victimization, fear of crime, reporting of crime — there is the facility for making comparisons over time, and therefore the basis for making assertions about social changes and social trends.

ACTIVITY 3

The following extract from Mayhew and Hough's article 'The British Crime Survey' (1982) details the research design of the initial survey conducted in 1982. While reading the extract, ask yourself the following questions:

• Was the sample drawn using random procedures?

• What was/were the sampling unit(s)?

• Was the sample stratified?

• Was proportionate sampling used?

• How good was the response rate, and could non-response affect the conclusions?

THE ORGANISATION AND DESIGN OF THE SURVEY

Sampling design

One person aged 16 or over was interviewed in each household. An issued sample of some 20,000 addresses yielded almost 11,000 interviews in England and Wales and 5,000 in Scotland — with a response rate of 80.5 per cent of eligible addresses. The survey used the electoral register as a sampling frame to yield an initial sample of addresses. This sample was then converted into one of households, and one person was selected from each household using a modified version of a random number grid. People living in institutions such as hotels, hospitals, barracks and universities were excluded from the sample.

The sample was designed to be nationally representative. However, inner city areas were over-sampled in England, partly to maximise the number of victims identified by the surveys, and partly to provide more precise information on inner-city areas than pro-rata sampling would have allowed. The classification of parliamentary constituencies developed by the Planning and Research Applications Group (PRAG) was used to define inner cities and to stratify constituencies in England and Wales. In Scotland stratification was based on local government divisions using 1971 census indicators.

(Mayhew and Hough, 1982, p.26)

The above extract outlines the sample design at point A in Figure 3, in this case 1982. At point B (1984) and point C (1988) the same items of information were collected from an equivalent sample selected using roughly the same procedures. This facilitates comparison between points A, B and C, and thus represents a major advantage of trend designs over one-shot designs. In terms of criminological research and criminal justice policy, the British Crime Surveys have made important contributions by measuring the level of victimization, by estimating the 'dark' figure of unreported crime, by measuring the extent of fear of crime, and by analysing explanations for non-reporting.

You should have noted, remembering the discussion of this topic in the previous unit, that the response rate will limit the interpretability of the results. A response rate of over 80 per cent is very good for a survey of this kind on so sensitive a topic; few surveys have achieved so high a rate of response. Nonetheless, 20 per cent or so of the sample did not respond, and we cannot assume that the experiences of this 20 per cent are necessarily the same as those of the people who did respond. It is likely, for example, that some people did not respond if they had been victims of a crime which made them feel 'ashamed' — for example, young men who have been beaten up — and so the true incidence of these crimes is likely to be higher than the survey suggests.

In methodological terms, although providing an analysis of trends over time, the surveys are best described as *descriptive* rather than *explanatory*. In essence, the surveys are descriptive studies which measure crime at particular points in time with no pretensions of providing explanations. However, there is the potential — as there is in all such trend designs — to use the findings from the surveys to theorize about the causes of changes in the incidence of social phenomena (in this case, crime levels). For example, throughout the 1980s and into the 1990s politicians and researchers alike speculated about the causal connection between changes in unemployment levels and changes in crime levels (see Jupp, 1989, pp.109–19). What is more, trend designs offer the potential to assess the efficacy of policy initiatives in relation to crime levels. For example, the 1980s witnessed a major push towards crime prevention, including neighbourhood watch schemes, factory watch schemes and car security campaigns. Crime levels, as indicated by surveys carried out at different times, can be examined prior to, and after, the introduction of such campaigns with a view to obtaining some measure of the effectiveness of those campaigns. However, the survey findings do not themselves provide a direct test of such theorizing nor a direct evaluation of such policy initiatives. In both examples it may well be the case that there is statistical evidence of a time-lagged relationship between a rise in unemployment levels and a rise in the crime rate, or between an increase in crime prevention initiatives and a decrease in crime levels. If so, there is evidence both of correlation and of time-ordering of variables. However, there is not complete evidence as to causality in so far as variables other than unemployment or crime prevention, which have not been controlled in the analysis, may well have brought about the changes in question.

What is more, time-ordered relationships which can be established at a societal level do not necessarily provide evidence as to causality at the level of the individual. This 'fallacy of the wrong level', or ecological fallacy, which you came across in Unit 6, is especially apposite with regard to the analysis of the relationship between unemployment and crime. A statistical relationship between unemployment levels and crime levels does not provide evidence that unemployed people commit crimes.

There is a related fallacy built into the design of the British Crime Survey and trend or time-series designs in general: namely that, although equivalent samples, generated by the same procedures, are selected at different points in time, this does not mean that the same individuals appear in each sample. In fact, the chance of this happening is very low. In other words, the samples at points A, B and C in Figure 3 are equivalent but comprise different individuals. The implication of this is that, although findings from trend designs can be used to generalize about changes and trends in society as a whole (or perhaps particular sub-sections of society), they cannot be used to make inferences about changes in particular individuals. To facilitate this, some variant of a longitudinal cohort study is required. This is the subject matter of the next section (Section 4).

Although we have used the British Crime Survey and victim surveys in general to illustrate trend designs and their strengths and weaknesses, such designs are not confined to the analysis of crime or to policy initiatives relating to it. We can briefly mention three other examples of surveys using trend designs: the General Household Survey, the National Food Survey and the Family Expenditure Survey.

General Household Survey

The General Household Survey is carried out by the Social Survey Division of the Office of Population Censuses and Surveys (OPCS, annual). It is based on an annual sample of approximately 20,000 people living in private (i.e. non-institutional) households in Great Britain. The sample is two-stage and stratified. The first stage is a selection of postcode sectors (roughly equivalent to electoral wards) and the second stage is a selection of addresses. The chosen addresses are subsequently converted to households. The survey collects data on the main variables with which social policy is concerned, including population, housing, health, employment and education. The survey also collects data from time to time on other topics of social interest: burglary victimization and smoking behaviour have been popular topics. New topics are introduced from time to time. The survey permits the monitoring of changes from one year to another on these variables and helps to fill information gaps between censuses, which are held every ten years.

National Food Survey

The National Food Survey (MAFF, annual) is another example of a trend design. The sample is a three-stage, stratified random sample, and comprises 7,000 private households. Different households are included at each point of selection. Each household records details of all items of food brought into the home for human consumption during the course of a week, and also of meals eaten outside of the home. The survey provides data on trends of expenditure on food of different kinds and also on the nutritional values of foods taken by households of different kinds.

Family Expenditure Survey

The Family Expenditure Survey (CSO, annual) is carried out annually by the Social Survey Division of OPCS. It is a two-stage, stratified sample organized around the section of postal-code sectors and then households. Seven thousand households participate annually, with different households chosen at each point of selection. The survey collects data on family expenditure and is used to provide data on spending patterns for the construction of the Retail Prices Index which measures the change in the cost of a shopping basket of goods and services representative of the expenditure of the vast majority of households.

4 STUDYING THE DEVELOPMENT OF INDIVIDUALS

In this section the features of longitudinal cohort studies will be examined in comparison with those of one-shot cross-sectional designs on the one hand, and time-series designs on the other. One-shot designs tend to collect contemporary data about current attitudes, actions and events, and so represent relatively quick and cheap ways of describing populations. They may also collect retrospective data about past attitudes, actions and experiences with a view to treating these as causal agents in explanations of how respondents think and act at present. As indicated in the preceding section, there are problems with this; for example, problems relating to the validity of retrospective data and problems of providing evidence of time-ordering of variables.

Time-series or trend designs take equivalent samples at different points in time and thereby provide a means for assessing changes and trends in society over time. However, because different individuals are chosen at each sampling point, time-series designs are not appropriate for examining changes in individuals or for studying individual development. It is the study of such changes and development at the level of the individual, and over a long period of time, which is the hallmark of the longitudinal cohort design. By studying the same group of individuals at different points in time, longitudinal surveys seek to provide a stronger basis for providing explanations in causal terms, in comparison with the designs considered earlier. Such explanations are often constructed in terms of relating change in individuals to initial characteristics of those same individuals (for example, personality), or to development variables (for example, family socialization), or to intervening events (for example, unemployment). This is facilitated by collecting data from the same individuals at different, often key, points in their lives. In terms of Figure 3, an initial sample is selected at point A, and the researchers return to the *same* sample members at points B and C. It is because of this procedure of following a group of individuals through the various stages of their development that longitudinal surveys are sometimes referred to as 'cohort studies'.

Longitudinal surveys have been used in a wide range of areas: for example, psychiatry (Rutter and Pickles, 1990), paediatrics (Zetterstrom, 1990), child development and health (Fox and Fogelman, 1990) and psychology (Arsendorpf and Weinert, 1990). A celebrated British example is the National Child Development Study, which selected a national sample of children born in one week in 1947 and followed them until they were in their late twenties (Douglas, 1964, 1976). Within British criminology, and the study of the causes of delinquency and crime in particular, the longitudinal or cohort study is typified by the Cambridge Study in Delinquent Development carried out by West and his associates. We shall examine this in some detail to illustrate the main features of longitudinal surveys and to consider some of their strengths and weaknesses, although it must be emphasized that longitudinal cohort studies can be found in many areas of social science.

The aims and broad strategies of the Cambridge Study were very much influenced by the previous work of the Gluecks in the USA, which had indicated the important influence of early family socialization and family circumstances on who did, and did not, subsequently become delinquent. In the 1940s the Gluecks had matched 500 delinquent boys with 500 non-delinquent boys on a number of variables such as ethnic background, intelligence, age and type of neighbourhood in which they lived, and then *retrospectively* collected data from parents, schools and local workers about the boys' upbringing and family circumstances (Glueck and Glueck, 1950, 1962). The Cambridge Study intended to follow these broad aims, although by the admission of its director, it 'began as a basic, fact-finding venture without strong theoretical preconceptions and without much clear notion of where it might lead' (West, 1982, p.4). Nevertheless, from the outset a number of broad explanatory variables were identified, influenced by the previous work of the Gluecks:

> We wanted to assess the relative importance of social pressures (such as low income), individual style of upbringing (manifest in parental attitude and discipline), personal attributes (such as intelligence, physique and aggressiveness) and extraneous events (such as mischance of being found out). As a by-product, we hoped to identify criteria, present at the early age of 9 or 10, that could be used to predict which individuals would be likely to become delinquent. The Gluecks had claimed that this was possible, but no similar prospective data were available on the predictability of delinquency in an English setting.

> (West, 1982, p.3)

Although it followed the basic research aim of the Gluecks, the Cambridge Study departed from its American predecessor by adopting a prospective (or longitudinal) design rather than a retrospective (cross-sectional) design. Retrospective and prospective designs are illustrated and compared in Figure 4. In effect, the Cambridge retrospective study involved examining which individuals, out of an initial sample, subsequently became convicted of delinquent acts, as opposed to studying retrospectively the backgrounds of those who have already been convicted of delinquent offences. The reason for this is as follows:

> Research with established delinquents can be misleading. Once it is known that one is dealing with a delinquent, recollections and interpretations of his upbringing and previous behaviour may be biased towards a preconceived stereotype. Moreover, deviant attitudes may be the result rather than the cause of being convicted of an offence. In spite of the length of time involved we decided to embark

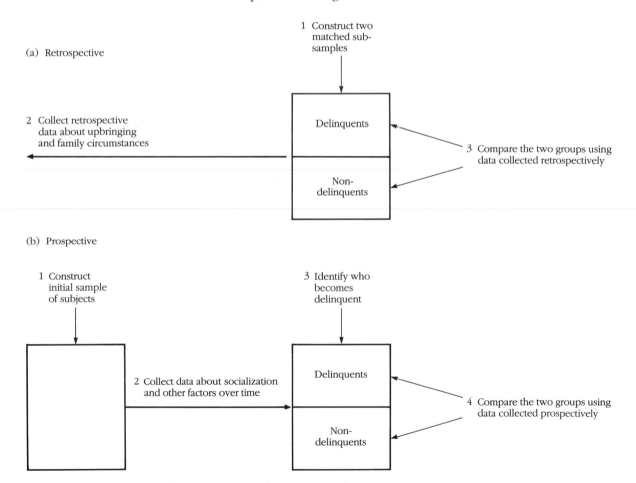

Figure 4   *Comparison of retrospective and prospective designs*

on a prospective study, collecting and assessing the sample while they were still below the legal age for finding of guilt by a juvenile court. Those who subsequently became official delinquents could then be compared with their non-delinquent peers, using unbiased assessment made before it was known to which group they belonged.

(West, 1982, p.3)

The Cambridge Study is a longitudinal study. In 1961 a sample of 411 working-class boys, aged about 8 years old, was selected from the registers of six state primary schools in an area of London. The area was chosen because it had a reasonably high delinquency rate but also because it was close to the researchers' London office. Girls were not included in the sample, and only twelve boys came from ethnic minority groups:

> In other words, it was an unremarkable and traditional white, British, urban, working-class sample. The findings are likely, therefore, to hold true of many similar places in southern England, but they tell us nothing about delinquency in the middle classes or about delinquency among girls or among immigrant groups.

(West, 1982, p.8)

The sample members were contacted at the ages of 8–9, 10–11, 14–15, 16–17, 18–19 and 21. Also, at the ages of 23 and 24 sub-sections of the sample were purposively selected and interviewed. These included persistent recidivists, former recidivists who had not been convicted of an offence for five years, and, for the purposes of comparison, a random sample of non-delinquents. Finally, the sample members were contacted when they were 32 years old to examine which of them had continued a life of crime into adulthood and why. This occurred in 1986.

A wide range of findings and assertions have emanated from the study as well as a multiplicity of research reports, three main books corresponding to different stages of the research (West, 1969; West and Farrington, 1973, 1977), and a book which brings together in summary form the main conclusions up to the 1980s (West, 1982). A central aspect of the findings pertaining to subjects up to the age of 18 years, relates to the identification at age 8–10 of five clusters of items which have some statistical relationship to subsequent delinquency. These clusters are summarized in terms of five key factors which, it is claimed, can be used as predictors of delinquency. They are:

- Coming from a low-income family.

- Coming from a large-sized family.

- Having parents considered by social workers to have performed their child-raising practices unsatisfactorily.

- Having below average intelligence.

- Having a parent with a criminal record.

Each of these factors is taken as having an independent effect on subsequent delinquency. However, analysis indicates a substantial overlap between these factors, and some sections of the sample had more than one such factor. For example, low-income families might also be large ones and have come to the attention of the social workers. Where this occurred it increased the likelihood of subsequent delinquency.

READING

You should now read 'The origins of crime: the Cambridge Study in Delinquent Development', by D.P. Farrington, reproduced in Offprints Booklet 2. The article describes the research design in greater detail and summarizes findings concerning delinquency, including the five predictors mentioned above. It also summarizes findings relating to subjects' subsequent criminal careers (indicated by convictions for criminal offences) up to the age of 32.

As you read the article consider how you would answer the following questions:

1   What key features of longitudinal designs are exemplified in the Cambridge Study?

2   What forms of data collection were used?

3   What strategy of analysis is used to explain delinquency and also subsequent criminal careers?

4   What explanations of delinquency and subsequent criminal careers are put forward? (You should consider this briefly because, in a course on methodology, the following related question is much more important.)

5   How is theory used in relation to data generated from the survey and interpretations derived from statistical analyses of these data?

The Cambridge Study typifies longitudinal (cohort) studies in a number of ways. First, it is *prospective*, as opposed to retrospective, following 411 boys from the age of 8 through to the age of 32. Second, in doing so, it focuses on *individual development* especially in relation to the generation of delinquent behaviour and subsequent criminal careers. Third, the study is *descriptive* in so far as it describes individual development and change; yet it is also *explanatory* in the way the analysis seeks to identify factors which can explain why some sample members became delinquents and others did not, and why some continued a life of crime into adulthood and others did not. Fourth, the study seeks to be *predictive* by investigating how far delinquent and criminal behaviour can be predicted in advance. For example, when the boys were aged 8–10 years old, five predictors of subsequent delinquency were identified: low family income, large family size, convicted parents, low intelligence and poor parental child-rearing behaviour. In subsequent stages of the research, six predictors of offending in later years, up to the age of 32, were identified:

> Statistical analysis revealed that these six most important childhood predictors were independently related to the likelihood of conviction, suggesting that each was important in its own right. Therefore, it can be concluded that the most important childhood characteristics that are predictive of later offending are poverty, poor parenting, family deviance, school problems, hyperactivity/impulsivity/attention deficit, and anti-social behaviour.

(Farrington, 1989, p.31)

Finally, the study illustrates a feature of longitudinal research which has not been emphasized so far in this text; namely, that it is often closely related to *policy formation*:

> The major policy implications of the Cambridge Study are that potential offenders can be identified at an early age and that offending might be prevented by training parents in effective child-rearing methods, pre-school intellectual enrichment programmes, giving more economic resources to poor parents and providing juveniles with socially approved opportunities for excitement and risk taking.

(Farrington, 1989, p.32)

During the summer of 1991 the then Home Secretary, Kenneth Baker, held a number of seminars with teachers, clergy, magistracy, social welfare professionals and others to discuss the rising crime rate and especially the problem of youth crime. Subsequently, the Home Secretary outlined, in general terms, policies to identify potential offenders at an early age and to introduce the kind of preventative measures outlined above. His decision was influenced not only by the seminar discussions but also by the conclusions of the Cambridge Study. The following extract from *The Guardian* illustrates the leading position of the Cambridge Study in the Government's 'hierarchy of credibility' (a phrase which owes much to the writings of Howard Becker, 1967), following major concerns about rising crime rates and also serious disturbances in the Meadowell estate on North Tyneside and in Elswick, Newcastle upon Tyne. This leading position stems from a number of factors; first, the Cambridge Study was resourced by funds from the Home Office; second, and more important, there is perceived validity in the findings and conclusions, which owes much to the longitudinal and predictive nature of the research; and third, the conclusions were attractive to a government which located the causes of social problems, including crime, within the family and the school rather than within wider social structural factors such as unemployment and inner-city decay. We shall return to this in Unit 21 when the Cambridge Study is subjected to a 'critical textual analysis'.

A BAD LOT

The Government's approach has been influenced by a mammoth academic study into the links between 'bad' parenting, juvenile delinquency and adult criminality.

For the last 30 years a Cambridge University research programme has been following the development of 411 boys born in the east end of London in 1953. They were almost all white and working class.

David Farrington and Donald West found that about a fifth of the boys were convicted as juveniles before they were 17 and a third by the age of 25. But half the total convictions were amassed by only 23 boys — less than 6 per cent of the sample.

Most of these chronic offenders shared common childhood characteristics. They were more likely to have been rated troublesome and dishonest in their primary schools. They tended to come from poorer, larger families and were more likely to have criminal parents and delinquent older siblings. They tended to be experiencing harsh or erratic parental discipline and family conflict.

Their parents endorsed authoritarian child-rearing techniques when they answered questionnaires, but tended to supervise the children poorly and were lax in enforcing rules or under-vigilant.

By the age of 10 these children were identified as daring, hyperactive, impulsive, unpopular and of low intelligence. By 14 they were aggressive and likely to have delinquent friends: it did not seem to make much difference which secondary school they attended.

By the age of 18 those who became offenders were more socially deviant in many ways. They drank more beer, smoked more cigarettes and were more likely to be heavy gamblers. They were more likely to have drink-drive convictions, to have taken prohibited drugs and to have had sex from a young age with a variety of girls, without using contraception. They tended to go around in groups of four or more and to use weapons in fights. Other characteristics were tattoos, bitten nails and a low pulse rate.

Farrington and West concluded that 'an anti-social tendency ... arose in childhood and persisted into the teenage years when it manifested itself in a variety of types of deviant behaviour, including offending.' A recent follow-up study found that the teenage offenders tended to go on to become social failures at the age of 32, with poorer housing, more marital break-up, more difficulties with their own children and more psychiatric disorder.

Surveys of this kind cannot extract any single factor of upbringing from the general soup of parental and environmental influences and proclaim it the 'reason' for subsequent delinquency.

But, according to Michael Rutter, professor of child psychiatry at the Institute of Psychiatry, research in this country and abroad consistently showed family circumstances to be the best predictors of criminal behaviour. Those circumstances involved all kinds of pressures upon parents which had a bearing on how they related to their children — such as unemployment, poverty or marital disharmony. The more adverse circumstances there were, the greater the risk. But what mattered was their impact on how parents behaved towards the child. 'Abusing, scapegoating or rejecting the child are more important than any variable', Rutter says.

(*The Guardian*, 19 September 1991, p.19)

With regard to the second question you were asked to address while reading 'The origins of crime' in Offprints Booklet 2, the data were collected by a number of means, including interviews with sample members and their parents, personality and intelligence tests, self-administered schedules completed by teachers, self-report interviews (where respondents are asked to report their criminal acts), and records held in the Central Criminal Office. The latter are important in so far as they remind us that surveys do not just involve the use of questionnaires and schedules, self-administered or by interview, but also involve secondary sources such as official records of convictions. This point will be illustrated in greater detail in the following section.

The strategy of analysis used to explain delinquency and subsequent criminal careers owes much to the logic of *comparison*. At the point at which two sub-groups within the sample were identified — delinquent and non-delinquent — these groups were compared on a range of variables to examine which of these variables are the best predictors of differences between them (in other words, by asking the question, 'Which factors do the delinquents share in common which are not shared to the same extent by the non-delinquents?'). This strategy of comparison was carried out at key stages in the respondents' careers. For example,

One of the most important findings of the study was that the more serious offenders at each age differed significantly from the remainder in many respects. For example, at age 18, the convicted offenders drank more beer, they got drunk more often, and they were more likely to say that drink made them violent ...

and:

At age 32, as at earlier ages, the convicted men differed significantly from the unconvicted ones in most aspects of their lives. They were less often home owners, more often moved house, more often divorced or separated, more often in conflict with their wives or cohabitees ...

(Farrington, 1989, pp.29–30)

The analysis is not only comparative but also *multivariate* in so far as a number of variables is introduced in order to explain the dependent variables 'delinquency' and 'subsequent criminal careers'. These are not only explanatory variables, they are also predictors of delinquency and crime.

The interpretations of the longitudinal data are explained by reference to an amalgam of established criminological theories which cluster around explaining, first, the *motivation* to offend, and, second, the existence of *internalized beliefs* and *attitudes* that crime is a legitimate activity. This is not a course on criminology and we shall not, therefore, dwell on the specifics or merits of these theories. What is much more relevant here is an understanding of the role which theory plays in

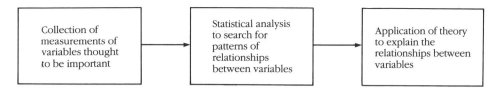

Figure 5 *Role of theory in* ex post facto *analysis*

explaining the results. In this case theory is not used from the outset to formulate a set of precise hypotheses to be tested against the data, although it will of course influence, in some general way, the initial choice of variables thought to be important. (As we have seen elsewhere in the course, theory always enters into the design of studies, whether or not the researcher is aware of it; 'atheoretical' research is informed by commonsense theories.) Rather, theory is introduced *ex post facto* to provide an explanatory gloss to patterns between variables which had been indicated by statistical analysis. Again, this is not a necessary element of cohort studies, but very many have approached their data in this way. The broad strategy is represented by Figure 5.

ACTIVITY 4

Now list the strengths and weaknesses of cohort designs, as you perceive them, before reading on.

The values of such designs are as follows. First, unlike one-shot cross-sectional designs, longitudinal research is not dependent upon the collection of retrospective data in seeking to relate past experiences to present-day attitudes and actions. It can collect a wide range of data about a wide range of variables at different stages of the individual subject's life. As Douglas, a leading exponent of longitudinal surveys, points out:

> A cohort study allows the accumulation of a much larger number of variables, extending over a much wider area of knowledge than would be possible in a cross-sectional study. This is of course because the collection can spread over many interviews. Moreover, information may be obtained at the most appropriate time: for example, information on job entry may be obtained when it occurs even if this varies from one member of the sample to another.

> (Douglas, 1976, p.18)

Second, the collection of data at the stages of an individual's life to which they relate reduces the invalidity associated with the collection of retrospective data. (This invalidity can arise, as we saw, from inaccuracies of memory, and telescoping or reinterpretation of the past in the light of intervening events and experiences.) The third value of longitudinal studies is that they can focus on individual development, not only in terms of describing such development but also in terms of providing explanations. The longitudinal dimension provides direct evidence of the time-ordering of variables, and so gives credence to causal inferences which link contemporary attitudes and actions to previous backgrounds, experiences and events.

On the negative side, however, longitudinal studies are very costly and they produce their results very slowly. They require key members of the research team to have a long-term commitment to the project, and they also require research funding bodies with patience and foresight as to the long-term benefits of such research. With regard to the sample, there is always a risk that members will change as a result of being part of the study, perhaps by responding in ways which they believe are expected of them. What is more, the sample runs the risk of being seriously depleted by drop-out over the years. This is sometimes known as 'sample attrition'. A survey of major American longitudinal studies found that the average attrition rate was 47 per cent (Capaldi and Patterson, 1987). Longitudinal research requires a long-term commitment on the part of sample members. Even where such commitment is provided, some respondents move their area of residence or emigrate without leaving evidence of their new whereabouts; others die. Sample attrition is a problem in all survey research but it is potentially a much greater problem in longitudinal studies because their *raison d'être* is the repeated contact of specified persons. Also, the problem of sample attrition in longitudinal research is magnified because, even with a relatively small drop-out at each stage of data collection, the number of subjects about which data have not been collected can be quite considerable by the time the final stage of research has been reached:

> Unlike cross-sectional researchers, longitudinal researchers do not have the luxury of selecting a random person at an address. The focus in longitudinal research on change and continuity means that specified persons have to be interviewed at every data collection point. Missing persons cannot be replaced. Because longitudinal researchers have to interview specified persons, this raises the major problem of tracing subjects. Longitudinal researchers also have to contend with death and emigration as reasons for attrition. Hence it might be expected that attrition rates would be greater in longitudinal surveys than in cross-sectional ones and that they would increase with the length of the follow-up because problems of tracing, death, and emigration are likely to increase over time.
>
> (Farrington *et al.*, 1990, p.123)

It is not just the size of drop-out which is important, but also the question of whether the representativeness of the remaining sample is seriously affected in relation to the subject matter of the survey. It may well be the case that the 'changers' whom researchers wish to study are more prone to drop out of research or to switch their place of residence on a regular basis. For example, research on children with severe adjustment problems showed that they tended to be over-represented in drop-out (Cox *et al.*, 1977). West and Farrington (1973) found that parents who were unco-operative or reluctant to participate in the survey when the boys were aged 8 were significantly more likely to have boys who were later convicted as juveniles. In addition, there is always the possibility that individuals who turn to crime are more likely to be difficult to trace as research progresses. It is for this reason that the Cambridge Study went to great lengths to trace sample members. However, this is a costly and time-consuming business. The study was extremely successful in reducing attrition. For example, at sample age 18 the researchers traced all respondents except one; at age 32 every man was eventually traced, and 94 per cent were interviewed or completed questionnaires (Farrington *et al.*, 1990). However, this involved detailed tracing methods, including telephone calls, letters and personal visits to the man's address, to his family's address and to his workplace; searches through the electoral register, telephone directory, criminal record office, and marriage records; and contacts with the then Department of Health and Social Security (DHSS), the National Health Service (NHS) and local housing departments. At age 32 it required a total of 2,915 attempts to trace 403 men, which is an average of 7.2 attempts each, and the average number of days taken to trace a subject was 36. To repeat a point made earlier, longitudinal research is a slow, costly business!

A further problem which can be encountered in longitudinal research is that variables about which data are collected at early stages may not anticipate theoretical developments at a later stage, with the result that crucial data relevant to such developments may not have been collected. This is sometimes referred to as 'the problem of fading relevancy':

> Because a long-term longitudinal study takes a long time to carry out, there is a risk that the theoretical framework that served as a basis for the design of the study, for the choice of variables, and for the con-

struction of indexes, and so forth, has become obsolete by the time the data collection is complete and the results can be published.

(Magnusson and Bergman, 1990, p.25)

Indeed, this fate has overtaken the Cambridge Study to some extent: theoretical criminology is now substantially *less* interested in personality variables as 'causes of crime', and *more* interested in people's understanding of their own criminal behaviour and in why some crimes are prosecuted more often than others. There are two potential pitfalls in trying to avoid the problem of fading relevancy. First, there is the danger of excessive eclecticism and empiricism where researchers attempt to collect data about as many variables as possible from the outset in the hope that one day they may be useful. Second, at the conclusion of the research, data may be squeezed inappropriately into theoretical categories in order to make them meaningful in relation to contemporary theoretical developments.

Another risk of cohort studies is the effect of *history*. Camberwell, where the Cambridge Study was carried out, has changed a great deal since the original sample was selected, so what was true of children then may not be true of the children who are there now. There have also been changes in educational opportunities, youth training, job opportunities and the organization, practices and resourcing of the schools, the hospitals and the police. The system of income maintenance for young unemployed people has also been radically reshaped. Any of these could be reasons why the experiences of the sample at a given age might not be typical of what people of that age experience today.

A final point to be made is that the strengths of longitudinal surveys in terms of demonstrating causality can be overrated. Even though it is possible to demonstrate temporal sequence by showing that certain actions and behaviours (for example, delinquency) are subsequent to initial characteristics, maturational features and intervening events, longitudinal surveys still rely on statistical evidence of relationships between outcomes and what are taken to be the explanatory variables. Such statistical evidence does not by itself provide conclusive proof of the causes of delinquency.

This point is recognized by Farrington and West and their researchers. The main focus of their research was on family background and early upbringing in relation to subsequent delinquency. However, they also collected data about employment status from individuals, and in the mid-1980s published a paper examining the connection between unemployment and criminal behaviour at the level of the individual (Farrington *et al.*, 1986). This was done against a background of high unemployment levels and high crime rates during the 1980s and political comment in some quarters that the two are related. Moreover, academic research using official statistics showed a connection between unemployment and crime at a societal level over the preceding twenty years (see, for example, Tarling, 1982). Farrington and his colleagues compared the offending rates of sample members while in employment with offending rates while unemployed. They estimated that the offending rate while unemployed was significantly higher than when employed. Statistical modelling techniques suggested that the offending rate was 2.41 times greater when a youth was unemployed than when he was employed. However, to reiterate the main methodological point of this paragraph, one should exercise caution in making assertions about causality. As the authors themselves indicate:

This research is highly suggestive but it does not prove that unemployment causes crime. This could only be demonstrated in a randomized experiment in which employment levels were systematically varied. For ethical reasons, such an experiment would need to consist of an attempt to reduce unemployment levels in an experimental group in comparison with a control group.

(Farrington *et al.*, 1986, p.352)

5 SURVEYING SECONDARY DATA SOURCES

The preceding section focused on a longitudinal survey which used standardized questionnaires and schedules to collect information from and about individuals. However, data sources other than interviews and self-administered questionnaires can be used. The focus of this section is upon other sources of data, especially, but not exclusively, secondary sources. We shall make use of a reading which, as with the Cambridge Study, is concerned with criminal careers. By holding the subject matter constant we can highlight differences in research design. Both surveys study individual criminal careers, but one does so primarily by collecting data at first hand from and about such individuals; the other relies upon secondary data sources.

READING

You should now read 'Criminal careers of those born in 1953, 1958 and 1963', by K. Shaw and D. Lobo, reprinted in Offprints Booklet 2. While reading the article you should write notes on the following questions:

1   What are the similarities between this study and the Cambridge Study of Delinquency?

2   What are the differences between the two studies?

3   What is the Offenders Index?

4   What problems exist in using the Index to study criminal careers?

5   What are the advantages of the design of this study in comparison with that of the Cambridge Study?

6   Is the study descriptive or explanatory, or both?

7   What use is made of theory?

The 'criminal careers' research and the Cambridge Study are similar in so far as they are both longitudinal, prospective cohort studies which allow an analysis of criminal behaviour over time. However, they differ in so far as the Cambridge Study involved direct contact with sample members in order to collect data, this being done primarily by interview. The study of criminal careers by Shaw and Lobo relies instead upon secondary data in the form of the Offenders Index. What is more, by collecting data from and about particular individuals, the Cambridge Study is primarily concerned with changes in individual behaviour, especially criminal behaviour; whereas Shaw and Lobo's study is concerned with criminal careers taking the cohort as a whole — considering, for example, average age of first conviction (although, as a careful reading of notes on the Offenders Index will demonstrate, the data would facilitate an analysis of individual criminal careers).

The Offenders Index is a database of named individuals convicted of an indictable offence in England and Wales since 1963. Indictable offences are those offences which can be tried only on indictment in a Crown Court, or those offences which may be tried in a magistrates court but for which a defendant may elect to be tried by jury in a Crown Court. They include 'violence against the person', 'sexual offences', 'burglary', 'theft and handling stolen goods', 'fraud and forgery', and 'criminal damage'. These are taken to represent the so-called serious offences, although, of course, within each category there can be variations in the seriousness of the offence committed and the length of sentence it can attract. The Index does not include the lower-level offences, such as traffic offences, which are dealt with exclusively by magistrates courts and which are by far the majority. The Index began in 1963 and provides histories of convictions of all persons convicted of serious offences since that date. By 1992 it included details of some six million individuals. Each individual entry includes surname, gender, date of birth, ethnicity and the sentence awarded for each conviction. For each court appearance, information is provided on age at date of conviction, date of conviction, and number of offences taken into consideration (Keith, 1991).

The advantages of using the Index, and therefore the value of Shaw and Lobo's research design in comparison with that of the Cambridge Study, are that there is no dependence on contacting individuals at first hand or of maintaining contact with them over the time-period of the study. We have already noted the difficulties which interview-based longitudinal studies face in relation to maintaining a satisfactory response rate. The use of the Offenders Index does not involve the costly and time-consuming tracing of sample members. However, there are problems.

The problems of using the Index relate to the gaps which exist in it. First, as Shaw and Lobo point out, it does not include information on cases where a crime has been committed, and an offender found, but only formally cautioned rather than charged in court. Second, because data on variables such as social and family backgrounds are not provided, it is not possible to carry out the kind of detailed analysis to be found in the Cambridge Study (where social and family backgrounds are related to subsequent delinquency or non-delinquency). Third, and crucially (though this is not mentioned by Shaw and Lobo), the Index includes only those individuals who are convicted of offences. The number of individuals in any given cohort who have been convicted of criminal offences does not necessarily represent the number of individuals who embark on and pursue a criminal career. This has important implications for the representativeness of any such study. In order to explain this further it is necessary to examine some of the social processes by which some individuals become, or do not become, criminal statistics.

Contemporary government statistics on crime represent key sources of secondary data. The main publication is *Criminal Statistics (England and Wales)* (Home Office, annual) which gives crime and court-proceeding statistics for England and Wales. An equivalent document is available for Scotland. *Criminal Statistics* includes data on two aspects of crime and criminal activity which provide ways of measuring the extent of crime and the numbers of people committing criminal offences. First, statistics are provided on the number of *notifiable offences* recorded by the police. The offences are the so-called serious offences which are also those covered by the Offenders Index. Second, statistics are provided on *known offenders*. In essence, these are statistics about individuals charged with offences which are 'cleared-up' by the police; that is, offences which have been proceeded against, irrespective of outcome. For this latter reason, and others, the numbers of known offenders and the numbers of individuals in the Offenders Index will not correspond. It is well recognized that official data on offences recorded by the police and on known offenders fail to reflect the true extent of crime or the correct number of offenders, as we have seen in earlier units in this block.

Two key points can be said to apply to most, if not all, secondary data: first, surveys can, and do, make use of such data; second, there are problems with the validity of secondary data *vis-à-vis* interviews. It is as a response to such problems that researchers have on occasion used surveys based on interviews alongside secondary data. One example of this is the use of self-report interviews and officially recorded crime data in the same study. With regard to self-report interviews, respondents are asked if they have committed any crimes within a time period specified by the interviewer. Sometimes respondents are prompted by the use of a checklist of crimes. This is not the place to enter into a detailed discussion of the validity and reliability of data generated by self-report interviews (for a detailed discussion see Box, 1981; Jupp, 1989). It is sufficient to note that there are weaknesses associated with such data, not least of which is the risk that respondents will be unwilling to admit to committing offences, especially serious offences such as rape and murder. However, as we have already noted, there are also gaps in officially recorded crime data. The value of using interviews and official data alongside each other in the same study is that there is the prospect of improving validity by balancing the strengths and weaknesses of different approaches, and by using data generated by one approach to check the data generated by another. The combined use of different methods to study the same phenomenon, thereby 'trading off' different strengths and weaknesses, is known as *triangulation*.

The final two questions associated with the reading are relatively easy to address. Shaw and Lobo's paper is essentially descriptive: it describes criminal careers within a particular cohort. However, the authors do suggest that the Offenders Index could be used in an explanatory fashion, perhaps to assess 'the effects of demographic changes in society on the incidence and prevalence of criminal convictions, or the effects on re-conviction rates of changes in the courts' sentencing policy and practice and other changes in penal policy' (Shaw and Lobo, 1989, p.25). As with most of the research output of central government departments, and the Home Office in particular, this paper has no explicit theoretical input. Hypotheses are not formulated at the outset for subsequent testing, nor is theory overlaid to provide *post hoc* explanations. The paper typifies what Young (1986) has described as 'administrative criminology', meaning that it is empirical, atheoretical and policy-related.

6 SURVEYING INTERACTIONS

The primary aim of this unit is to extend our understanding of the varieties of social surveys by outlining ways in which a time dimension can be added to the research design: for example, by the use of time-series or trend designs and longitudinal cohort studies. However, a subsidiary aim is to demonstrate that social surveys can also vary in terms of the types of cases which they sample.

The popular image of a social survey is of a form of research which samples individuals and collects data from and about them by means of interviews and self-administered questionnaires. However, it does not have to be like that. It is perfectly feasible, and often highly desirable, to sample other units of analysis and to use other forms of data collection. To illustrate this we can draw upon the work of a group of sociologists who were concerned with examining the ways in which the police resolve disputes. Their research was conducted against a background of a whole range of issues which emerged in the 1980s, and developed during the 1990s, concerning police policies and practices in dealing with the public (especially ethnic minorities) and in relation to the collection of evidence and the subsequent disposal of offences known to the police. Two main strands can be found in the research. One of these concerns an analysis of ways in which police intervene in, and deal with, interpersonal disputes between two or more parties (for example, domestic disputes or disputes between neighbours). The main conclusions of the researchers are cast in terms of the negotiation and bargaining processes into which police officers are drawn when called upon to resolve a dispute. The researchers analyse — often quantitatively — aspects of this process, as well as the end product of negotiation and bargaining. The end product is usually to 'negotiate nothing':

> Disputes are downgraded and often 'lost' to, and in, the organization. This is, not least, because they are almost invariably taken over by the police and recast in terms of police expectations and priorities. Hence, among other things, victims are 'made absent' or even criminalized.
>
> (Kemp *et al.*, 1992, p.118)

In other words, once the police are asked to intervene in a dispute they tend to set their own agenda by which the dispute is 'resolved', and this may have little to do with the complainant's wishes.

Methodologically, the principal form of data collection was field observation of interactions between police and disputants, supplemented by semi-structured interviews and analysis of internal police documents. This form of data collection is consistent with a theoretical focus on interactions and the negotiating and bargaining which takes place within them. The researchers accompanied relief and community constables in London and Surrey for three eight-hour shifts per week during the period of fieldwork. In all, they observed 1,200 encounters between police and public, of which 60 were classified as disputes. Although the observational methods used by the researchers are described as unstructured, field notes were organized and processed in such a way that made them amenable to elementary statistical analysis in order to produce basic cross-tabulations. In this sense the data collection and processing were geared to the production of a 'rectangle of data' (see Figure 1) within which the cases (i.e. rows) were disputes and the variables (i.e. columns) were key features of these disputes.

The second strand of the research also produced a rectangle of data but by means of a more structured approach. This strand was concerned with interactions between individuals and police officers after the individuals had been 'stopped' by the police. The main conclusion of the research is that black people (especially black adolescents) are more likely to be stopped by the police than white people for the same types of incidents. The researchers also suggest that black people are stopped on more speculative grounds than white people. However, their data indicate that there is no significant differential or discriminating police action or interactions subsequent to the 'stop' (or, as the authors put it, 'once a stop is underway') (Norris et al., 1992, p.210). The data were collected in a much more structured fashion than in the disputes research. The researchers joined routine patrols in inner-city London and observed 213 police stops involving 319 members of the public. An observational schedule required each researcher to collect, in a systematic and formalized manner, data about three main features of each stop: first, *background* variables — rank of officer, time of day, nature of incident; second, *interactional* variables — manner of stopping, ways of processing, characteristics of exits from interaction; and third, *actor* variables — appearance, demeanour, sobriety. The team held regular meetings to discuss coding conventions with a view to improving inter-rater reliability.

The data concerning each of the stops were coded and organized in such a way that made them amenable to analysis using a computer statistical package known as SPSSx (Statistical Package for the Social Sciences, version 10), the most popular statistical package available to social scientists. The basic analysis involved the production of cross-tabulations, mainly concerned with examining relationships between the ethnicity of the 'stopped' citizen and key features of the interactional process; subsequent analysis proceeded towards multivariate analyses whereby the relationships between a number of these variables were examined simultaneously.

Two key features of the above example add to our understanding of the varieties of surveys. First, the sampling units in surveys are not necessarily individuals, although this is often the case. The theoretical and methodological thrust of the study of disputes and of police–citizen encounters led to the sampling of interactions rather than individuals. Indeed, the range of sampling units in surveys can be much wider than this and can also include institutions, social groups, communities, geographical and administrative areas, and countries. Second, surveys are not solely reliant upon interviews with individuals or self-administered questionnaires. As we have seen, other forms of data collection — such as observational methods, structured and unstructured — can be used.

Documents and texts are further types of case that can also be sampled, and these are discussed in Unit 21, 'Critical Analysis of Text'. A wide range of documents and texts is available, including diaries, letters, newspapers and other media, stories, essays and other writings, biographies and autobiographies, and institutional documents and records. The systematic and quantitative analysis of such documents is usually termed *content analysis,* and will be examined in greater detail in Unit 21. Here it is sufficient to note that content analysis is akin to the kinds of social survey we have already described in so far as it produces a rectangle of data. The rectangle comprises a sample of cases (the rows) — newspaper editorials, for example — and items of information (the columns) about these cases. Where the documents are sampled over a period of time (say, newspaper editorials over a period of two years), a longitudinal element can be added to the design.

Documents such as those listed above can be useful on a number of counts. For example, they do not suffer from the kinds of reactive effects which can be associated with interviews, in which subjects respond to the interview in a way they believe is expected of them, or in a fashion they think shows them in the most socially desirable light. Further, for certain kinds of research questions, documents, rather than individuals, are the most appropriate unit of analysis. This would be true, for example, of the question, 'How are street crimes portrayed in the tabloid newspapers in comparison with so-called "quality newspapers", and how has this changed over the past five years?' Documents are also helpful where researchers are denied access to individuals whom they might like to interview. For example, in a study of the effects of imprisonment, analyses of letters sent by prisoners to their friends and relatives can replace face-to-face interviews when the Prison Department denies access to inmates. Finally, surveys of documents play a vital role where respondents are dead! It is for this reason that documentary analysis is at the heart of *historical research.* It should always be remembered, however, that the range and value of documentary research is limited by the availability of appropriate documents, and, of course, that documents are not totally immune from reactive effects. Such secondary sources are produced by people other than the researcher and for their own reasons, and it is often difficult to uncover these reasons and the ways in which they affect the contents of the documents.

7   CONCLUSION

This unit has been concerned with examining the variety of surveys and their problems. This examination has proceeded by establishing the one-shot cross-sectional design as a benchmark against which to judge variations in survey design, and as a means of illuminating the ways in which the weaknesses of the typical one-shot survey are the strengths of other designs.

The one-shot cross-sectional design provides a relatively quick and cheap means of collecting data from large samples with a view to describing attributes of the population from which the samples are drawn. The fact that such a design represents a particular slice through time means that it is not appropriate to an examination of social changes and social trends. Repeated cross-sectional studies or trend designs, where data are collected from equivalent samples at different points in time, offer ways of overcoming this 'instamatic' feature of one-shot designs. In effect they increase the representativeness of surveys by sampling individuals *and* time. The British Crime Survey was used as an example of this. By taking equivalent samples at different points in time, trend designs permit an examination of social trends, say, in terms of crime and victimization. However, because different individuals are chosen to represent each of these equivalent samples, there is no scope for examining changes to, or changes within, specific individuals. Where the latter are the main research aim, alternative research designs need to be utilized. The one-shot design does provide one means of examining changes in particular individuals and in the sample as a whole (or a sub-section of it). It does so by collecting retrospective data from individuals, say, about their past experiences, perhaps with a view to making inferences about the causal connection between such experiences and contemporary attitudes and behaviours. However, there are problems with the collection of retrospective data (for example, deficiencies of memory, and telescoping) as well as methodological difficulties in making causal inferences on the basis of statistical correlations established between variables about which data have been collected in a one-shot survey. What have been described as longitudinal cohort designs counteract some of the problems of collecting retrospective data and also provide a much stronger basis for making causal inferences about individual development and change. However, longitudinal cohort studies are not without their own problems. For example, they are time-consuming and costly and there is the danger that representativeness can be seriously affected by sample attrition.

A number of points emerge from the preceding discussion and from the unit as a whole. All designs have strengths and weaknesses, so that it is inappropriate to refer to designs as being either 'right' or 'wrong'. Deciding on a research design is a matter of balancing a design's strengths and weaknesses in relation to the central aims of the research. These aims will have dimensions to them which will tilt research decisions in favour of one type of design rather than another. Typically, these dimensions include whether the research is primarily descriptive or explanatory; whether it is intended as 'instamatic' or longitudinal; whether the focus is on individual development or social change; and whether the unit of analysis is the individual or something else, such as interactions, social groups, or institutions. There is, however, no perfect fit between what is methodologically desirable and what is possible in terms of research design. Deciding on a design is always a balancing act in which trade-offs have to be made between strengths and weaknesses of different designs. What is more, such decision-making is not immune from the realities of scarce resources. Even if a perfect fit can be found between research design and what is methodologically and theoretically desirable, important questions of cost can intervene. For example, longitudinal studies may be desirable to study individual change and development, but their prohibitive cost may lead the researcher to the relatively quick and cheap one-shot design despite its flaws in relation to this form of research.

A further point to note is that research designs, or aspects of designs, do not represent rigid alternatives. Indeed, they can be brought together within the same study. For example, the Cambridge Study of Delinquency was primarily interview-based, but it also made use of secondary data relating to criminal records of sample members. As in all research which brings together different design features to focus on the same problems, the intention was to balance strengths and weaknesses and thereby improve validity. Indeed, the pursuit of improved validity lies behind all research decisions. It is by understanding the strengths and weaknesses of different designs, and by being inventive and creative in balancing these, that research can increase the validity of conclusions. What is more, an evaluation of an already completed research study requires an understanding of the implications of design decisions and the impact they are likely to have had on the validity of conclusions. The assessment of research designs and the evaluation of research reports are discussed in detail later in this course (in Units 10 and 22 respectively).

ANSWERS TO ACTIVITY

ACTIVITY I

(a) This is a clear-cut 'cross-sectional' or 'one-shot' survey: single sample inter-viewed on a single occasion.

(b) This is a 'time-series' design or 'trend survey': repeated measures are taken over time, but on different samples.

(c) This represents a panel study, involving repeated measures over time taken on *the same* sample.

(d) See (e).

(e) Like (d), this is a 'before-and-after' study, involving measurements taken before and after some event. (The first, (d), is obviously the more effective of the two in terms of evidence of change, because the same subjects provide both sets of measurement.) These are the most minimal kinds of time sampling: you can think of (d) as a minimal panel study and (e) as a minimal time-series study.

(f) A cohort study. (We tend to use the term 'panel study' when an adult sample is interviewed repeatedly, and 'cohort study' when a group of children or new entrants to, for example, an institution are 'followed up' repeatedly, but the basic design is the same.)

(g) This is a cohort study combined with a trend survey. A cohort is followed through, but the study also investigates samples of people corresponding to earlier points at which data were collected from the cohort. In the current example, this would control for the effects of changing history — the fact that different kinds of shoes have become available over the years at an affordable price. However, as you can see, it would be an expensive study to run: by the time the cohort reached the age of 30 we would need nine further samples to complete the design.

REFERENCES

Arsendorpf, J.B. and Weinert, F.E. (1990) 'Stability patterns and patterns of stability in personality development', in Magnusson and Bergman (1990).

Becker, H. (1967) 'Whose side are we on?', *Social Problems*, vol. 14, pp.239–47.

Box, S. (1981) *Deviance, Reality and Society* (2nd edn), London, Holt, Rinehart & Winston.

Capaldi, D. and Patterson, G.R. (1987) 'An approach to the problem of recruitment and retention rates for longitudinal research', *Behavioural Assessment*, vol. 9, pp.169–77.

Cox, A., Rutter, M., Yule, B. and Quinton, D. (1977) 'Bias resulting from missing information', *British Journal of Preventative Social Medicine*, vol. 31, pp.131–6.

Crawford, A., Jones, T., Woodhouse, T. and Young, J. (1990) *Second Islington Crime Survey*, Enfield, Middlesex Polytechnic.

CSO (Central Statistical Office) (annual) *Family Expenditure Survey*, London, HMSO.

Dingwall, R. and Fox, S. (1986) 'Health visitors' and social workers' perception of child care problems', in White, A. (ed.) *Research in Preventive Community Nursing*, Chichester, Wiley.

Douglas, J.W.B. (1964) *The Home and the School*, London, MacGibbon & Kee.

Douglas, J.W.B. (1976) 'The use and abuse of national cohorts', in Shipman, M. (ed.) *The Limitations of Social Research*, London, Longman.

Ennis, P. (1967) *Criminal Victimization in the United States: A Report of a National Survey*, Washington, DC, President's Commission on Law Enforcement.

Farrington, D. (1989) 'The origins of crime: the Cambridge Study of Delinquent Development', *Research Bulletin*, Home Office Research and Planning Unit, no. 27, pp.29–33 (reproduced in Offprints Booklet 2).

Farrington, D.P., Gallagher, B., Morley, L., St. Ledger, R.J. and West, D.J. (1986) 'Unemployment, school leaving and crime', *British Journal of Criminology*, vol. 26, no. 4, pp.335–56.

Farrington, D.P., Gallagher, B., Morley, L., St. Ledger, R.J. and West, D.J. (1990) 'Minimizing attrition in longitudinal research: methods of tracing and securing co-operation in a 24-year follow-up study', in Magnusson and Bergman (1990).

Fox, J. and Fogelman, K. (1990) 'New possibilities for longitudinal studies of inter-generational factors in child health and development', in Magnusson and Bergman (1990).

Glueck, S. and Glueck, E.T. (1950) *Unravelling Juvenile Delinquency*, London, Routledge & Kegan Paul.

Glueck, S. and Glueck, E.T. (1962) *Family Environment and Delinquency*, London, Routledge & Kegan Paul.

Home Office (annual) *Criminal Statistics*, London, HMSO.

Janson, C.G. (1990) 'Retrospective data, undesirable behaviour and the longitudinal perspective', in Magnusson and Bergman (1990).

Jones, T., Maclean, B. and Young, J. (1986) *The Islington Crime Survey: Crime, Victimisation and Policing in Inner-City London*, Aldershot, Gower.

Jupp, V. (1989) *Methods of Criminological Research*, London, Allen & Unwin.

Jupp, V. (1992) *Sport, Recreation and Attitudes to Police*, Northumbria Police.

Keith, S. (1991) 'The Home Office Offenders Index', *Research Bulletin*, Home Office Research and Statistical Department, no. 31, pp.41–2.

Kemp, C., Fielding, N. and Norris, C. (1992) *Negotiating Nothing*, Aldershot, Gower.

Kinsey, R. (1986) 'Crime in the city', *Marxism Today*, May, pp.6–10.

MAFF (Ministry of Agriculture, Fisheries and Food) (annual) *Household Food Consumption and Expenditure* (annual report of the National Food Survey Committee), London, HMSO.

Magnusson, D. and Bergman, L.R. (eds) (1990) *Data Quality in Longitudinal Research*, Cambridge, Cambridge University Press.

Mayhew, P. and Hough, M. (1982) 'The British Crime Survey', *Research Bulletin*, Home Office Research and Planning Unit, no. 14, pp.24–7.

Norris, C., Fielding, N., Kemp, C. and Fielding J. (1992) 'Black and blue: an analysis of the influence of race on being stopped by the police', *British Journal of Sociology*, vol. 43, no. 2, pp. 207–24.

OPCS (Office of Population Censuses and Surveys) (annual) *General Household Survey*, London, HMSO.

Robins, D. (1990) *Sport as Prevention: The Role of Sport in Crime Prevention Programmes Aimed at Young People*, Occasional Paper No. 12, Centre for Criminological Research, University of Oxford.

Rutter, M. and Pickles, A. (1990) 'Improving the quality of psychiatric data: classification, cause and course', in Magnusson and Bergman (1990).

Shaw, K. and Lobo, D. (1989) 'Criminal careers of those born in 1953, 1958 and 1963', *Research Bulletin*, Home Office Research and Planning Unit, no. 27, pp.25–8 (reproduced in Offprints Booklet 2).

Smith, D.J. and Gray, J. (1983) *Police and People in London*, vols 1–4, London, Policy Studies Institute.

Sparks, R.F., Genn, H.G. and Dodd, S.J. (1977) *Surveying Victims: A Study of the Measurement of Criminal Victimization*, New York, Wiley.

Tarling, R. (1982) 'Unemployment and crime', *Research Bulletin*, Home Office Research and Planning Unit, no. 14, pp.28–33.

Walklate, S. (1989) *Victimology: The Victim and the Criminal Justice System*, London, Unwin Hyman.

West, D.J. (1969) *Present Conduct and Future Delinquency*, London, Heinemann.

West, D.J. (1982) *Delinquency: Its Roots, Careers and Prospects*, London, Heinemann.

West, D.J. and Farrington, D.P. (1973) *Who Becomes Delinquent?*, London, Heinemann.

West, D.J. and Farrington, D.P. (1977) *The Delinquent Way of Life*, London, Heinemann.

Young, J. (1986) 'The failure of criminology', in Matthews, R. and Young, J. (eds) *Confronting Crime*, London, Sage.

Zetterstrom, R. (1990) 'Data in paediatric longitudinal research', in Magnusson and Bergman (1990).

ACKNOWLEDGEMENTS

Grateful acknowledgement is made to the following source for permission to reproduce material in this unit:

TEXT

pp.17–18, 'A Bad Lot', *The Guardian*, 19 September 1991.

UNIT 10 ASSESSING RESEARCH DESIGNS

Prepared for the Course Team by Ruth Finnegan

CONTENTS

ASSOCIATED STUDY MATERIALS

Reader, Chapter 14, '"It's great to have someone to talk to": ethics and politics of interviewing women', by Janet Finch.

1 WHAT THIS UNIT IS ABOUT

So far this block has focused on issues to do with problem formulation, logic and case selection within social research. Another way of putting this is to say that you have been considering and evaluating some contrasting strategies of research design, together with their respective strengths and weaknesses. The present unit follows this up to focus more directly on the topic of research designs, with special emphasis on their *assessment.*

This means going back over some of the same ground already touched on in earlier units — one way of reviewing the material anew in this concluding unit of the block. However, the treatment here will also complement the earlier units by providing a somewhat different perspective on research and the processes by which it is assessed. You will also be getting further experience of applying your understanding to the assumptions often lying behind both research reports and research proposals at the planning stage. You should end up not only with some deeper awareness of the complex processes at work, but also with a list of key questions to draw on when assessing research designs.

You have already seen that the strategies used to plan research are of crucial importance to its outcome. Following this through in the actual evaluation of research and its designing raises certain complex issues. It is worth making these explicit at the start.

First, there is the problem that, as already hinted in earlier units, the actual processes of research planning and implementation are usually messier than the often idealized final statements — or indeed than the models in most textbooks. This messiness, however unappealing, has to be taken on board in any serious assessment of a given research design.

A second point is that both designing and assessing research take place in specific social contexts. These in turn influence how research plans are translated into practice as well as how these are represented by both the researchers themselves and the assessors. Thirdly, since social research is not just an aseptic and uncontroversial pursuit but a process involving actual human beings, there are also social, ethical and political issues to consider.

This unit will alert you to some of these 'real world' issues which are essential for any down-to-earth, rather than idealized, analysis of actual research designs. In other words, it is not so much about assessing the strengths and weaknesses of the differing types of research design in formal terms (though there will be something on this, picking up points made in earlier units), nor just about how research *ought* to take place or *ought* to be assessed. It is more directed to how such designs are *actually* proposed, used and evaluated, and the kinds of strategies you can develop for assessing them in relation to their overall plan. Additionally it will consider the related issues of *who* is likely to be making this assessment and for what purpose — and how this in turn also takes place in a social context. And if at times this means a rather sceptical assessment of researchers' (and assessors') claims, looking at what they *do*, not just what they *say* they do — well, that is not an uncharacteristic stance for the social scientific investigation of any social activity.

To summarize, then, this unit starts with a brief review of some of the research designs that have already been discussed (adding some further ones) and the criteria commonly used in their assessment. It then goes on to take a closer look at some of the detailed processes within research, for these too need to be considered in any full evaluation — as is well illustrated in the article by Janet Finch associated with this unit ('"It's great to have someone to talk to": ethics and politics of interviewing women', in the Reader). Since no research strategy is neutral, ethical and political issues demand attention too: these are considered in Section

4. Finally, some questions are raised about the *purposes* of any assessment, and about *who* carries it out — again leading to some crucial issues for you to follow up. The unit's aims are to help you to:

1   Review and pull together material in earlier units in the block and relate this to the overall course and block aims (particularly the aim of evaluating research critically).

2   Complement the discussion of the formal design features by a consideration of the wider strategies and processes which in practice often shape research design in the wider sense of the term: its selection, planning, outlook and implementation. This means attention to the *actual processes* not only of designing research but also of its assessment: their social and political contexts, the related ethical issues, and the differing purposes both of research designs and of those assessing them.

3   Gain experience both in applying the points discussed in the unit (and the block), and in reflecting on the principles and problems in such assessments.

4   Develop a set of questions which you can draw on to assess research designs and research proposals.

2   SOME GENERAL POINTS ABOUT RESEARCH DESIGNS AND THEIR ASSESSMENT

Before plunging directly into the assessment questions, we need to pause briefly to draw together some relevant threads from the previous units — both what has been included already, and some further points that can now be added.

2.1   RESEARCH DESIGNS: VARIETIES AND MIXTURES

Let us start by just looking at what is meant by 'research design'. This is a term widely used within social research, and is often to the fore both when a research proposal is being assessed (for funding or support for example) before the event, and in evaluating the final report of that research afterwards. Basically it just means the plan or strategy shaping the research. The term is sometimes used quite narrowly, referring merely to prior technical choices between different sampling options or about experimental and control groups. But it also often has the broader meaning — and the one followed here — summed up succinctly in Hakim's statement that

> Design deals primarily with aims, purposes, intentions and plans within the practical constraints of location, time, money and availability of staff.

> (Hakim, 1987, p.1)

A longer but similar statement is to be found in another recent book:

> Completing successful research depends on having a clearly defined purpose and access to useful data pertinent to that purpose. Certainly, various problems require that different strategies be employed in successful research. The strategy employed, the approach, or the particular research tools involved relate to the idea known as design or research design. A *research design* refers to a plan, blueprint, or guide for data collection and interpretation — sets of rules that enable the investigator to conceptualize and observe the problem under study.

> (Adams and Schvaneveldt, 1985, p.103)

Certain aspects of research design have been considered in this block so far, chiefly those to do with problem formulation, logic and case selection. But as will be clear from the quotations just given, research design in the broad sense has a wider coverage than just the initial plan, for it can also extend into questions of how the blueprint is and can be translated into practice, and the practical constraints which in turn help to shape this. Assessing research designs and research proposals demands some consideration of these other issues. Many of them are treated more fully in their place in Block 3, but some brief preview is needed here in the context of design. (The account here can thus also be taken as a bridge leading into the next block.)

There are a number of different types of designs which social researchers commonly employ and distinguish. It is true that there is no definitive and fully agreed list, and they are classified in a number of different ways in the literature. But it is useful to be aware of the distinctions between some (arguably) contrasting categories of research strategies when you are considering possible criteria for their assessment.

You have already encountered some of these contrasts, for the earlier units have contained reference to what could (in one way or another) be considered examples of what are widely recognized as some of the most important types of research design:

1   *Experimental* designs — see Unit 6.

2   Various types of *survey* designs, both 'one shot' and longitudinal — Units 8 and 9.

3   A *case study* strategy, in the sense of a detailed and in-depth investigation of a particular social phenomenon — a group, situation, community, life history, episode. Note that this sense of 'case study' is that explained near the start of Unit 7 (Section 1); the term is used in a narrower sense in the rest of the unit. It is worth adding that the use of a case study strategy can be found not only in research within anthropology and sociology, but also in political and administrative studies and in psychology (see e.g. Hakim, 1987, Chap. 6; Murray, 1974; Abramson, 1992).

Each of these well-recognized strategies has its sub-varieties and, as will have come out in earlier units, its particular strengths and weaknesses. These strengths and weaknesses must therefore be among the prime reference points in any consideration of assessing research designs.

A couple of further points need to be added however, for these three types between them do not cover all forms of research design. Nor does all research necessarily fall neatly within just one or another of these categories.

First, then, there are also other strategies for social research besides those based on experiments, surveys and case studies.

ACTIVITY I

What other strategies can you think of, whether from your reading in this course or from your own observation and experience?

Here we enter into a somewhat controversial area. This is partly because researchers in some traditions are less likely to describe their approaches as 'designs' than in others, with the result (among other things) that terminology is less agreed. This is partly because the stock designs that tend to be highlighted in 'social research methods' books and courses (including this one) tend to favour the terminologies and traditions within certain of the social science disciplines principally sociology and psychology — rather than others. Additionally, few of the possible categories are mutually exclusive, and there is no single continuum along which they can be neatly divided. That said, however, it is worth taking note of some further strategies that are commonly used in social research which you may well come across and should thus be aware of.

1 *'Emergent' and exploratory research strategies*

These are usually based primarily on observation (participant or otherwise) and/or on in-depth unstructured interviews. (This is sometimes also referred to as 'qualitative research', meaning its *design* features, rather than its necessary lack of quantitative methods; see Hakim, 1987, p.26.)

This is a form most commonly used by anthropologists, but also now increasingly by sociologists, and sometimes by psychologists. It may or may not (depending on the research aims) overlap with case study strategies. Further details about interviews and observation as methods will be found later (Units 11 and 12), but the relevant point to notice here is not so much the precise method of data collection but rather the open-ended nature of this type of research strategy. The outcome may form the basis for further research questions, but it can also be seen as a complete strategy — an end in itself. The aim tends to be stated in terms of 'discovery' or 'insight' rather than of 'testing' or 'prediction'.

In one sense the final design here is only settled as the research unfolds rather than being set up tightly beforehand: as Martyn Hammersley explains in his comments on 'qualitative' research (leading up to his analysis of the specific 'case study' strategy) 'There is minimal pre-structuring of the data collected.' (Unit 7, Section 1, point 5.) So, for example, Dick Hobbs' *Doing the Business* (1988) emerged out of his own experience growing up in the wheeler-dealing world of the East End, while Whyte's classic *Street Corner Society* (1943) developed from open-ended exploration in certain areas of Chicago rather than resting on a pre-prepared blueprint. The same general pattern applies in much document-based research where the nature of the sources as they are explored reacts back iteratively on to the overall research strategy. Hakim comments on one variant of this in the context of using administrative records where, as she says

> The design ... has to be back to front. Instead of designing the study, and then collecting the necessary data, one obtains details of the contents and characteristics of a set of records and then identifies the corresponding research model. The builder, and the materials he has available, take a stronger leading role in the design than in the usual architect-designed study.
>
> (Hakim, 1987, pp.37–8, also reproduced in the Reader)

In another sense, however, there often *is* a clear structure to this type of research: and this is precisely that very strategy of leaving many of the questions, aims and formulation of problems in the research to be developed in the 'data collection' phase, interacting iteratively with the researcher's initial ideas or hunches; the final design thus 'emerges' throughout the research. It is worth stressing that this is one reputable and widespread form of social research and one which — like any other — can be carried out well or badly.

2 *Descriptive analysis*

This heading is something of an over-simplification and in fact covers a multitude of approaches. But some such category is needed to highlight what is a common research strategy among some social scientists, even though often not signalled as such (it is sometimes included under the general heading of 'descriptive strategies' or 'design based on description', for example in Adams and Schvaneveldt, 1985, pp.106ff.). What these approaches have in common is the aim of producing an analytic description founded in the sources, which are often of a documentary nature, rather than through a pre-designed test or prediction, with the 'problem' formulated often being to understand the nature or working of some particular institution or process. Examples range from sociologists' research on, say, family obligations (e.g. Finch, 1989) or the conduct of the mass media in time of war (e.g. Glasgow University Media Group, 1985) to document-based research by political scientists aiming to produce accounts of political parties, governmental institutions or constitutional developments (for example the comparative account of the structure of local government in 81 countries by Humes and Martin, 1969, or the research into public enquiries published in Wraith and Lamb, 1971), or perhaps economists' analyses of existing survey data. In particular cases this overall strategy may or may not have something in common with the 'emergent' or the 'case study' strategies (it quite often does) and may be more, or less, analytic and/or related to explicitly theoretical questions.

3   *Analysis with a historical dimension*

An analysis set within some kind of narrative framework, relating the subject matter to its wider social context and development, is more frequent among social scientists than is often acknowledged. It is particularly used among political scientists, and among historical geographers and sociologists — for instance, Cohen's work on the growth of the British Civil Service (1965); research into changing patterns of work over the centuries (Pahl, 1984); research by historical demographers and sociologists on the history of the family, e.g. Anderson (1971, 1983) and other examples cited in Hakim (1987, p.38) reproduced in the Reader. The 'problem', in so far as it is explicitly formulated, is to explore the background of particular institutions, processes, etc. as they have developed through time, and hence reach a deeper understanding of their workings in the past or present.

These three additional types of strategy perhaps sound less glamorous or 'scientific' than experiments, surveys or case studies. But they do between them comprise a good proportion of social research, so they cannot be excluded when we consider issues to do with assessing research designs and proposals.

The second general point is an obvious one but, perhaps for that reason, easy to overlook. This is that typologies of research design, however phrased, almost inevitably give the impression that these are 'pure' and mutually inconsistent types. In practice a large number of social research projects use a mixture of methods to such an extent that it maybe near-impossible to classify them under just one type of 'research design'.

You can check this for yourself by looking through the offprints and Reader articles associated with this course. Let me give just one other example to illustrate this. It is taken from my own research on the social aspects of amateur musical groups and music-making in an English town — the reason for selecting this example being that I can vouch personally for its messiness from my own first-hand experience!

In one way this was a case study about just one town — Milton Keynes. It also fell squarely within the 'emergent' research style: relying heavily on participant observation and on a few mainly unstructured interviews with key figures, and developing new approaches and questions as I learnt more about the local people and institutions, read more in the wider literature, reformulated my initial assumptions and approaches, and felt out different methods. But in another way it started out not *just* as an open-ended attempt to do a local ethnography round the topic of amateur music, but also from a fairly clear question (or it seemed clear at first) about how much amateur music-making there really was locally, given current views about the dominance of the mass media and the common image of Milton Keynes as a 'cultural desert': my hunch (rather than clearly enunciated hypothesis) was that the answer might be 'a lot'. The strategy developed as I went along but I had also vaguely anticipated from the outset the possibility of drawing in other methods too. These included internal comparison between different musical worlds *within* the field area; the use of both local and national documentary sources, especially the systematic scrutiny of local newspapers; and some reliance on more quantitative methods as the research developed, like a mailed questionnaire to schools, a survey of pubs, churches and social clubs about their musical activities with the help of a research assistant, and structured interviews with 50 or so local bands. The result was a mess as far as neat typologies of research design go, and overwhelmed me with data to sort out. But it brought results. And though looking back I can see lots of mistakes and omissions, I wouldn't ultimately adopt a radically different strategy if I could do it all over again. (If you want to see the results — or criticize the design — it is published in Finnegan, 1989.)

So, research 'designs' are neither easily classifiable nor always, in practice, pure or mutually incompatible types. Still, it is useful to be aware of their disparate nature — 'trends', rather than distinct 'types' might ultimately be the better term — as a background to any attempt to assess the strengths or weaknesses of particular strategies and proposals, and the varying criteria that might be useful in this.

2.2 SOME STANDARD CRITERIA IN ASSESSING RESEARCH DESIGNS

After that preamble we can turn more directly to the issue of assessing research designs, both when looking back at these after the event or (the primary focus here) at the planning and proposal stage. You have already had the chance to consider the strengths and weaknesses of the different types of research designs discussed, one by one, in previous units. Now is the time to pull together some of these points by taking a different perspective and looking at key factors which to varying degrees run *across* several (perhaps all) of these designs.

ACTIVITY 2

Look back briefly over the types of research design discussed in this block (including the examples just given) and the discussions of assessing research in Unit 3/4 and Unit 5, and see whether, despite the disparity of examples and strategies, you can identify any recurrent underlying factors that keep being mentioned in assessing research designs. If you can:

1 identify about six recurrent questions or criteria mentioned as relevant for assessing research designs,

2 list them in order of priority in terms of their apparent usefulness in assessing the value of research, and

3 indicate which *you* consider to be the most important, and why.

Then read on after referring to the comments on this activity given at the end of the unit.

This exercise doubtless proved both easy and difficult. To take the easiest part first, the recurrent questions you identified probably included some or all of those listed at the end of this unit.

But you may also have found that you had some difficulties in trying to list them in order of 'priority' or deciding which were the 'most important'. Or if you did not, then I certainly did. 'Important' for what? For whom? For which kind of research design? In what context? Maybe in tackling the exercise you tried to anticipate the kind of answer you thought a standard 'methods' textbook (or a DEH313 examiner) would think right? That is certainly one possible yardstick — and indeed leads to a set of criteria often employed in teaching prescriptive methods courses or in research applications to academic funding councils. They are well worth remembering in that context, as part of the vocabulary of social science methodology.

However, might there be other contexts? If so, the criteria just mentioned might not be the first to spring to mind.

ACTIVITY 3

Recall or imagine some research proposals in your own line of work or private life: some problem, say, that you or others would like to see investigated. Then imagine that you have the power to decide between several contending proposals. Which if any of the criteria just listed would you immediately think of in making your decision — or would it be quite different ones? Be *honest*.

No doubt you also thought of other down-to-earth matters: questions say, of cost, availability of personnel, need for a rapid decision (or alternatively a smokescreen for no decision), desire for status or for academic advancement, action, internal politics. Not all of these are necessarily cynical criteria. But whatever their desirability or otherwise, they do form the often unavoidable background to how choices about research and its assessment are made in practice, whatever the overt vocabulary in which these decisions are outwardly expressed: the 'practical constraints' that Hakim mentioned in her definition of research design (Section 2.1 above).

This should not be taken to suggest that the criteria of validity or representativeness no longer apply. They remain essential questions which social scientists can and must continue to ask about research designs. But it does mean that anyone assessing research needs to be aware not just of the rhetoric of the researchers and their supporters, but also of the other considerations that may move them — the differing purposes for differing people, the hidden agendas, the often contending interests. To ignore all this is to move in an unreal world.

Assessing research design, too, is not just a matter of some asocial set of scientific principles, the same in all situations. As with the question of purpose, it has to be considered in actual social context. These contexts may be extremely variegated and complex. For in addition to the initial purposes to which the research was directed — and even these may vary according to *which* participant is considered — there may well be yet other purposes among those many (and again diverse) people who come to assess it. The 'audiences' for research, in other words, are not just single and self-evident, and there may be unintended as well as expected audiences.

Who you are and what you expect of a particular piece of research will thus directly affect how you are likely to assess it, and the criteria you use. This is a point to which we will be returning.

3 PROCESSES OF PLANNING AND IMPLEMENTING RESEARCH

So far in the block the discussion has focused on different types of research design and some of the standard criteria that are frequently referred to in their assessment. But it is also possible to take yet a different slice again through the material. This time the focus will be looking in more detail at each of the different but comparable *phases* which tend to be found within research designs (in the broad sense of that term). Our purpose is to draw attention to some recurrent questions that can be asked about each of *them*.

In taking this approach the argument will necessarily have to be presented on two levels, sometimes one after the other, sometimes simultaneously. First, commenting on the different research phases themselves; and then, on the second level, pointing to the relevance of *each* of these phases for the research strategy, and hence, of course, for its assessment.

The discussion here thus takes the sense of research design indicated in the earlier quotations as meaning, not just some idealized plan, but its interaction with the constraints of time, access, and cost; its appropriateness to particular circumstances; and the degree to which it is (or is judged likely to be) used, developed or changed in its actual application. Assessment at the end of the research would thus imply looking back to see how the blueprint actually developed (or perhaps changed) over time; while assessment at the start would mean making some informed judgement as to how the plan was likely to work out in practice. It is this longer process of research designing that is considered in this section.

3.1   LIFE CYCLES IN RESEARCH DESIGN

As soon as one thinks about it, it becomes obvious that a particular piece of research cannot be *fully* described by classifying it under a single, once-and-for-all label ('experimental', 'survey', 'case study' or whatever), for it is developed through a series of stages. No serious research, in other words, is planned, pursued and completed in one moment; research depends on a series of decisions and actions, taken over time.

The precise stages and their importance vary according to the project, and (depending both on the type of strategy and the particular history of the research) may not follow in neat chronological sequence. Furthermore, iteration between them is often an essential feature. So these different 'stages' should not be taken too literally. However, with that proviso, it will be helpful for the purposes of this unit to identify the following commonly found phases:

1   The initial stages of thinking about the possibility of the research.

2   Settling the research strategy or approach (including aims and methods).

3   Preparing the ground.

4   Implementing the main phase(s): data collection, field work, consulting the sources, or whatever.

5   Analysing or reflecting on the results.

6   Writing up or communicating the findings/conclusion (in various forms, perhaps including action).

As you know from earlier portions of the course, such a list is somewhat simplified. The significance of each stage depends on the style of the research, its circumstances, and the personality of the researcher. The amount of iteration and of overlap between the stages also varies (arguably most marked in ethnographic or document-based research). But despite these complexities, it can focus one's mind to regard these phases as key decision nodes to take note of when assessing how the research design has, in practice, worked out or is likely to do so in the future (as you will see below, there is a point here to adding the qualification 'in practice').

So let us look at likely points in this life cycle of a piece of research — the points about which you may need to raise questions. No research design comes ready-made: it is always developed through a series of decisions. And since each of these decisions might have been otherwise — they are seldom self-evident or neutral ones — they each deserve attention from anyone wishing to assess that research.

Some understanding of *all* these phases of research is necessary for a full assessment of the design in its broader sense. However, the later stages are only touched on lightly, since they will be elaborated in later blocks.

3.2 RESEARCHERS' ASSUMPTIONS AND ATTITUDES: SOME QUESTIONS AND COMMENTS

In any piece of research decisions are always made, either consciously or (equally if not more influential) by default. Here are some of the questions that often have to be decided. What kinds of topics are to be studied? What are the purposes? — in practice often quite fuzzy at first, and often later too, despite precise-sounding vocabulary about 'aims' or 'hypotheses'. What kind of outcome is expected: a set of generalizations in an academic context?, a narrative?, a policy proposal?, action of some kind? How far are the questions being asked answerable ones (or even ones that *ought* to be answered)? What hidden political agenda (perhaps) lies behind the research? What attitudes will be adopted to the sources for data (which will often be *people*), and how they are to be treated? And finally (if perhaps only unconsciously) what is the fundamental motivation behind the research, to whom is it (implicitly) directed, whose authority or canons are being invoked, and, ultimately, for whose benefit?

These early decisions — assumptions might be a better term — flavour the whole character of the research. For this reason they too deserve careful scrutiny in any assessment of that research. Some of the issues relate to questions which will already be very familiar to you: about validity, reliability, relevance and case selection. But it *is* worth noting that precisely these questions need to be asked not just of the *stated* 'research design', but also of those prior implicit phases of formulating the research. Such choices, furthermore, will affect the research procedures and findings in ways which have not just technical but also intellectual implications — and often political and ethical ones too (on the latter, see Section 4 below).

So in assessing a particular research proposal it would be reasonable for you to make judgements about these prior choices too. For example, you may consider the aims of the research quite misconceived, perhaps treating as a 'social problem' something which you see rather as just a set of social practices to investigate. Or you may believe that the focus of attention — on national 'averages' for example, on one particular area of the country or on respondents in particular power positions — is somehow unbalanced. Or you may consider that basic concepts in the proposed research ('the family', say, 'households', 'work' or 'community') are used so uncritically as to make the planned research valueless.

ACTIVITY 4

1   Look back at any one example of research read or discussed earlier. Can you pick up any impressions which indicate anything about those earlier decisions/assumptions? If so, how does this affect your judgement of that research?

2   Then repeat the process, if you can, for any further examples of research you know of from your own experience or have read about outside the course.

Comments on this activity are given at the end of the unit.

In one sense, asking questions like the above leads to an impasse. When it is so much more straightforward to ask about the formal design features — topics on which most researchers are relatively articulate and most methods books wax eloquent — why muddy the waters by raising these often unanswerable questions?

There *is* an important point here however. And this is that both the earlier choices which underlie research design, and the actual way that the design is manifested in the research process, are more than just technical questions (though they may have a technical side). They relate intimately to the underlying assumptions of the researcher. These underlying choices, furthermore, are likely to affect not only the overall plan, but also how empirical evidence is represented and co-ordinated, or the sources approached. The latter are not asocial 'data' just waiting there to be collected by some mechanical and neutral process, but are constructed according to the original selection of research topic and aims of the researcher. It is not that researchers are to be *blamed* for this: some such choices are inescapable. Given this, the more we can discover about the researcher's attitudes and beliefs the more we can understand the direction taken by the research.

One useful hint for winkling out the underlying attitudes that are likely to be shaping the research is to look at other work by the same researcher(s). Since it is only common sense to use every route to disentangle attitudes influencing the research design both in its initial formulation and in how it is actually applied, it can be illuminating to ask *who* is responsible for it. In practice this is a commonly-used strategy in assessment (though not always one explicitly admitted by assessors).

Such information may not be available of course, and it is not always possible to work out what the original choices and assumptions were. But reminding our-selves that there always will have been *some,* should at least make us sensitive to any evidence we can detect. How were they formulated? What were the alterna-tives to the actual way the research was designed and implemented? Are over-dogmatic claims being made about the objectivity or finality of the research? In *each* case the initial (and continuing) choices might have been otherwise — and the nature of the subsequent research, even its precise findings, could therefore have turned out differently.

Evaluating underlying preconceptions of this kind is ultimately a matter of judge-ment rather than just a technical matter. Some of the reactions can be linked, in turn, to differing attitudes held by the critics and assessors.

A light-hearted example (see extracts on following pages) can illustrate how differ-ing assessments can be linked with differing presuppositions. Light-hearted, that is, in that the quotations are from newspaper accounts (one common medium, of course, for the reporting and assessment of research). The subject matter is serious enough. It concerned research on 7-year-olds' knowledge of mathematics, widely reported in the press in October 1991. The disagreements implicitly focus not just on the detailed wording of the question but, more strategically, on the *appropri-ateness* of a research design relying on pencil-and-paper tests. This in turn links with a series of other assumptions and convictions about, for example, the nature of education, status of teachers, or role of the government.

Some of the above discussion really just rests on common sense, i.e. on the kinds of judgements we tend to make every day, following our normal practice of look-ing behind people's claims and conclusions (something not to be lightly given up, incidentally, in spite of the way specialists sometimes claim to supersede it). But it also links into some of the continuing debates about the nature and philosophy of social research, which you will already have encountered elsewhere in the course (especially in Block 1). For example, critics and counter-critics may invoke differ-ent sides in the arguments about 'objectivity' and 'truth' (see Unit 1/2, also for a handy recent discussion of these issues, Kimmel, 1988, pp.126ff.), or alternatively arguments about the effects of the researcher on the people, situation, or insti-tutions being 'researched'. Older assumptions about the possibility of 'non-inter-vention' and 'objectivity' in research are now very much in question, and there is currently greater awareness of researchers not as detached outsiders but as them-selves social actors within social situations. In this light, a researcher's implicit assumptions and attitudes run through and affect not just the early choices in planning and selecting the research, but also how the design is actually formu-lated and implemented throughout — and for this reason are increasingly likely to be challenged as part of the evaluation of their research.

Further critical questions draw on more general disagreements over the nature and role of differing kinds of research. These often surface explicitly or implicitly in the actual assessment of research designs and aims. One set of debates relate to some of the post-modernist and feminist critiques of traditional claims to 'objec-tivity' and 'scientific rigour', stressing instead the instability and relativity of texts, conclusions, etc. There are also the disagreements between those who emphasize

Scandal in our schools: one in three can't count

Tests reveal nationwide ignorance

'Back to basics' in education

by Charles Hymas
Education
Correspondent

ALARMING and widespread ignorance of basic mathematics and English has been revealed in the first national test results for seven-year-old pupils in state schools. Fewer than one in seven can do simple multiplications such as five times five, and up to a quarter are unable to spell simple words such as car, man and hot.

The unpublished results show that about one in three cannot count up to 100, and know the meaning of a half and a quarter. Only one in 30 can master figures to 1,000, read the temperature using a thermometer, and understand the decimal system for money. More than a quarter have not learnt to read accurately and demonstrate knowledge of the alphabet.

Yesterday the results, contained in a confidential report commissioned by government advisers on testing and assessment, prompted calls for a back-to-basics approach by teachers accused of neglecting the three Rs.

A study by the National Foundation for Educational Research, based on a sample of 3,400 pupils who took last summer's tests in England and Wales, has shown that 44% were unable to do a series of sums such as five plus four and work out, for example, how much change is left from 20p after buying a 10p doughnut and an 8p currant bun.

Only one in seven was able to answer a series of questions including the cost of three 50p loaves of bread, and how many 25p packets of crisps could be bought for £1.50.

Leading educationists said the results of the first tests taken by more than 600,000 pupils in England and Wales — based on written tests and teachers' assessments — had exposed worrying gaps in children's knowledge.

Hilary Steedman, a former member of the government-appointed School Examinations and Assessment Council, described them as horrifying: "It's inexcusable that children should have been in school for two years and not have learnt to add up or subtract."

'Is that good or bad?'

The questions that puzzled our seven year olds
page 3

Steedman, a senior research fellow at the National Institute of Economic and Social Research, said that Kenneth Clarke, the education secretary, should tackle the problem immediately.

Ministers, who are due to publish a full analysis of the results by the end of the year, had hoped as many as one in five seven-year-olds would reach the highest levels of achievement laid down in the government's national curriculum. The results show that fewer than one in 20 reached the target, with more than a quarter in the lowest of three ability bands.

In basic geometry, more than six in 10 are not up to the standards expected of the average seven-year-old, such as understanding angles. Only one in 50 was put in the top band, which requires knowing the points of a compass and distinguishing between clockwise and anti-clockwise movements.

About one in three appears incapable of using common measurements such as metres, miles, litres and pints; fewer than one in 20 can use more difficult metric units such as kilometres or grams.

Pupils, however, performed better when applying mathematical knowledge in classroom experiments, with more than one in four reaching the highest standard.

In English and science, results were better, with nearly one in five reaching the highest level of achievement. But many pupils failed to excel, with only one in six capable of spelling longer words, such as teacher, because and animal; fewer than one in 25 is starting to produce legible joined-up writing.

Nearly one in three does not know magnets attract some materials and can repel each other. Only one in 50 could complete tasks such as interpreting common meteorological symbols.

Sir John Kingman, who has advised ministers on mathematics, said Britain desperately needed a better-educated workforce capable of "simple calculations in shops to putting men on the moon".

Kingman, vice-chancellor of Bristol University, said the mathematics results were very disturbing: "It ought to be possible for young children to reach quite a good standard.

"If they are not, it shows that there's something wrong.
Continued on page 3

CONTINUED FROM P.1

It may be with the tests or it may be the teaching in schools that needs attention."

Demands for a return to basics were supported by Chris Little, executive officer of the Schools Mathematics Project, who said there was a danger that teachers were being diverted from arithmetic to other topics such as data handling.

"What we are getting is kids who can't add two decimals or can't say which of two decimals is larger. There should be

THE QUESTIONS THAT PUZZLED SEVEN-YEAR-OLDS

● Find the difference between seven and three.
● If six pencils are taken from a box of 10, how many are left?
● Work out the change from 30p when two cakes costing 15p and 6p are bought.
● How many jam rolls costing 40p can be bought for £3.20?
● If you had three £1 coins plus six 1p coins, how would it be written?
● What is half of eight?
● Name as many standard units as possible used to measure milk and water, length, the weight of an object and time.
● Add 5+2, 4+3, 1+6 and 6+4.
● Subtract 10-3, 7-2, 8-4, 6-3.

a concentration on this elementary number work in primary schools," he said.

Some academics, however, felt that the standards for the new tests had been drawn up arbitrarily, with some being too high and others too low.

Professor Ted Wragg, of Exeter University, said: "It may not be whether the children are better at maths or science, but how accurately the

people who developed the tests pitched the level."

Chris Whetton, who headed the team that carried out the research, rejected suggestions that the failure of children to reach certain levels implied poor standards in schools. "They are goals to which people should aspire. They reflect elements of maths that it was felt desirable that children should learn, but were not being taught," he said.

The results coincide with moves to simplify classroom targets after criticism that some were ambiguous and too complex. New streamlined tests for seven-year-olds are to be introduced next year, with the emphasis on pencil-and-paper exercises.

Draft maths papers, obtained by The Sunday Times, show that pupils will have to write down the answers to simple sums, such as 4 + 4, or 10 - 7, as they are read out by the teacher. They have five seconds to answer each question.

Above-average children will get more difficult sums, such as 15 + 2 and 19 - 13, as well as multiplication questions, such as 2 x 7. The brightest will be able to aim for a higher level than this year, by taking further tests, including questions such as 404 + 167.

Sir Rhodes Boyson, the former education minister and Conservative MP for Brent North, welcomed greater rigour and said that Britain's economic future depended on improving school standards. He was pleased that parents were getting clear evidence for the first time of standards in the state system: "This is bringing to light what the man in the street and ordinary parent have known for the last 20 years. Standards have to be improved. Unless we do, we can't remain a major economic power in the world."

The Sunday Times, *27 October 1991*

Sums that do not add up

Margot Norman says tests failed our seven-year-olds

Everyone must be shocked by the first results of our ambitious, unprecedented and ruinously expensive attempt to test the mathematical competence of all the 600,000 or so seven-year-olds in the country.

According to a leaked report in *The Sunday Times*, of a sample of 3,400 children who studied simple arithmetic for two years, 44 per cent were still unable to do a series of sums such as 5 + 4, or work out, for example, how much change would be left from 20p after they had bought a 10p doughnut and an 8p currant bun.

Disgraceful, we fume. Or do we? How many people are really surprised to find that, at seven, children are not ready to be put to work serving behind the counter in the cake shop?

A glance at a selection of the questions given to seven-year-olds in state schools to test their knowledge of basic mathematics should provoke similarly mixed reactions. I tried, as conscientiously as possible and with juvenile assistance, to approach them from the vantage point of a seven-year-old Alice in Numberland.

Question: "Find the difference between seven and three." Answer: "One is made up of straight lines and the other of curves." Wrong, of course. But if you haven't been taught that coy phrase "find the difference", you will no more realise that it means "subtract" than that grandpa has died when you are told that he has "passed on".

Next question: "Subtraction: 10 - 3, 7 - 2, 8 - 4, 6 - 3". Answer: "7, 5, 4, 3, of course, easy," Moral (for Lewis Carroll said everything had one, if you could only find it): it's easy when you know what the question means.

Question: "Name as many standard units as possible used to measure milk and water, length, the weight of an object and time." Answer: Silence. Moral: as above.

Question: "What is half of eight?" Answer: "If you give me eight beads I'll show you, but I can't do it in my head." Subsidiary question: "Why don't you just divide by two?" Answer: "We haven't done division yet. But if you give me those beads I'll show you." Questioner again: "Sorry, the secretary of state says that in future these have to be simple pencil-and-paper tests, so beads are out." Moral: if you want to discover whether a seven-year-old understands the concept of half of something, you will have to give him things — beads, bits of string — to divide in half physically. Pencil and paper won't do.

As we proceeded, this Snark began to appear a real Boojum. The question, though, was whether it was the national curriculum or the testing that was the Snark. After all, we know that our maths teaching is, to put it politely, uneven. We know that British children are less numerate than German and Japanese children, and we brought in a national curriculum because we thought it was time to become systematic, orderly and standardised about teaching numbers.

The same applied to the teaching of letters, words, and a host of other things, but because we are British and so morbidly glad to hear ill of ourselves, we have paid a lot more attention to the National Foundation for Educational Research's maths results than to those in English and science, which indicate that the state of affairs in those subjects is broadly as the government expected.

Unfortunately, as a nation we seem to have lost the art of being systematic and orderly about anything (look at our road signs, or indeed the direction signs in any public place, and count the number of despairing foreigners nearby), so it is not surprising that we have made a mess of our first attempt at a national curriculum in this, the subject that must above all others be approached systematically. We do not yet have a national curriculum, in the sense that there is one in Japan, where there is no need of national testing because the people know that their system works. We still have only a grandiose and waffly set of documents.

We have overcrowded the menu in junior maths and then compounded the mistake by devising over-ambitious tests to see if the meal is up to scratch. No doubt, in our intemperate way, we shall swing too far in the opposite direction and over-simplify, with the Education Secretary's simple paper-and-pencil tests.

Surely it would be better to test a few thousand children sensibly, with beads, bits of string and whatever else is required, than to test the whole lot badly.

The Times, *29 October 1991*

the study of historical and cultural specifics (as in some ethnographies or narrative accounts) and those supporting more comparative, generalizing or quantitatively-based research designs, raising questions of what is research *for* and *about*? (see discussion in Block 1). Which side of these various fences you are on may have implications for design and thus for your assessment of its appropriateness.

It is also worth noting that despite some convergence across the social science disciplines, the *characteristic* approaches within disciplines do tend to differ. An assessor from psychology (say) would be less likely to be sympathetic to case-study, narrative or ethnographic research proposals, while most anthropologists would look critically at large-scale surveys or hypothesis-led experimental designs.

In such arguments, then, the criteria for assessment go beyond such formal features as validity, generality or representativeness. In the end they extend to questions about the ultimate *appropriateness* of particular philosophical (and perhaps moral) underpinnings for the strategies and aims planned in designing the research.

Finally, it is worth remembering that it is not just the researchers themselves, but also those assessing the research, who are likely to differ in how far they accept the researcher's unspoken assumptions. So one of the lessons must be that it is not just the *researcher's* obligation to be explicit about the hidden preconceptions behind the research. It is also the responsibility of those assessing it to be aware of *their own* assumptions.

READING

For a well-written and usefully explicit account of how underlying methodological, intellectual and ethical attitudes affected a piece of research, read and make notes on the article by Janet Finch '"It's great to have someone to talk to": ethics and politics of interviewing women', reproduced as Chapter 14 of the Reader. (This will be useful throughout this unit.)

3.3   PRACTICAL CONSTRAINTS AND INDUCEMENTS IN RESEARCH PLANNING

So far we have considered decisions made in the early phases of research planning and their implications for evaluating that research. There is also a second set of questions which in practice often interact or overlap with the first. These concern the effect on the overall research strategy of such practical and down-to-earth factors as access, funding, personnel, or the powers of explicit or implicit sponsors. For, contrary to what might have been implied in the last section, researchers are seldom completely free agents, but are necessarily influenced by the practicalities of their situation: the 'constraints' pointed out by Hakim (Section 2.1 above).

Some issues centre on quite straightforward questions. Thus people involved either in planning their own research or in assessing a research proposal at the start of the process would also want to ask about such practical points as:

1   The availability and competence of the researcher(s) and who they are.

2   The timescale: is it feasible for the researcher(s) and acceptable for the sponsors?

3   Availability of, and access to, the necessary sources and data.

4   Management of the research, e.g. relations between different personnel involved (for research of a customer-contractual nature this might include an explicit written contract).

5   Ownership and control of the researcher's results, e.g. reporting to whom, when, how and under what sanctions.

6   Costs (money and other).

And perhaps:

7   Convenience and acceptability, e.g. within an organization will the benefits of the research outweigh the likely intrusiveness and 'time wasting' it might cause? Will it upset certain parties whose good will is needed?

Whatever the precise situation the answers to the questions arising from these points inevitably impose constraints on both researchers and, where applicable, their sponsors. Knowing about such factors must inevitably, therefore, play a part in the assessment of any research proposals.

Although they sound simple, these questions can have quite complex answers. This can be illustrated from just a couple of them: questions about the sources/data, and about the personnel and funding of research.

First the availability of sources and (the crucial point here) of access to them. Any serious social researcher has to some extent to consider this question in drawing up research plans. How centrally it is treated, and with how much care, varies along a continuum ranging from little or no consideration in the initial stage to the other extreme of the research strategy emerging from, rather than guiding the approach to, the sources or data.

The placing on this complex continuum is yet another factor to take into account in assessing research design. Adopting one extreme (little or no prior consideration) is not unknown, if usually an unconscious or undeclared position. It carries the dangers that whatever the *stated* strategy, the initial aims will later have to be changed, twisted or even in essence abandoned to fit the practicalities (perhaps without this being admitted). When researchers are open about this, such factors can be taken into account. Sometimes, however, the original aims or questions are quietly changed to something else or alternatively the planned *methods* followed blindly despite turning out to be impracticable for the initial *aims* — the research design proceeds in formal terms, but no longer with the same meaning. The final report may still make a show of consistency to the original plan by quietly camouflaging the changes. These are possibilities to which anyone assessing a research design needs to be alert (they are not as infrequent as the more traditional methods textbooks would lead us to suppose).

The other extreme also raises questions: starting from the sources/data which *are* in practice available and superimposing some overall research design after the event. This sometimes results in *anything* that is 'discovered' getting loaded into the research report without any clear strategy or overview: a result with which few people assessing the research may be satisfied. But it can also lead into genuinely debatable issues about whether, for example, planning one's research should be aiming at insight arising from a particular case study (as against a representative sampling approach), or how far problems should be formulated *after* in-depth steeping in the sources rather than prior to the data-collection phase. Which position you take on these controversies might affect how you assess this kind of research design. So too might the basic research design. A piece of research which claimed a rigorously experimental or sample survey design but in practice had to adapt its strategy and hypotheses as it went along because the data could not be collected or manipulated as had been expected would call for more critical scrutiny than one conducted from the outset in the more ethnographic tradition, other things being equal.

Whatever the style, however, investigating the effect or likely effect of the data-collection or source-consultation phase on the original plan is always a relevant question. So when assessing a proposal, questions about sources and data are central ones. Has the researcher intending to use government statistics, for example, taken account of the ways they may or may not be dependable sources (see Unit 5, Section 2)? Once again things may not be what they seem in the stated research design. It is also easy to assume later on that the people, sources or data to which the researcher in practice did gain access were the 'real' and 'intended' ones in the plan (with the others somehow slipping out of memory as peripheral) — on the same lines as the non-respondents to which attention was rightly drawn in Unit 8 (Section 5.2). Once again, one measure to apply here is how open the researcher is about such (not unfamiliar) problems, and how far they have been anticipated in the early planning stage.

Issues about the availability of sources and access to data can often not be answered just in numerical terms, or by a simple 'yes' or 'no'; they can also have qualitative implications for the overall research strategy. What *kind* of access there is to sources of information may be crucial. A researcher may claim to have access to particular people or written sources — but is he or she competent in the language used there?, acquainted with the background and assumptions of the sources?, or accepted as trustworthy by those being interviewed? Questions about access need to be raised for *any* research involving contact with people but are particularly significant in ethnographic or similar research involving in-depth interviews or extended participant observation. Here the role taken (or perceived to be taken) by the researcher may also have direct effects on the 'findings', all the more radical where, as not infrequently, the researcher is in a position of power as against those being 'researched on', or seen to be a representative of a particular interest or organization such as the DHSS, a colonial government or the police. Such aspects are treated in more detail later, in Block 3 on data collection and construction (especially in Unit 16). The point here is merely that since such issues are bound to come up in any research in which the researcher is interacting with people, one necessary aspect of the assessment of the research proposal is to ask how far they have been recognized and planned for.

Other questions to look to are decisions about *who* is doing the research, in what kinds of relationship, and for whom? These points too can be of strategic importance to the actual outcome of the research.

There is, first, the straightforward matter of the organization of the research personnel. Is the research to be carried out by a single researcher? A 'principal' researcher together with assistants at various levels? A 'junior' researcher doing the work under the umbrella of an already entrenched academic? A group of researchers in a collaborative project? There is a huge range of possibilities from single scholars working on their own at one end to large collaborative projects, sometimes with a national or even international scope.

You might think that this is fairly trivial, or that the same basic principles about research design can be applied whatever the precise division of labour between the individuals who happen to be involved. In one sense this is true. Irrespective of who does what, issues of validity or reliability or competence still arise. But beyond that, the relationships between the people involved in the inception and the carrying through of the research plans are a relevant factor to consider. Some quite commonly-heard criticisms of particular pieces of research can run, for example: 'Well, the plan sounded fine in theory, but of course it was all really done by meagrely-supervised graduate students', or 'There was a change of personnel in the middle, so though the original design was overtly followed, in practice the emphasis changed', or 'The collaborative strategy was impossible to implement because of lack of communication or disagreement between the researchers'. The personal and power relations among the relevant parties to the research usually receive little publicity either in the initial proposal or the final report. Their relevance is often all the more worth scrutinizing, drawing on what little information may be provided.

Among these various parties must also be reckoned the sponsors of the research. They too may have a crucial — but undeclared — influence on the research design, and one it is worth reflecting on.

One kind of sponsorship is of course from those who provide money to support the research. The effect of such funders — whether from government institutions, business, charitable foundations, institutions of higher education, employers, clients or whatever — is clearly one factor to consider in assessing constraints on particular research designs. These may well be influenced by the funders' expectations, even when these are not fully shared by the researcher. Not all research plans are tailored to sponsors' perceptions, but that this is one factor to consider is widely accepted. The general import here is neatly summarized in Cullingworth's lecture on the politics of research:

> There was a young lady of Kent
> Who said that she knew what it meant
> When men took her to dine
> Gave her cocktails and wine
> She knew what it meant — but she went.
> (Quoted in Cullingworth, 1970, p.18)

Sponsorship does not just end with money, nor is all research planned on the researcher-applies-to-funders model. Questions also need to be asked about sponsors in the broad sense of all those who support or guarantee the research in less tangible but sometimes equally influential ways. These could be academic superiors, employers, patrons, peers, gatekeepers — indeed everyone who allows their time, name or implicit promise of future support to enter into the transaction. The researcher's intended audience — his or her reference group — is usually another important factor into which we should enquire, to the extent that we have the information to do so. All these parties and their expectations help to model the researcher's conception of what kind of research strategy should be adopted and how it should be applied. And it has to be remembered that non-monetary inducements and sanctions can sometimes be even more effective than those consisting of cash, and can work in subtler ways.

Since *all* research is likely to be affected by the social context in which it is conceived — and that context includes the often-powerful parties who sponsor it — it is insufficient just to assert that this should not happen. The key is to be alert to the complexities of that process and, rather than just be embarrassed into ignoring it, try to work out its implications for the actual shaping of specific research designs. In other words, to emulate that young lady of Kent in at least knowing what the score is.

As with the previous questions there is no one comprehensive litmus test for assessing this phase of research design. It is an art, not a science, and the particular circumstances of each piece of research always have to be considered. In some cases, furthermore, it is nearly impossible to discover just why certain decisions were taken and whether the researcher had in fact really weighed up their pros and cons or planned for likely complications. Perhaps in the end it comes down to just two overriding questions to ask of this phase of the research planning:

1   How far *does* the researcher — or, indeed, the sponsors or the intended audience — seem to have actually weighed up and assessed the implications of the particular planning decisions made in relation to the various points discussed in this section? In general terms, one might be sceptical about a plan which involved rushing into research, however technically 'correct', without having considered such implications explicitly.

2   How much information does the researcher give about the process of reaching these decisions, and the background and reasons for them? The more open researchers are about this process the more likely one is to have confidence in their research planning. If the necessary information is not present we would not dismiss the report out of hand, but we might treat it with some caution.

ACTIVITY 5

Although, as just stated, there is no definitive code of questions, recapitulate the points in the previous section by spending a short time (say 20 minutes) on one or other of the two following 'games' (useful, if not to be taken over-seriously):

1   You must at some time have seen examples of very bad research, whether at work, in the newspapers or even in this course. Try to recall one of them.

2   Make up a fictional worst case 'horror story' illustrating as many as possible of the issues discussed above.

Whichever you choose, then give yourself the easy task of writing a critical assessment of their research designs. (You will probably find you can elaborate this as you go on, not only by comparing notes with other students, but also by keeping your eyes open for similar issues in actual research.)

3.4 PRESENTING THE RESEARCH STRATEGY: TERMINOLOGIES AND SMOKESCREENS

Deciding on the basic approach or strategy for a particular research project is one thing — and a necessary phase — in any piece of research. But how this is presented to colleagues, potential funders or eventual readers may be quite another thing. And what people say (or even perhaps think) they are doing or have done may be rather different from what actually happens in practice.

This discrepancy is common enough in social research to deserve some specific attention here. Though it is not always so easily detectable at the research *proposal* stage, being aware of this possibility is still important for research assessment, for taking certain claims uncritically could result in a very misleading impression of the actual structure of the research. After all, we all know from our own experience that action does not always match what people say about it. The importance of this in assessing social research has been highlighted by recent writing on how social researchers construct the 'texts' of what they write following particular currently fashionable conventions.

One powerful model here presents social research as taking place in a 'hypothetico-deductive' framework (see discussion in Unit 1/2). Whether from the influence of (supposed) natural science models or for some other reason, this vocabulary was for a long time considered the accepted one for dignifying one's investigations as social science, for presenting both applications and final reports to academic funding bodies, and for structuring accounts of the planning and processing of research. Using this vocabulary seemed to identify the research and the researchers with the specialist research community in social science.

For many years then, this was the major model for research presentation. It was never the only one, however, and there were still large numbers of researchers who used neither the vocabulary nor the procedures of the hypothetico-deductive model. But because it was thought to be the dominant one, these researchers too sometimes expressed themselves in this vocabulary when speaking publicly and officially, even if it did not at all match their actual procedures (e.g. in many 'case study', 'emergent' or 'historical' research designs).

In searching out the *actual* plan and genesis of a piece of research, therefore, you cannot always take researchers' statements at their face value. Although it can be hard to detect this at the prior planning and proposal stage, knowing about the kinds of ways researchers write afterwards can help to forewarn one and induce a more sceptical attitude. So one prior question always has to be how far a researcher is giving an honest account, how far she or he is engaging in a cosmetic exercise to meet the perceived canons of formal presentation. Andrew Greeley of the National Opinion Research Centre of the University of Chicago talked about this kind of camouflage in a provocative article in *The American Sociologist*:

> We have observed that the most creative of our colleagues do not seem to work according to the strict rules of the scientific method. They form explicit hypotheses only when they are ready to write up the account of their work, and generally they worry about specifying their formal theory only as they try to figure out how to begin their article. I am not suggesting that theories or null hypotheses are absent from their works but that theories, hypotheses, scholarly footnotes, and familiarity with the literature are present in implicit and fundamentally unimportant fashion. What the creative scholars are doing when they are working in a project has nothing to do with anything that fits in the neat paradigm of scientific method. What they are doing is dreaming, speculating, playing with the variables in the model, following their hunches and instincts, and puttering with their raw materials. None of these activities gets into sociological reports because they are not 'science'. However neat and precise the professional tone of articles, papers and monographs, are they really honest descriptions about how our colleagues

went about their work? No, they are using the approved literary form for communicating with each other and can escape the charge of dishonesty with the plea that nobody really believes that the analytic process described in an article is in fact the one that went into its preparation.

(Greeley, 1971, p.224)

(For further discussion of actual procedures as against 'scientific' terminology in the social sciences, see also Shipman, 1988; Bell and Roberts, 1984; Hammond, 1964; Burgess, 1984, 1992.)

A touch of scepticism, then, about researchers' *own* statements of their research strategies is essential. Sometimes they are relatively honest, sometimes not.

On the face of it, you have a simpler job where researchers are open about their research or confess the down-to-earth ways in which they actually designed or failed to design their research, or the muddles through which they in practice modified their original plans or are likely to do so in the future. Such frank accounts used to be infrequent — it was dangerous to reveal such 'faults' even if widely surmised that they were actually quite widespread. Recently, however, they have been increasing even to the extent of its becoming fashionable to 'reveal all', particularly but not exclusively in ethnographic work, including coverage of the misunderstandings, false starts, limitations and doubts about claims to reliability or validity.

Part of the background to this is the so-called post-structuralist challenge to 'objectivism', i.e. to the once-assumed objective or independent status of knowledge. This has been further reinforced by our increasing awareness of the part played by 'rhetoric' rather than just detached 'science', particularly in the stylistic conventions according to which research claims are presented in writing (see, e.g. Clifford and Marcus, 1986; Simons, 1990, also the comments in Unit 1/2). Whatever your judgement about the various theoretical controversies involved here, the plain fact is that it is now more common than in the past to reveal the politics and human fallibilities of our research processes, perhaps as a supplement or addition to some final report on that research, perhaps even as a substitute for it.

In one way this openness makes assessing research designs much easier. You are apparently told what the plans *really* were and how they actually developed, rather than just the cover story. But we have to look between the lines here also. Revelatory accounts too have their own rhetoric, their own political and philosophical positions, and their selections about what is put in, what is left out. And — to take the more extreme cases — reports which assert that they are not making authoritative truth claims while at the same time conveying their interpretations in the powerful medium of academically-framed print may need as careful scrutiny as more 'scientist' forms of presentation.

Whatever format is used by researchers to present their research planning, therefore, you will need to engage in some critical analysis to uncover the 'real story' — if indeed there *is* one real story (another set of controversies). There is no simple answer as to how to get at this, although following up the kinds of questions discussed in this unit will help. But that there always is *some* such conventional format, both for presenting research proposals and for summing them up after the event, is another of the many factors which you need to be aware of in assessing research designs.

3.5 PREPARING THE GROUND: SOME FURTHER QUESTIONS TO CONSIDER

There are also decisions about early processes such as pilot studies, literature searches, or negotiations with gatekeepers. Though not necessarily separate in every way from the phases just discussed, these need some special consideration in assessing a research design. They are also points to which many funding bodies pay particular attention. So, although the detailed consideration of specialist aspects of these processes comes later (especially in Block 3) some more general questions about practical planning can be considered briefly at this stage.

It is commonly said that a 'literature search' should come before or near the beginning of planning any piece of research (it could therefore equally have figured in the previous sections). Consulting the relevant available information can in fact enter into all stages of the research, including the final writing up. Its relevance here, however, is that one common measure for assessing research plans is the researcher's acquaintance with other comparable or related research in the same area. This is important as it gives the opportunity to build on others' research and to avoid repeating naïve mistakes or merely discovering an already often-invented wheel. Competence can be evidenced by mastery of the written literature on the subject, supplemented as appropriate by personal knowledge of on-going work and other available information.

Various reasons are given for the importance of this stage, and thus for checking on its successful conduct. One is to ascertain whether and how far the research is repeating what has been done before. Replication may or may not be considered a 'good thing' (for the concept of 'originality' is not the same in social research as in natural science) but it is widely assumed that researchers and those assessing their plans should at least *know* about related work. If the main research aims have already been accomplished by someone else, or the data are cheaply and readily available in some other form, are the proposed research aims and strategy as valuable as if they were breaking new ground?

A second reason is that it is often only by learning about comparable research in an area that a researcher gets some insight into likely controversies and pitfalls (even if this does have the complementary danger of following the accepted wisdom, rather than thinking out possible issues afresh). Plunging into planning research *without* this background, or without allowing for some time to gain it, could certainly be open to criticism. So too would planning a research strategy without the researcher having made an effort to gain some understanding of the strengths and weaknesses of the planned methods — for example the differing forms of sampling (Unit 8) or the alternative ways of administering questionnaires (Unit 11).

An acquaintance with comparable research methods and findings thus often affects the research strategy; indeed, it sometimes changes the arguments for the research being conducted on particular lines at all. A researcher's failure to carry out that phase competently — and the consequently uninformed decisions at an early stage — has to be yet another factor in assessing the research plan.

There are also questions to ask about the research plans for preparatory stages like selecting sampling techniques, negotiating access, piloting a questionnaire and so on. Detailed consideration of these processes comes elsewhere, but since planning such arrangements is an essential part of the research design they need to be mentioned briefly here.

Arranging access can be a crucial stage in *planning* research, and often a delicate and time-consuming one. Many parties are likely to be involved, both institutional and personal, ranging from participants in questionnaires or in-depth interviews, to custodians of private records or gatekeepers guarding the right of access to particular institutions. Researchers also need strategies for presenting the aims of their research to those involved (perhaps in more than one way), and for considering what social role(s) they and/or their colleagues/assistants will be taking up (or perhaps have foisted upon them). This can be an issue not only in explicitly 'participant observation' methods but in any kind of research involving personal contact. These procedures may just be allowed to emerge as the research unfolds rather than being precisely pre-planned. But *some* issues are extremely likely to arise at some point and in assessing a research plan it is always fair to ask how far they were, or will be, explicitly provided for.

Similar questions arise about other preparatory but necessary steps in planned research strategy. These include the kind of topics well discussed in earlier units, such as making arrangements for choosing a 'representative' case (if desired) and for developing the necessary sampling procedures; ensuring that the chosen units for comparison really *are* comparable; co-ordinating the timing so as to minimize repetition or unhelpful delays; training assistants, interviewers, etc.; and so on — all perhaps rather mundane steps, but often essential for the overall planning. So another question to ask in assessing the design is how far such procedures have, or will be, explicitly planned for.

Piloting can be another important phase. This does not *have* to be a stage in every research plan, and it can take various forms — from an early feasibility study of an exploratory nature to give familiarization with the field as an aid (among other things) to conceptual analysis, or prior sampling of particular sources, to a trial run of experimental arrangements or of reactions to a questionnaire.

This last item — piloting of questionnaires — is commonly held to be of particular importance but, equally, can easily be neglected in research planning. The researcher 'knows' what the questions mean and so is confident that 'respondents' will understand them in the same way. As you will see in Unit 11 — and will anyway know from your own experience as soon as you think about it — this is an unwise assumption. Stanley Payne's classic *The Art of Asking Questions* (1951/1980) emphasizes the importance of ambiguities and misunderstandings in questions, quoting in illustration an assessment made by a sample of researchers earlier this century on what they saw as 'the principal defects of commercial research'. He lists their most frequently mentioned criticisms:

Improperly worded questionnaire	74%
Faulty interpretations	58%
Inadequacy of samples	52%
Improper statistical methods	44%
Presentation of results without supporting data	41%

(Payne, 1951, p.5)

You will, of course, by now be quick to raise questions about the samples and the research design behind *that* investigation before taking it too literally — it is of course only a piece of vivid illustration in Payne's otherwise lengthy and detailed analysis. But it *is* a vivid illustration of the importance in any research design that involves questioning people of paying attention, not just to statistical methods, but also to such factors as the framing and testing of the questions — the *non*-sampling issues, as Schofield puts it in Unit 8. The former frequently loom large in stated research plans, the latter less often. But since providing some plan for discovering possible ambiguities and connotations in the questions may be crucial for the overall research strategy, asking questions about the plans for this phase could be equally crucial in its assessment.

3.6 THE RELEVANCE OF SOME LATER STAGES FOR ASSESSING RESEARCH DESIGNS: A BRIEF PREVIEW

These later stages are discussed in subsequent blocks. But some short comments are needed here to point up relevant questions for assessing research designs, whether at the start or finish.

The key question is, of course, what happens to the plan? 'Was the research carried out on the lines originally proposed?' is the way the Economic and Social Research Council (ESRC) puts it in its checklist for 'end-of-award assessment'. Sometimes there are good reasons for changing the original design — in terms of, say, data collection, consultation of specific sources, personnel, selection of cases, timescale, scope, even perhaps the aims. Sometimes these changes could, maybe should, have been anticipated in the initial planning. But since social research after all takes place in the real world, equally they sometimes may not. Indeed a research plan that admits no flexibility to respond to unforeseen circumstances or findings could itself be open to criticism. Either way, the questions need to focus on the reasons for the changes, how ingeniously they are accommodated, and how explicitly the researcher faces and explains their implications.

How the completed research is to be communicated is another factor to consider. Are arrangements for this explicitly built in from the start? Questions might indeed be raised about the design if the plan seemed merely to end when the *researcher* is satisfied, without any further dissemination or action. There are controversies here — including ethical as well as intellectual ones — but whether or not dissemination is built into the design, as well as to whom and how, are certainly questions to consider in assessing proposals.

4 ETHICAL AND POLITICAL QUESTIONS

This section moves away from questions about specific design phases to some more general underlying issues. The discussion needs only to be a brief one, since it does little more than remind you that ethical and political issues, which arise in all stages of research (see, e.g. Units 16 and 22 and Part 2 in the Reader), have also to be considered in assessing the planning facets too.

We are now more sensitive than in the past to the ethical implications of research, above all of social research, the more so as older models of the 'neutral' researcher are challenged, and the participatory role of researchers in the social world around them more clearly recognized. This comes out clearly in the article you read by Janet Finch in the Reader (see also, e.g. Kimmel, 1988; Bulmer, 1982; Kidder and Judd, 1986, Chap. 18). Increasingly codes of practice are being developed and researchers expected to make their positions clear. Depending on your viewpoint these are issues which you may wish to consider in your assessments of any research design. Some will be relatively widely agreed — if not always practised — as matters of professional ethics. Others are more a question of personal judgement.

The discussion here will not attempt to cover these issues, with which anyone intending to *do* research would surely have to acquaint themselves in some detail. It merely gives some hints to alert you to the general lines of questioning that can be useful in assessing research plans.

As indicated earlier (Section 3.2, also Unit 1/2) setting research aims is seldom if ever merely a technical matter, so that assessing a research design soon leads into questions about the assumptions behind its selection or formulation. These may turn out to be ones which you may, or may not, accept on moral or political (not just theoretical) grounds. The same may apply to the researchers' moral convictions, if you can disentangle them. As you no doubt noticed in the article by Janet Finch, these may give you a clue to underlying commitments likely to affect the basic plans and how they are carried through.

It is not so much the details of a particular design that matter here, as the fundamental values and attitudes of the researcher(s). Who do they ultimately answer to in their research planning, and what moral responsibilities — and to whom — do they recognize? Do their obligations extend to people at different levels within their organization, to some imagined 'research community', to colleagues and competitors, to fund-givers, to the general public, to those researched 'on'? Is the research envisaged as a top-down asocial act from the outside, or as a collaborative activity by people interacting on a basis of human equality with other people? And when, as almost always, there turn out to be conflicting obligations to differing parties in the process, are the kinds of solutions the researchers adopt ones with which you can ultimately sympathize?

Terminology can, as we saw above, be misleading, but one clue to a researcher's attitudes can sometimes be found in the vocabulary used. If you are one of those who feels uncomfortable about any tendency to depersonalize those being researched 'on' — particularly if the researcher is in a position of power in relation to them — then it may be worth considering what words are used. Some people are nowadays uneasy about terms like 'interviewee', 'respondent', 'sample', 'object', even 'subject', as demeaning the human qualities of those involved, arguably indicative of a tendency to ride roughshod over *their* susceptibilities or convenience. (Not that the practical problems of terminology are easy to solve, and alternative terms like 'colleague', 'collaborator', 'consultant', 'citizen', or 'partner', have their difficulties too.) Similar issues may emerge over the attitudes to research assistants and colleagues, and what recognition if any they are to receive in the final outcome.

There are also the ethical or political implications of any constraints on the research, whether conditions imposed by sponsors, limitations of access to particular sources, or limits on the right to publish the findings. There are almost always some such constraints on the research plan, but more often implicit than explicit — all the more worth being alert to. A particularly important question to ask about research can be who is going to control — even 'own' — the final outcome, and to whose benefit. Depending on your own particular commitments you may find that the answer to this raises ethical or political problems.

These are tangled issues, and they become even more so when explicitly political controversies are confronted. Clearly there can be political overtones in particular social theories both at a generalized level (think of Marxist as against more conservative functionalist terminologies for example) and in the way these are formulated in specific research projects. Similarly labels used to select cases and formulate problems in particular pieces of research — e.g. 'ethnic minorities', 'working class', 'underdeveloped countries', 'criminals', 'the homeless' — may be far from politically neutral, and can be the basis for real *political* disagreement, not just theoretical controversy.

It is often hard to sort out just what the political implications of a particular research design might be and how far such issues should be allowed to affect one's assessment. Dogmatic assessments resting *just* on political grounds or following whatever the current politically 'correct' fashions might be are scarcely fair to all the other complex criteria that need to be considered. But political preconceptions often do in practice enter into assessments, if only because particular approaches are judged (depending on the viewpoints) as likely to be misleading in ways which have political as well as scientific implications.

As you will already have noticed in Janet Finch's article (which you would find it useful to review again), these are not trivial issues. There is no neat solution beyond merely restating the need to be alert to their significance and to the role they sometimes play in the actual assessment of research.

Further points to consider are those specifically directed to the interests of those whose lives, beliefs or actions are being investigated. The basic principle is usually taken to be that they should not in any way suffer harm from the research — a guideline worth holding to, even if not always easy to interpret in practice. Familiar issues here include those to do with confidentiality, secrecy, and anonymity. Arguably of equal importance are people's rights to the credit for or ownership of their own productions (in many senses of that term). This has less frequently been discussed in the past but is now increasingly coming to researchers' attention through the recent stress on the democratization of the research process and on the concept of intellectual property rights.

Many controversies cluster round such ethical issues. Some hold that all research is essentially exploitative, with the power held in the researchers' hands. Others that the aim should be dialogue *with* rather than research *on* the research 'subjects'. But even the most 'democratic' of ideals here will not remove the need for difficult ethical choices among the *contending* interests of different groupings of those whose lives are being investigated, or between competing obligations to respect, say, both anonymity and the attribution of rights (further discussion on these points can be found in, for example, Kidder and Judd, 1986, Chap. 18; Akeroyd, 1984; Bulmer, 1982; Barnes, 1977; Schröck, 1991).

Most research designs involving any interaction with human beings will be susceptible to being assessed in the light of the kinds of questions briefly indicated above. What answers you give to them — and how much weight you attach to them in your assessment of the design whether at a proposal or a final report stage — may largely depend on your own moral or political position. This is a perfectly proper line of evaluation to take, although it also of course has to be balanced against other criteria too, and how far you should push it may be a matter of opinion. It could be that in the end you will want to lay as much weight on such qualities as, say, humility, honesty or integrity as on more formal requirements. That has to be a judgement left to you to make.

5 WHO ARE THE ASSESSORS?

It will by now be obvious that while there are certainly technical points to consider in assessing a research plan, they are not the whole story. The planning and conduct of research does not take place in a social vacuum, but like any other social activity can be formulated and perceived differently according to varying viewpoints, conflicting obligations or contending sets of interests.

But there is also a further implication of this: as will by now be obvious, nor does the *assessing* of social research take place in a social vacuum. There too — if we are to be realistic — different interests and perceptions will inevitably be in play, and it would be naïve to conclude that (despite some element of concurrence on the kind of criteria discussed already) there are fully agreed objective or universal standards which can be invoked.

This is sometimes obscured by the common stress in many types of social research and among its academic sponsors on the ideal that research, in both its plan and its outcome, should 'advance knowledge'. That is an aspiration most of us on this course would probably share, whether as students, tutors or course team members. But once one starts applying this, it turns out to be less clear-cut than it sounds, for it quickly leads into complex issues of 'knowledge for what?', 'for whom?' and 'how used?', issues which attract much discussion (as, for example, in Lindblom and Cohen, 1979; see also the discussion of 'truth' in Unit 1/2). So *just* to speak of 'advancing knowledge' still leaves questions about who is judging this 'advance of knowledge' and with what sanctions. Even within the blanket terms 'research community' or 'scientific community' there are many different interest groups and contending intellectual traditions. The definition and control of 'knowledge', furthermore, is in any culture likely to have overtones of power. In this respect assessment even of the purely 'knowledge'-outcomes of particular research designs can seldom be a *fully* objective procedure, without at least some influence from the position and interpretation of those doing the assessing.

This also applies to the question of 'relevance'. This sounds easy until one asks 'relevant for whom?' — a question first raised in Unit 3/4 but which needs some further amplification here. A central issue here must be *who* is doing the assessing and from what viewpoint?

ACTIVITY 6

1   Spend a few minutes considering how many participants in a piece of research you can think of (my own suggested list will be found at the end of this unit).

2   Having made your list and/or consulted mine, reflect on whether you have yourself been involved in any piece of research in any of the above (or similar) roles? If so, how did/would you assess it either at the time or in terms of any of the questions raised in this unit?

The list of possible participants and roles in research could be extended almost *ad infinitum*. Within each category, too, there are likely to be many different purposes, depending, for example, on the circumstances, the precise roles and the individuals. The point, however, is not production of a specific list but the awareness that there *are* different interested parties and they cannot all be assumed to have the same viewpoint on the research design.

So what questions you consider most important in assessing research strategies may essentially depend which of the many possible roles you currently come under. Each has a right to its own viewpoint. Here are some examples.

Academic fund-givers may emphasize one set of criteria. You may be interested, for example, to consult the checklist for referees' comments in research applications to the Economic and Social Research Council (ESRC), given below. This formed the framework for assessments by experienced social scientists of research plans in a high-level academic context (not excluding some interest in policy questions). But even in such assessments there can easily be disagreements. What counts as 'originality'? What is a 'significant contribution to theory'? Finally the question of how far the methods are suitable to the aims and objectives may well attract a consensus evaluation — but equally can lead to heated dissension, particularly among those speaking from the viewpoint of differing disciplines.

CHECKLIST FOR REFEREE COMMENTS

GRADING: You are invited to indicate your overall judgement of the research proposal using the following definitions:

Alpha: Research of high scientific merit, i.e. of such novelty or timeliness and promise as is likely to make a significant contribution to knowledge.

A+ Outstanding; A Important; A– Significant

Beta: Research will add to understanding and is worthy of support but which may not be of such quality or urgency as to have a significant influence on the research area.

Reject: Research which is flawed in its scientific approach, or is repetitious of other work, or judged not worth pursuing, or which, though possibly having sound objectives, appears seriously defective at a technical level.

COMMENTS: You may wish to use the following checklist as guide to the points on which we would welcome your advice. Some points may not be relevant to a particular research proposal and you may wish to comment on additional aspects, which are not included in this checklist.

1.   **Originality**

Is the proposed research likely to make an original and significant contribution to theory, methods or knowledge? Is there similar or related work, not mentioned in the proposal of which the applicant(s) should be aware? If so, please specify.

2. **Methods and Timescale**

   Are the methods suitable to the aims and objectives?: Are they clearly defined, rigorous and feasible? Is the timescale and scheduling of the work appropriate and realistic?

3. **Value for Money**

   Are the staffing levels appropriate? Could they be reduced without damaging the project? Are the equipment, travel and other costs necessary as far as you can judge, or could they be reduced? Does the project represent good value for money?

   You are asked to bear in mind that, in the case of independent institutes qualified to undertake research, ESRC will meet up to 20% of the cost of overheads.

4. **Outputs**

   Is the planned output of the research appropriate? Have the applicants made adequate plans to disseminate the results of the research?

   (Economic and Social Research Council)

However, there are also other situations. With commissioned research in the 'customer/contractual' model those assessing both the research design and its outcome might be little concerned with 'originality', more (perhaps) with cost, timing and precise specification of agreed objectives. For others, again, questions of 'knowledge' or 'theory' might be of no interest compared with the identification of particular problems, or proposals for their solution. The term 'practitioners' is sometimes used as a generalized category, pointing perhaps to some implied, if problematic, contrast between 'pure' and 'applied' research — practitioners being supposedly the consumers of the latter, academic researchers of the former. But even this is a bit too general, because people 'practise' in a whole host of ways and are likely to stress a variety of different criteria for assessing research depending on their situation, the type of research and what they hope to get out of it.

Other possible assessors yet again might be as much concerned with enhancing certain values as with 'academic' knowledge for its own sake. Fund-givers in the various charitable bodies — who between them support a great deal of research — necessarily, and properly, pay a great deal of attention to such aspects in assessing research proposals and their results. The influential Nuffield Foundation is an example:

Social Research, Experiment and Welfare

Grants are made to fulfil one of the Trust Deed's objects — the *advancement of social well being*. Trustees are prepared to fulfil this object in a flexible and open-minded way, but their preference is for *experimental or developmental projects which, if successful, can serve as a model for others*. An early example was the Bristol Courts Family Conciliation Service, which the Foundation funded when it was the only service offering divorce conciliation. Now that conciliation is an accepted part of the scene, it remains an interest of the Foundation as an element within the theme of Family Law/Child Protection.

Trustees also support research which *looks critically at statutory arrangements and current practice*. The purpose of such research might be to throw light on the unintended or unrecognised consequences of a current policy or to suggest ways in which a practice or provision might be improved, in however small a way.

(The Nuffield Foundation, 1990, *A Guide for Applicants*, p.8, my italics)

Or again ethical and practical considerations may be to the fore as in the checklist of factors to consider in research plans produced by the Royal College of Nursing of the United Kingdom:

1 The research must be necessary and must contribute to further knowledge.

2 The subjects must receive full explanations of what their participation might entail and must be told explicitly that they have the right to refuse.

3 Consent must be obtained, if necessary, from a relative or legal guardian.

4 Subjects must be protected against physical, emotional, mental, or social injury.

5 Confidentiality must be assured and maintained.

6 The researcher must be qualified to carry out the investigation, must make public the results of the inquiry, and must attempt to prevent their misuse.

7 The contract between the sponsor of the research and the researcher must make explicit their mutual obligations and must state clearly the remit for the work to be undertaken.

8 Clear arrangements must be made as to the researcher's duties and responsibilities in the place where the research is carried out.

(Quoted in Cormack, 1991, p.34)

Finally, those at the 'receiving end' of the research or approached as gatekeepers certainly have some interest in possible applications or insights brought by the potential findings. But they may equally well be moved in their assessment by political or ethical questions — and quite reasonably so — or by such factors as the degree of inconvenience, disruption of other valued activities, or personal intrusion. There is also the important point that some research findings — and questions — may be painful for some or most of those assessing it. Some 'truths', it may be felt, are best left hidden and researchers who reveal these may sometimes find their research not evaluated highly by the very people whom it concerned or to whom it was directed.

Another question about relevance is of course 'relevance for what?' In assessing research plans or reports, the 'what' is presumably the *purpose* of that research. It is easy to jump again to the simple conclusion that the only purpose is necessarily that supposedly neutral thing called the 'advancement of knowledge'.

ACTIVITY 7

In many discussions of research design the model that comes across most strongly is that of an activity with the aim of a disinterested search for the truth and/or of reporting on the facts. But is this in practice always the sole purpose of research? Looking back at earlier units *and* exercising your own critical sense as a social scientist and a citizen, see how many other purposes you can list.

Here are some other real, but not always stated, purposes (do any of them link in with your own experience?):

• Research to *avoid* action ('we're doing research on it' is a notorious alibi in an organization unwilling to take action — or a dumping ground for someone who is otherwise a nuisance).

• Power politics (research designing and the giving or receiving of funds, may be closely entwined with enhancing someone's reputation or position).

- Finding out the facts on a *specific* point without too much expenditure of time or money.

- Exploring the potential market for some product or service.

- Giving a voice to the voiceless.

- Training students.

- Selling services and justifying one's job — or one's existence.

- A mixture of these (or yet others) held severally by *different* participants in the research and/or its assessment — or at different times.

If the purposes of a piece of research include any of the above (perhaps overlapping with more 'academic' aims), then obviously if those evaluating that research at its start or finish share those aims, their assessments are going to be affected by them. Not all their criteria will fall under notions like 'reliability' or 'validity', but may turn on questions of cost, of convenience, of who-knows-whom, of a hoped-for *lack* of clear findings (often the best result for the alibi-type purpose), of career-building, of practicability, of who is available when.

The assessment of a particular piece of research is not necessarily always a permanent and once-and-for-all judgement either, even by any one of the interested parties. It can vary over time with changing fashions, perhaps, or changing situations. This is well illustrated in the many 'gallows-humour' stories told about research designed for implementation. One (extremely cynical!) account of the sequential stages of the reception of such research by others runs:

1 Wild enthusiasm

2 Disillusionment

3 Total confusion

4 The search for the guilty

5 The punishment of the innocent

6 The promotion of the non-participants.

(Hakel *et al.*, 1982, p.120)

Such stories should not to be taken too literally of course. But they do encapsulate one aspect of the truth: in practice assessment cannot be assumed to be either an absolute nor necessarily a 'just' procedure.

Examples like these, together perhaps with others from your own experience, suggest yet again that there is no such thing as *the* right assessment of any given research design. Certainly there are recurrent questions, some more commonly applied than others. But since the assessing will be in relation to particular interests and contexts — and these will vary — so too the criteria on any given occasion are necessarily relative to those, not absolute.

So we end up with the simple but uncomfortable fact that assessing is a social process, conducted by people acting in a social context. And though it may not sound very 'academic' to say this, in practice the process of assessing research plans can also therefore be affected by such things as the researchers' reputation or status, the old boys' network, or the potential use of the findings in local power politics. As will now be clear, assessment is not a purely technical or neutral matter; and in any act of evaluation people are moved by a number of different motives. It is also always worth thinking back to some of the possible aims of research mentioned above: the hidden agenda that might be understood by (some of) the parties in the transaction but would emphatically not figure in public statements and applications. These too are likely to play a (perhaps veiled) part in the actual assessing of specific research designs, both before and after the event.

It is not that laying weight on such factors in your own assessment is being recommended: far from it. But in so far as you may be engaged with others in the process of assessing — whether as decision-maker in funding, gatekeeper, evaluating someone's achievements or prospects, or merely as 'consumer' — you need to be aware that such motivations in practice often play an important role, perhaps along with, or concealed behind, more apparently 'scientific' criteria. To accept all the publicly-stated assessments (including your own perhaps) at their face value would be to take a naïve approach to the essentially social act of assessing. Understanding these complexities need not, however, contradict an ultimate aim of exercising informed and independent judgement in the assessing of research designs — something this unit is designed to assist you in doing. Indeed it could help you to spot pitfalls to avoid, and so to make such judgements with greater integrity and self-awareness.

6 CONCLUSION: OVER TO YOU

The questions that could be asked in assessing any given research design, whether before or after the event, are thus near-endless — as extensive as those we could ask about any aspect of human social activity (which of course is what researching is). So you will not be surprised if I stress once again that there can be no simple definitive checklist which could be applied equally to any and every piece of research or be equally acceptable to the different personalities or interests involved in the process of assessing.

However, rather than just leaving these questions totally open — which *ultimately* perhaps they have to be — let us tie them down just a little by a mutual attempt to pick out some key ones.

ACTIVITY 8

1   Suppose someone you knew was put in a position of having to assess a social research proposal, was not allowed to show you the actual proposal or tell you about the circumstances in which it was to be assessed, but did very much want quick advice from you — knowing your expertise from DEH313 — about how to go about it. What main criteria (say, up to a dozen) would you highlight for them? (Think back quickly to this block as a whole as well as to this unit and to the list of questions you have already been developing in previous examples and activities.)

2   Having done this look at my own personal list at the end of this unit, compare notes and consider arguments for and against both my, and your own, selection.

Even more important than any summary list of questions, of course, is the realization, first, that drawing up and following through a research plan is not just a technical process, for there are always a whole series of decisions involved, *all* of which may need to be evaluated; and second, that a research plan is not always what it seems. Being aware of this, and applying it, is more important than any simple list of criteria.

ACTIVITY 9

Here are some optional suggestions to come back to if you wish to gain further practice in assessing research designs.

1   Look back at the examples of research you have read so far in the course and for at least two of these sketch out a preliminary assessment of their design (in the broad

sense of that term) by applying as many as possible of the questions raised in this unit (draw on your own summaries of these made as you worked through the unit and, if you wish, my own list prepared for Activity 8 at the end).

You will no doubt find that you are not able to discover all the information needed to answer some of these questions. This too is worth noting. As so often, a *full* assessment may not in practice be possible. Here, as on other occasions, part of the battle is being aware of where the gaps may lie and of the need for following up such questions wherever possible if you are to fully understand and assess a piece of research.

2   Look again at your assessments and consider how far answers to some of the questions might have differed if *different* people had been doing the assessment: e.g. two academics with differing methodological viewpoints; a practitioner of a particular profession in a particular role; an employer; a fund-giver; a member of the group being researched 'on' (these are only some suggestions — think of whichever ones you like).

3   Repeat both the above processes for some piece of research with which you have some personal contact. This need not necessarily be an example of high-powered academic research — it could be a small-scale investigation into something to do with your work or the report of a public opinion poll in a newspaper.

Once again you may not be able to get all the answers you want. But — the aim of this unit in a nutshell — the process will make you alert to your need and right to ask the questions.

4   Draft a brief research plan on some topic that interests you (a really brief one — the outcome of 5 minutes writing down first thoughts in skeletal form in half a page or so). Then go back and assess it as critically as you can, drawing attention to all the issues that might be misleading, controversial, omitted, etc. (also say what you still like, and why). Think of different roles you could take up in this assessment exercise and see if the criticisms differ according to these differing viewpoints: e.g. your competitor for the same research funds/opportunities, a journalist (publisher) looking to get an article (book) out of it in a week's (three years') time, a superior only too glad for you to be side-lined into 'research', a gatekeeper to whose institution you will be needing access, any of those mentioned in Activity 6 above.

The final point to make, then, is that in assessing the process of research planning, social scientists need to apply their usual scepticism in asking how far people are always actually doing what they say, write, or perhaps believe that they are. Such issues are all the more important to raise when those controlling the design and its presentation are of high status or hold powerful positions which enable them to directly affect its reception — sometimes indeed (to put an extreme view) to collude in fixing the conventional wisdom about its assessment. From this viewpoint too, not only as a social scientist but also as a citizen, do not let yourself be browbeaten by apparently authoritative wisdom about research designs whether put forward by academics (who, perhaps fortunately, also often disagree), the mass media, government departments, computer manufacturers or whoever. You should rather have the confidence — and the right — to make your own assessment of research plans and achievements in the light of the kinds of questions discussed in this course. This need not mean invoking some cynical conspiracy theory, merely an informed and moral capacity to read between the lines, appreciatively as well as critically.

ANSWERS TO ACTIVITIES

This section gives answers and comments on selected activities, and through this mounts up to a list of possible questions and factors to consider in assessing research designs. This can complement the lists *you* have drawn up — and will doubtless need amplifying as you go further.

ACTIVITY 2

The general questions can be listed under a number of headings, but here is one possible set (there are obviously overlaps and differing ways of stating much the same points). They are not elaborated here, as most will already be familiar to you from earlier units and/or are taken up for further discussion later in this or following units. As you will by now be aware, some are more important than others for particular types of research design:

Validity (or likelihood of producing accurate or true findings)

Reliability

Representativeness and sampling

Formulation of clear problem, aim or hypothesis

Discovery of new information not already pre-structured by the research design

Control and/or standardization

Degree of generalizability

Effect of the researcher

'Relevance'

Appropriateness of methods to the research aims

Relation of the evidence to the conclusion: the logic of the argument.

ACTIVITY 4

Obviously your answers will depend on which example(s) of research you chose, but you may well have had one or more of the following reactions:

(a) that alternative choices might have been made,

(b) that you often do not have the full information in practice to tell you about these crucial underlying decisions, and

(c) that you are not quite sure what is wrong but do not feel quite comfortable about some basic attitudes in the research — or, alternatively, that you do.

Even if you reached no clear conclusions it is always worth looking hard for the basic assumptions behind a research design: not an easy task, but one you can carry out more effectively the more you practise it.

ACTIVITY 6

Here are some of the possible participants and roles I can think of in a given piece of research. All will be likely to have legitimate viewpoints on implications of the research design.

1   Sponsors — academic fund-givers.

2   Sponsors and/or contractors — governmental.

3   Sponsors and fund-givers — charitable organizations.

4   Employers/controllers within a particular organization.

5   The principal researchers themselves.

6   Research 'assistants' of various kinds.

7   Academic and/or specialist readers (including professionals; policy makers; academic researchers).

8   More general readers (including through the mass media).

9   Those responsible for allowing access to particular data, sources or institutions.

10 Those being in some sense researched 'on'.

ACTIVITY 8

Since, as I have constantly stressed, assessing research is a matter of *judgement* not just a technical procedure with 'correct' answers, the following should not be taken as definitive. Here, however, is my own list, not in any particular order of priority.

• *Aims and outcome* (is it worth doing, e.g. will it result in 'new' knowledge or important action?, for whose benefit?, nature of feedback or communication?, relevant for whom or what? — see especially Sections 3.2 and 5).

• *Validity* (will the findings be true?).

• *Practicability* (do the methods look sensible, practicable and appropriate to the aims/claims of the research?; and what are the costs? — see Section 3.3).

• *Reliability* (for certain types of research design).

• *Discovery, insight, new understanding* (for certain types of research design).

• *Technical competence* (*not* the whole story, but definitely one factor: how far does the research demonstrate competence in the kinds of points discussed in Units 5–9? — as appropriate for the specific type of research design).

• *Openness* (i.e. how open about the *actual* approach being used — see Section 3.4 — and its likely strengths and weaknesses?).

• *Sensitivity to possible ethical dimensions* (see Section 4).

• *Basic assumptions underlying the research strategy* (intellectual, methodological, and perhaps also ethical and political — see Sections 3.2 and 4).

• *Relevance* (but you will have to decide for whom or what — see Section 5).

• *The researcher(s)* (how well positioned in relation to the points above?, track record on previous research, if any?, personal assumptions where relevant?, likelihood of actually completing the research?).

REFERENCES

Abramson, P.R. (1992) *A Case for Case Studies*, London, Sage.

Adams, G.R. and Schvaneveldt, J.D. (1985) *Understanding Research Methods*, New York, Longman.

Akeroyd, A. (1984) 'Ethics in relation to informants, the profession and government', in Ellen, R.F. (ed.) *Ethnographic Research: a Guide to General Conduct*, London, Academic Press.

Anderson, M. (1971) *Family Structure in Nineteenth Century Lancashire*, Cambridge, Cambridge University Press.

Anderson, M. (1983) 'What is new about the modern family?', Occasional Paper OPCS, *The Family*, vol. 31, pp.2–16.

Barnes, J.A. (1977) *The Ethics of Inquiry in Social Science: Three Lectures*, Delhi, Oxford University Press.

Bell, C. and Roberts, H. (eds) (1984) *Social Researching: Politics, Problems, Practices*, London, Routledge & Kegan Paul.

Bulmer, M. (ed.) (1982) *Social Research Ethics: an Examination of the Merits of Covert Participant Observation*, London, Macmillan.

Burgess, R. (1984) *The Research Process in its Setting: Ten Case Studies*, Brighton, Falmer.

Burgess, R. (ed.) (1992) *Learning About Fieldwork*, London, JAI Press.

Clifford, J. and Marcus, G.E. (eds) (1986) *Writing Culture: the Poetics and Politics of Ethnography*, Berkeley, University of California Press.

Cohen, E. (1965) *The Growth of the British Civil Service 1780–1939*, London, Cassell.

Cormack, D.F.S. (ed.) (1991) *The Research Process in Nursing* (2nd edn), Oxford, Blackwell Scientific Publications.

Cullingworth, J.B. (1970) *The Politics of Research: an Inaugural Lecture*, University of Birmingham, Centre for Urban and Regional Studies, Occasional Paper 7.

Finch, J. (1984) '"It's great to have someone to talk to": ethics and politics of interviewing women', in Hammersley, M. (ed.) (1992) (DEH313 Reader).

Finch, J. (1989) *Family Obligations and Social Change*, Oxford, Polity Press.

Finnegan, R. (1989) *The Hidden Musicians: Music-making in an English Town*, Cambridge, Cambridge University Press.

Glasgow University Media Group (1985) *War and Peace News*, Milton Keynes, Open University Press.

Greeley, A. (1971) 'Sociology as an art form', *The American Sociologist*, vol. 6, no. 3, pp.223–5.

Hakel, M.D., Sorcher, M., Beer, M. and Moses, J.L. (1982) *Making it Happen: Designing Research with Implementation in Mind*, Beverly Hills, Sage.

Hakim, C. (1987) *Research Design: Strategies and Choices in the Design of Social Research*, London, Unwin Hyman [Chap. 4, 'Research analysis of administrative records', is reproduced in Hammersley, M. (ed.) (1992) (DEH313 Reader)].

Hammersley, M. (ed.) (1992) *Social Research: Philosophy, Politics and Practice*, London, Sage (DEH313 Reader).

Hammond, P.E. (ed.) (1964) *Sociologists at Work*, New York, Basic Books.

Hobbs, D. (1988) *Doing the Business: Entrepreneurship, the Working Class, and Detectives in the East End of London*, Oxford, Oxford University Press.

Humes, S. and Martin, E. (1969) *The Structure of Local Government: a Comparative Survey of 81 Countries*, The Hague, International Union of Local Authorities.

Kidder, L.H. and Judd C.N. (1986) *Research Methods in Social Relations* (5th edn), New York, CBS Publishing Japan.

Kimmel, A.J. (1988) *Ethics and Values in Applied Social Research* (Applied Social Research Methods Series, vol. 12), Newbury Park, Sage.

Lindblom, C.E. and Cohen, D.K. (1979) *Usable Knowledge*, New Haven, Yale University Press.

Murray, D.J. (1974) 'Case studies as a form of enquiry', in *Public Administration* (D331), Block II, Part 4, pp.165–72, Milton Keynes, Open University Press.

Pahl, R.E. (1984) *Divisions of Labour*, Oxford, Blackwell.

Payne, S.L. (1951, reprinted 1980) *The Art of Asking Questions*, Princeton, Princeton University Press.

Schröck, R. (1991) 'Moral issues in nursing research', in Cormack, D.F.S. (ed.) (1991).

Shipman, M.D. (1988) *The Limitations of Social Research* (3rd edn), London, Longman.

Simons, H.W. (ed.) (1990) *The Rhetorical Turn: Invention and Persuasion in the Conduct of Inquiry*, Chicago, University of Chicago Press.

Whyte, W.F. (1943) *Street Corner Society*, Chicago, University of Chicago Press.

Wraith, R.E. and Lamb, G.B. (1971) *Public Inquiries as an Instrument of Government*, London, Allen & Unwin.

ACKNOWLEDGEMENTS

Grateful acknowledgement is made to the following sources for permission to reproduce material in this unit:

TEXT

Hymas, C. (1991) 'Scandal in our schools: one in three can't count', *The Sunday Times*, 27 October 1991, © Times Newspapers Ltd 1991; Norman, M. (1991) 'Sums that do not add up', *The Times*, 29 October 1991, © Times Newspapers Ltd 1991; 'Checklist for referee comments', courtesy of the Economic and Social Research Council; The Nuffield Foundation: A Guide For Applicants 1990, The Nuffield Foundation.

CARTOON

p.151: Newman/Courtesy *The Sunday Times*.